TOP LEADERSHIP, U.S.A.

TOP
LEADERSHIP, U.S.A.

By
FLOYD HUNTER

CHAPEL HILL   1959
THE UNIVERSITY OF NORTH CAROLINA PRESS

To

JAMES EDWARD DINSMORE

ROBERT LONG FOUST

CONTENTS

TABLES

FIGURES

INTRODUCTION

THE study, or more accurately the series of studies, presented in these pages is an array of logical statements compounded of research abstractions, for although the frame of reference for study—the exploration of the hypothesis that a power structure exists in concretely definable terms at the national level of affairs—was a theoretical statement that guided the research in part, actual visits with national leaders, observations of them, and analysis of their statements and behavior in relation to each other guided the research more than all else. The major elements of power relations have been pointed out by an unfolding series of leads in the empirical process. Following these elementary leads, I have been able to trace major configurations of power groups, and by relating various groups to each other in terms of the development of specific policy matters, I have traced a living model of United States power.

Examined as a social system, the model of power consists of several coordinate parts, among which are community base, inter-community relations, association ties, state leadership orientation, regional policy requirements, commodity complexes, service configurations, national power structures, and, sketchily, international networks of influence. These have been the major categories in which data on the ways in which men habitually relate themselves to policy-making and power groups in the United States have been presented. I believe that the categories align themselves with the actual activities of men who go about the business of national policy-making, and further that a structure of national power is revealed in this alignment.

Methodological steps are listed below in approximate order employed. Some of the work had to be done when funds for special studies were made available, and backward and forward skips characterized some of the work, but the objective remained steady throughout and the research order presented here was held firmly in mind.

1. A list of 1093 national associations was gathered, and a panel of persons assumed to know about national associational activity was asked to weigh the relative influence of each association with others. In this process the judgment resulted from considering an association's influence in terms of its stated national policy purposes, its size, and its public reputation as a policy-making organization. Out of this judging, the first list was cut to a shorter list of 106 organizations, or roughly to ten percent of the original listing (see pp. 13-15).

Subsequently, a questionnaire was sent to the leaders of the 106 organizations. They were asked (1) to judge the power and influence of their own and other policy-making associations, (2) to give the names of five national leaders (exclusive of elective and appointive officials) considered to be of top influence in national policy-making, and (3) to add comments and send materials related to their association's activities as a policy-making body.

2. Thirty association secretaries, principally in New York, Chicago, and Washington, D. C., where most of the national associations are located, were interviewed to substantiate the materials collected, to get firsthand information on methods of association activities, and to expand knowledge of the national leaders.

3. A letter of inquiry was sent to Chamber of Commerce and Community Chest secretaries in all cities in the country with populations exceeding 100,000. The secretaries were asked to give five names of persons in their communities considered to be at the top level of local influence in policy matters.

4. Leaders whose names appeared in a sample of a listing of unduplicated names gathered in step 3 were visited in the first cross-country trip to get their opinions on the adequacy of the list nationally and to ask their opinions on policies of national significance.

5. Studies in some depth were made of policy development in two Southern states.

6. An intensive study was made of the private clubs in a large city on the West coast.

7. A study was made of the development of the housing industry, which touches all citizens directly and indirectly, to determine precisely its policy-making actions.

8. Supplementary community studies of power and status factors were made in selected areas of different sizes.

9. A questionnaire to find out who knew whom was sent to a composite list of nearly 500 leaders named by others as national figures, and biographical sketches, copies of public speeches, and policy statements were solicited.

10. A second cross-country trip was made, during which at least three leaders each in a sample of thirty towns (large to small) were interviewed regarding their role in national policy development.

11. A third cross-country trip was made, during which a sample one third of the leaders who had been previously designated by their peers as number-one policy makers was interviewed.

12. An examination of policy relationships within the United States textile industry was made.

13. A fourth cross-country trip was made to interview various corporate management persons. The trip was extended to world cities outside the United States, including Tokyo, where exploratory interviews were held with power structure leaders concerning textile export policies.

14. The last of four annual polls for nominations of top national leaders was completed.

15. State leadership lists of North and South Carolina were revised.

16. National elected and appointed officials were interviewed with general reference to the over-all structure of policy development and with specific reference to textile policy decisions.

17. A questionnaire was designed and circulated among leaders at all levels of power to reveal and document interaction in policy development.

18. A special questionnaire was sent to a cross-section of the textile industry.

19. A telephone panel was used to follow policy in the making.

20. Printed materials, notes, processed interviews, and a few books related to the subject were analyzed for content and condensed for this writing.

21. The work manuscript was read for criticism.

Besides the use of personal resources and monies received from three pieces of individual contract research that made travel and study possible, I have also received grants from the Research Council of the University of North Carolina and the Political Behavior Committee and the Urban Studies Program of the Institute for Research in Social Science of the University of North Carolina.

Part I

FINDING THE LEADERS

1 COMMUNITIES AND THE NATION

IN the course of a field study in Atlanta, Georgia, in 1950 I noticed several photographs of General Dwight D. Eisenhower in the office of Francis X. Baffin of the Coca Cola Company.[1] I inquired about the pictures and was told that they were informal shots taken of the General while he was hunting on an estate owned by Mr. Baffin. I was also told that Mr. Baffin had been among the men who had urged General Eisenhower to take his post-war European assignment as an aid in grooming him for the presidency.

This statement surprised me a little for two reasons. The first: the ground-swell, so called, of the people's "liking Ike" had not yet got fully underway, so I had no firm notion, news knowledge, that the General was being made ready for The Call. The second reason for mild surprise was that I had read and heard rumors about the General to the effect that he had Republican leanings, although he had not said so publicly. Working in an area that had been traditionally Democratic, I had assumed, perhaps wrongly, that Mr. Baffin was a Democrat. I still do not know whether Mr. Baffin is a Democrat

1. It should be stated at once that all names in this study were gathered in a strict social science method. At any point where the interrelations of persons acting on policy matters have been described, pseudonyms have been used, indicated by an "X" middle or first initial. Individual choices of specific men at all levels of leadership have been kept strictly confidential.

or a Republican, but I do know that he was a strong supporter of Eisenhower and I also understand that he worked quietly at the national level of affairs in helping to make a President of his choice of candidates. This was, as I have said, in 1950, and I was in no position to know how strongly the currents of opinion were running in the General's favor nor how many Democrats would support a Republican candidate in 1952.

In a subsequent conversation with Mr. Baffin, he indicated that many of his interests brought him into contact with people at the national level of policy- and decision-making. Contrary to the image held of him by many of his townsmen, he disavowed knowing too much about purely local affairs in Atlanta. He spoke, in illustrative remarks concerning his activities, of a specific interest in the program of the National Safety Council and of a general interest in several other civic and corporate groups of national significance.

He called persons of national prominence by their first names, not as a name-dropper but as one with the assurance of knowing personally those of whom he spoke. In this he differed, I have come to learn, from some of the new-rich oil people who like to impress New York bankers with the fact that they have had a phone call from the White House, or who produce an effect in their home towns by casually mentioning the names of New York bankers with whom they have talked. Mr. Baffin spoke easily and offhand of conversations with "Young Henry" Ford and others of his caliber in relation to national committee work.

A few months after this interview, Mr. Baffin's picture appeared on the cover of *Time* magazine, and the story on the inside pages gave him national recognition as an astute businessman. His role in the developing Eisenhower boom was not mentioned, but in due course, brief news releases over the national press wires did refer to it.

In spite of Mr. Baffin's protestations of knowing little about internal affairs in Atlanta, it was evident that he had considerable influence there. His picture hung in the office of the mayor, and on every hand I was told that "Frank Baffin has had a great deal of good influence in policy determinations affecting the city—some of it indirect, of course." There also were a few other men in Atlanta who were mentioned as both local and national leaders.

The dual roles of local and national leadership began to interest me, and as I talked with people in Atlanta and later in other cities in which I have made a series of power leadership studies, I began to collect notes on persons who were considered to be of national stature.

Small bits of information, when pieced together, indicated that there might be an informal pattern of opinion leadership and policy-making at the national level of activities comparable to the sort found in any large community. It was a hunch anyway, and one that now I have followed out systematically. I have become convinced that a good seedbed of national study is community study, because patterns of policy development parallel, in many ways, those found in local areas. There are, however, very great differences between the processes of local and national policy-making.

In every community in which I have visited, worked, or studied, there has been a well-defined, relatively small group of people whose activities, related to policy-making, constitute a social power structure. A few men, community by community, are recognized as leaders—top leaders, as the Community Chest and Chamber of Commerce secretaries call them—and around them cluster other men who have the ability to move, in coordinated ways, still other men to "get things done" or, negatively, to stop things from getting done. The whole pattern of power in action is a fan-out affair.

A small group of men in any particular community become known as top leaders, policy makers, opinion leaders, or decision makers. As a top-drawer circuit of influential persons, they most often represent the largest local industries, banks, law firms, commercial houses, and newspapers. A fringe group of ranking politicians, educators, clergymen, and occasionally one or two labor leaders may be called upon to sit in council with the nuclear group when a community-wide project or issue is up for policy discussion.

Rarely, if ever, would any major project in a community get underway and pass to successful conclusion without at least informal sanction of a majority of the policy makers. This does not mean to say that every member of an informal policy group must sit in discussions related to every project concocted in a community. Nor can the policy-making structure of a community be described as a single pyramid of power. There are revolving committee clusterings of leaders who link with other committee clusterings on matters of major policy concern, and representatives of these various groups help to hammer out a line of action for the community in general. The informal policy-making structure is self-appointed, and unanimity is the rule in successful undertakings.

Final decisions of a policy-making group may take into account many opinions, professional and otherwise, before a project is publicly launched. Studies are made, outside experts consulted, costs computed, civic committees formed, luncheon associations tuned up, newspapermen alerted, and church organizations activated. One or several of the names of community prime movers may appear in the early publicity of a major undertaking. In the city of New York, in the early 1950's, one might have seen in print, along with others, such names as Winthrop Aldrich, Clarence Francis, John McCloy, Sidney Weinberg, Lucius Clay, David Sarnoff, or Thomas Watson, Jr.; in Detroit, Henry Ford II, Harlow Curtice, James B. Webber, Jr., or Walter Reuther; in Chicago, Laird Bell, Clarence Randall, Meyer Kestnbaum, John McCaffrey, or Edward E. Brown; in San Francisco, Charles R. Blyth, J. D. Zellerbach, or W. W. Crocker. The men named in but four of the major cities of the country are cited merely to illustrate concretely the type of men who are considered top leaders in the communities in which they live and work. They are, each after his fashion, a part of the power structure of the cities mentioned. Their counterparts, as top leaders, may be found in any city across the nation.

If some of the men at the community level of power patterns are oriented to national affairs, are these men in touch with similar men in other key cities and do they provide the nation with a pattern of policy-making and decision-making that is comparable to that found at the local level? This was a basic question guiding the present research. Other questions rode in the train of this one, and a number of them were turned into assumptions and assertions to provide a backdrop, guide, or frame of reference for the study.

What I am about to say could possibly be summed up by saying that at the beginning of this work I assumed that the most influential men in national policy-making would be found residing in the larger cities, manning the larger corporate enterprises, and using their influence to get the government to move according to their interests. Such a simple assertion would not be nearly precise enough, however, to satisfy the requirements of science, and a more orderly array of statements was developed.[2] The assertions made at the beginning of the study (and subject to modification as this writing progresses) were as follows:

1. At the national level of affairs, as in a local community, there is a power structure inside and outside government (but not synonymous with government or any other formal organi-

2. I am indebted to the Political Behavior Committee of the Institute for Research in Social Science of the University of North Carolina and to Professor Alexander Heard, in particular, for constructive criticism of the hypotheses in their governmental dimension. The criticisms of political scientists have been helpful to me in many ways during the course of the present study, and while I have remained independent of many of their judgments, I have come to appreciate their concern for the development of political theory. Not being a theorist, I am glad to leave the rigors of the developmental task to them.

zation) acting in relation to policy development. The national power structure can be identified in various ways: (a) While it is not a single pyramid of influence and authority, it is a kind of informal circuit (not circle; not group) of representatives of many of the major influence groups. (b) It is representative of geographic segments of the economy, and different formally organized groups. (c) While disagreements may occur in relation to specific issues, the basic values and aspirations of dominant interests, traceable most often to the larger corporate interests, will bring about a workable unity within the total power structure.

2. Dominant cities containing concentrations of major industries are anchor points of power and furnish a large proportion of the individuals who may be identified in the national power structure. The national power structure is held together, city by city, in large measure by a network of informal communications.

3. Decisive actions are brought to bear in national policy formulation and power execution by men who are identified with dominant urban centers.

4. National policy-making associations reflect in their formal decisions matters that have been agreed upon, informally, by men of decision in dominant urban centers.

5. Because of its unique authority, government is of special concern to the rest of the power structure, and segments of the informal structure, tacitly supported by the whole structure, act through and upon government in relation to specific policies.

6. A large portion of the total power structure is not seen in operation because of its diffuse and informal characteristics.

After settling on these assumptions, the next step was to come to terms on how to examine them—how to go about seeing people who could give answers to the questions raised by such assertions. At moments, after I had determined to make the study, I was overwhelmed with the size of the task. John McCloy of the Chase Manhattan Bank, as a man who is used to thinking in rather large terms and figures, after I had asked whether one could think of the nation as a community, put the matter this way, "Yes, I think you may be partly right." Then as I prepared to leave the interview in which we had discussed this idea at some length, he thought a moment and added, "It's something like a community, but it's sure a mighty big one!"

On the other hand, even a metropolitan community is a big area for study, if one thinks of it as a whole; but if one isolates the factors he wishes to study, the concept of community is manageable enough. In the present case, it was not contemplated that everything related to the country as a complete, operating social system would be studied, but rather the intention was to isolate and study the ideas of and about those persons who might be considered policy makers and opinion leaders at the top level of national policy development. Thus some limit of coverage was placed upon the study.

I have long admired the anthropologists for their persistent efforts to see social phenomena as cultural wholes. As they study a culture, they may observe parts, yet their cultural frame of reference holds them to the task of integrating partial findings to larger social wholes. I would say that this study, following the suggested method of the anthropologists, has been related to the desire to see the whole of policy-making groups. The nation, however, is too large a social unit to grasp as a cultural whole within the limits of this study. I do believe, on the other hand, that large segments of the nation's power structure can be separated for special analysis that will reveal and help us to understand American society as a total, functioning social system.

Obviously our country is a national and coordinated system of activities. As a system it produces goods and services for vast numbers of people and defends itself from external attack and from internal disintegration. Through its institutions it has a democratic value system. As a whole it can be identified and distinguished from a larger community of national states. To effect its collective purposes the exercise of power is imperative.

Since these correlated elements of the system of national activities must be coordinated and guided by men, some men must be able to conceive of and see the system, to a considerable extent, as a whole. Systems of law, legislation, execution, and adjudication are some of the primary means developed to minimize the conflict of diversity and to achieve coordinated unity, but all know that the institutions erected to achieve legal cohesiveness are only a part of the whole system of the channeling of power. When one thinks of the nation as a power system, there is always the feeling present that there are groups of men who operate behind the scenes of the governmental bodies to achieve their ends—ends that may be in the interest of the nation, but ends that are not always clearly stated or universally understood.

Decades of muckraking, of laying the blame for economic and social troubles at the doorsills of Wall Street or wealthy families, and of name-calling the politicians have convinced many that the exercise of power carries within itself an inherent evil. It becomes easy to project frustrations on a vaguely imagined complex of malevolent forces "out there somewhere" that are bent on a course of individual and national injustices. We have all read treatises to this effect and, in some degree, believed them. We believe them partly because they seem to make sense and partly because they help to make comprehensible a vast whole. They simplify our thinking.

If Wall Street is to blame for our troubles and if one or two men on Wall Street can be identified as leaders there, then the answer to all our problems seems simple. These are real villains. But such scapegoat reasoning, of course, leaves a void. We know that the answer is too simple. Yet, as often as not, we let the whole matter go at that. We are busy with many things, and so long as the villains on Wall Street do not invade our homes, we will live and let live. We are, however, left with many unsatisfied questions.

My own feeling has been that it is possible to try to get answers to some of the questions of power, and I have felt that the best possible way to begin was to ask questions of those who are presumed to have power. I also have determined to try to lay aside some of my preconceived notions as to the evil of power by saying to myself that power is exercised as a vital function of the social system, that it is necessary— not a necessary evil, but just plain necessary. Given this definition, where then does one begin to look for men who might help with the answers to questions about power manipulations?

The first place to look for answers, it occurred to me, was among men who have habitually thought of the nation as a whole. The executive secretaries of some of the national associations might be considered such persons. Like secretaries of Chambers of Commerce and Community Chest directors in local communities who see their cities in larger perspective than the average citizen, the national association secretaries should be able to see the country more as a whole than many. It was assumed also, and I now think rightly, that the national association secretaries, like local secretaries in a more limited sphere, would have a working knowledge of some of the most influential leaders at the national level.

The first step taken in field study was to visit some of the association secretaries and ask them to help in judging the relative influence of other national associations; from the vantage point of some of the more powerful national groupings I moved as quickly as possible to interviews with those persons considered to be powerful and influential leaders.[3] The whole process of study also simultaneously took many other factors into account, but the first major step was to consult manage-

3. For other methodological steps, see Introduction.

ment personnel of the national organizations. I began by calling upon secretaries in the U.S. Chamber of Commerce, the American Medical Association, the American Bankers Association, the American Farm Bureau, the American Meat Institute, the Congress of Industrial Organizations, the National Association of Manufacturers, and the National Federation of Business and Professional Women's Clubs. I moved from these groups and their secretaries to others.

As a matter of fact, in the execution of the study I finally took into account several areas of investigation. Besides the materials in Part One of this writing related to community and associations—materials that are the building blocks of the action patterns of national policy-making groups—it soon became apparent that study of state and industrial groupings would be needed, as in Part Two, in order to come to the conclusions of Part Three. This then is the logical structure of the chapters to follow.

2 ASSOCIATIONS, LEADERS, AND PROFESSIONALS

HAVING determined to ask national associations to nominate their choices of candidates for a nucleus of policy makers and decision makers, I then had to weed out those organizations that might waste time, so my next step was that of arbitrarily eliminating a great mass of names from a tentative list of 1,093 organizations. It seemed quite possible that one could ask help of the top influential organizations of the nation, as I had previously asked help of influential community organizations in local studies, to lead to a large number of top power leaders in the country, whereas minor associations might be of little help.

With the aid of four other persons who had a working knowledge of national organizations, the list was pared to 106.

106 NATIONAL ORGANIZATIONS POTENTIALLY INFLUENTIAL IN
NATIONAL POLICY DEVELOPMENT, 1953 *

Advertising Federation of America
Aeronautical Chamber of Commerce of America
Amateur Athletic Union of U.S.
Amer. Agricultural Editor's Assoc.
Amer. Arbitration Assoc.

Amer. Assoc. Advancement of Science
Amer. Assoc. Advertising Agencies
Amer. Assoc. Med. Social Workers

* Numbers in parentheses indicate the rank order of the top 20 organizations, compiled from answers to a questionnaire sent to the secretaries of these 106 associations.

Amer. Assoc. Social Workers
Amer. Assoc. Univ. Professors
Amer. Assoc. Univ. Women
Amer. Bankers Assoc. (11)
Amer. Dental Assoc.
Amer. Farm Bureau Federation (7)
Amer. Federation of Labor (2) †
Amer. Federation of Teachers
Amer. Forestry Assoc.
Amer. Gas Assoc.
Amer. Hotel Assoc.
Amer. Inst. Accountants
Amer. Inst. Planners
Amer. Jewish Congress
Amer. Legion (3)
Amer. Meat Inst.
Amer. Med. Assoc. (4)
Amer. Nat. Red Cross
Amer. Nat. Retail Jewelers' Assoc.
Amer. Paper & Pulp Assoc.
Amer. Petroleum Inst.
Amer. Public Welfare Assoc.
Amer. Retail Federation
Amer. Trucking Assoc.
Amer. Veterans' Committee
Amer. Veterinary Med. Assoc.
Assoc. Junior Leagues of America
Automobile Mfrs. Assoc.
Brotherhood of Railroad Trainmen (20)
Carnegie Endowment Internat. Peace
Chamber of Commerce, U.S.A. (1)
Civitan International
Clothing Mfg. Assoc. of U.S.A.
Community Chests & Councils, Inc.
Congress Industrial Organizations (5)
Council of State Governments (15)
Federal Bar Assoc. (17)

Ford Foundation
Foreign Policy Assoc.
General Education Board
Grocery Mfrs. of America
Investment Bankers' Assoc. of America
Kiwanis International
Knights of Columbus
League for Industrial Democracy
Limited Price Variety Store
Lions International
Motion Picture Assoc. of America
Nat. Aeronautic Assoc.
Nat. Assoc. Advancement Colored People (13)
Nat. Assoc. Amer. Railroads
Nat. Assoc. Broadcasters
Nat. Assoc. Chain Drug Stores
Nat. Assoc. Cotton Mfrs.
Nat. Assoc. Food Chains
Nat. Assoc. Insurance Agents
Nat. Assoc. Insurance Brokers
Nat. Assoc. Manufacturers (6)
National Assn. Mutual Insurance
Nat. Assoc. Mutual Savings Banks
National Assn. Real Estate Boards
National Assn. Retail Druggists
National Assn. Retail Grocers
National Assn. State Univ.
National Assn. Wool Mfrs.
National Better Business Bureau
National Canners' Assn.
National Coal Assn.
Nat. Congress Parents, Teachers (16)
National Consumers' League
National Council of Churches of Christ in the U.S.A. (8)
National Dairy Council
National Education Assn. (9)
National Federation of Business and Professional Women's Clubs
National Grange (10)

† Not yet merged with C.I.O.

Nat. League of Women Voters (14)
National Livestock & Meat Board
National Municipal League
National Recreation Assn.
National Research Council
National Restaurant Assn.
National Retail Credit Assn.
National Retail Dry Goods Assn.
Nat. Retail Furn. Assoc.
National Retail Hardware Assn.
National Safety Council, Inc.
Nat. Shoe Mfrs. Assoc.

National Small Bus. Men's Assn.
National Urban League
National Y.M.C.A.
National Y.W.C.A.
Optimist International
Portland Cement Assn.
Rotary International
U.S. Conference of Mayors (18)
U.S. Junior Chamber Commerce (19)
U.S. Wholesale Gro. Assn.
Veterans of Foreign Wars, U.S.A. (12)

I am not sure at the date of this writing, 1958, how much significance the rank order, obtained from a tally of the number of votes each association as a power organization received from all others for a place in the top twenty national policy-making bodies, has. At the time of the poll in 1953, for example, the American Medical Association had been recently joined by many other national associations in its fight to keep the Truman program of extended medical insurances from becoming law. I have heard little of the American Medical Association since, and in general the doctors are individually and collectively not considered a power-laden group—nor do they want to be.

The rating of organizations in some kind of power status scale was, however, a research necessity in order that a manageable number of organizations could be approached as nominators of top national leaders, and while I believe that time might change the rank order of one or another of the organizations listed, I also believe that the top twenty associations are consistently high status organizations in American civic life. The names of national leaders they provided to this study have stood several rigorous tests of analysis quite well.

The associations listed in the poll represented a broad cross-section of organized national life, including women's organizations, veterans', civic, minority, and fraternal groups, and professional, welfare, youth, education, religious, and business associations.

Other organizations presumed to have considerable influence, but less than the twenty listed, are the following: National Association of American Railroads, National Association of Real Estate Boards, National Better Business Bureau, Rotary International, Automobile Manufacturer's Association, Foreign Policy Association, American Petroleum Institute, and the American Jewish Congress. Organizations that did not rate in the top brackets of power prestige were mainly fraternal, civic, commercial, and professional in character.

The 106 associations polled were asked to nominate the names of influential organizations that we might have overlooked and to nominate the names of persons known to them who might be considered top policy makers at the national level.

Several association names were added to the list by this process, and these were also polled, but this polling did not basically change the ratings of the top associations as given above. The names of persons given in response to the question of nominating top national leaders provided a basic list of leaders, nearly 500, to whom a questionnaire was eventually addressed and with whom I had a sample of interviews designed to relate the activities of individual leaders to other leaders, and leader groups, in turn, to the development of public policy.

It must be said, for emphasis, that the names identified on the list to follow were those of persons nominated by association leaders in the *first* poll of the study. In subsequent polls many of the names listed were eliminated by those who ranked or rated them. As the study progressed, other names were added to the primary list. The first list thus represented only a crude array of nominations. Nevertheless, a core of names contained on the first listing continued to be nominated year after year and it was from this group that study tests of leadership interaction were finally made.

The first list of names was as follows:

NAMES AND IDENTIFICATIONS OF PERSONS NOMINATED IN FIRST POLL BY NATIONAL ASSOCIATION LEADERS AS TOP NATIONAL LEADERS, 1953

Name	Brief Identification
Chris Abbott	Rancher
C. E. Adams	Harborside Warehouse & Terminal
Charles Francis Adams	Raytheon Mfg. Co.
J. B. Adams, Jr.	Nat. Bank of Commerce, Dallas
Horace M. Albright	U.S. Potash Co.
Mrs. DeLeslie Allen	Junior League volunteer
William M. Allen	Boeing Airplane Co.
Stanley C. Allyn *	Nat. Cash Register Co.
Jacob M. Arvey	Arvey, Hodes & Mantyband
Frank Avery	Amer. Farm Bureau
Edith M. Baker	U.S. Children's Bureau
Melvin H. Baker	National Gypsum Co.
William R. Baker, Jr.	Benton and Bowles, Inc.
Roger Baldwin	Amer. Civil Liberties Union
Thomas A. Ballintine	Louisville Yellow Cab Taxi Co.
Frank Bane	Council of State Governments
Bernard M. Baruch *	Financier
Louis H. Bauer	Amer. Med. Assoc.
Arthur R. Baxter	Civic volunteer
Thomas H. Beacom	First Nat. Bank, Chicago
Stephen D. Bechtel *	Bechtel Corp.
Daniel W. Bell	Amer. Security & Trust Co., Washington
Laird Bell *	Bell, Boyd, Marshall & Lloyd
Edgar Bellis	Civic volunteer
Dana Bennett	Farm Film Foundation
Harriet M. Bertlett	Social worker
Howard Landis Bevis	Nat. Comm. Development Scientists and Engineers
Allen L. Billingsley	Fuller, Smith & Ross, Inc.
Barry Bingham	*Louisville Courier-Journal*

* Named again in first exploratory cross-country research tour as top national policy leader, and name was included on a list used as a point of reference in interviews. See pp. 30-31, 57-59.

Name	*Brief Identification*
James B. Black *	Pacific Gas and Electric Co.
Eugene C. Blake	Nat. Council Churches Christ, U.S.A.
Sarah Gibson Blanding	Vassar College
Jacob Blaustein	Pan-Am. Petroleum & Transport Co.
Joseph L. Block	Inland Steel Co.
Charles R. Blyth *	Blyth & Co. Inc.
Erwin W. Boehmler	George Washington Univ.
Harold Boeschenstein *	Owens-Corning Fiberglas Corp.
Julian B. Bondurant	Armored Motor Service Co. Inc.
Louis J. Borinstein	A. Borinstein & Co.
Richard L. Bowditch	Sprague Steamship Co.
Lloyd D. Brace	First Nat. Bank of Boston
Albert Bradley	General Motors Corp.
Mrs. Hannah Brady	Civic volunteer
Otto William Brandhorst	Dentist
T. E. Braniff	Braniff Co.
Ernest R. Breech *	Ford Motor Co.
W. Harold Brenton	Brenton Bros., Inc.
A. W. Brickman	Illinois Meat Co.
Detlev W. Bronk	Rockefeller Inst. Med. Research
Thomas D'Arcy Brophy	Kenyon & Eckhardt, Inc.
Bruce K. Brown	Petroleum Chemicals, Inc.
Edward E. Brown *	First Nat. Bank of Chicago
Leo Brown	Amer. Med. Assoc.
Prentiss M. Brown	Detroit Edison Co.
Mrs. Rollin Brown	Civic volunteer
Charles A. Bruce	E. L. Bruce Co.
Howard Bruce	Maryland Shipbuilding and Drydock Co.
Ralph Budd *	Colorado & Southern Railway
Harry A. Bullis *	General Mills
Ralph J. Bunche *	United Nations official
W. Randolph Burgess	Nat. City Bank of New York
Eveline M. Burns	N.Y. School of Social Work
August A. Busch, Jr.	Anheuser-Busch, Inc.
Vannevar Bush *	Mass. Inst. Technology
Edward H. Butler	*Buffalo Evening News*
Karl D. Butler	AVCO Mfg. Corp.
Harry F. Byrd	U.S. Senator from Virginia
Mrs. Evelyn S. Byron	Civic volunteer
William J. Cabannis	Southern Cement Co.
Charles C. Cabot	Herrick, Smith, Donald, Farley & Ketchum

Name	Brief Identification
George Cameron	Civic volunteer
L. C. Campbell	Eastern Gas & Fuel Associates
Herbert J. Case	City Bank Farmers Trust Co.
William J. Casey	Maryland Trust Co., Baltimore
Bertram J. Chan	Kupenheimer Clothing Co.
Norman Chandler *	*Los Angeles Times*
Walter Chandler	Chandler, Morgan, Manire & Chandler
Colby M. Chester	General Foods Corp.
J. Hamilton Cheston	Philadelphia Saving Fund Society
Edwin M. Clark	Southwestern Bell Telephone Co.
Evans Clark	*New York Times*
Mrs. James Lee Clark	Junior League volunteer
Lucius Clay *	Continental Can Co.
William L. Clayton *	Anderson, Clayton & Co.
Francis C. Cocke	First Nat. Exchange Bank of Roanoke
L. L. Colbert *	Chrysler Corp.
John S. Coleman *	Burroughs Corp.
John L. Collyer *	B. F. Goodrich Co.
Hugh M. Comer	Comer-Avondale Mills
Arthur H. Compton	Washington University
Karl T. Compton	Mass. Inst. Technology
James B. Conant *	Ex-U.S. Ambassador
Fairfax M. Cone	Foote, Cone & Belding
(George Coppers)†	(Nat. Biscuit Co.)
S. A. Cosgrove	Margaret Hague Memorial Hospital
John Cowles *	*The Minneapolis Star & Tribune*
Charles R. Cox *	Kennecott Copper Corp.
Cleo F. Craig *	Amer. Tel. & Tel.
David Crawford	Pullman Co.
Frederick C. Crawford *	Thompson Products, Inc.
W. W. Crocker	Crocker Nat. Bank
Nelson H. Cruikshank	AFL-CIO economist
E. H. Crump	E. H. Crump & Co.
Hugh Roy Cullen	Texas oil
John P. Cunningham	Cunningham & Walsh, Inc.
Harlow H. Curtice *	General Motors Corp.
Robert Cutler *	Old Colony Trust Co.
Samuel T. Dana	Univ. of Michigan
Donald K. David *	Ford Foundation
Chester C. Davis	Ford Foundation
E. Asbury Davis	U.S. Fidelity & Guaranty Co.

† Name did not appear on list culled from associations but was later suggested in first cross-country research tour. See pp. 57-59.

Name	Brief Identification
Waters S. Davis, Jr.	Nat. Assoc. Soil Conservation Districts
Donald C. Dayton	The Dayton Co.
Cecil B. de Mille	Paramount Studios
Frank R. Denton *	Mellon Nat. Bank & Trust Co.
Richard R. Deupree *	Procter & Gamble Co.
Joseph Devero	N.Y. Life Insurance Co.
Thomas E. Dewey	Dewey, Ballantine, Bushby, Palmer & Wood
Charles P. Dickey *	J. P. Morgan & Co.
Charles H. Diefendorf	The Marine Trust Co. of Western N.Y.
Howard Doane	Doane Agricultural Service
Joseph M. Dodge *	The Detroit Bank
Mrs. Ruth Dodge	Civic volunteer
Dain J. Domich	U.S. Chamber of Commerce
Benjamin R. Donaldson	Ford Motor Co.
Herman L. Donavan	Univ. of Kentucky
James H. Doolittle *	Shell Oil Co.
James H. Douglas	Gardner, Carton & Douglas
Lewis W. Douglas *	Mutual Life
Thomas Dowling	*Queen's Work*
Mrs. Jacob Eckel	Civic volunteer
Dwight D. Eisenhower	President of U.S.
Milton S. Eisenhower *	Penn. State College
Leroy M. Ennis	Dentist
D. C. Everest	Marathon Corp.
Benjamin F. Fairless *	U.S. Steel Corp.
Fedele F. Fauri	Univ. of Michigan Sch. of Social Work
J. Ralph Fenstemaker	Hugh J. Baker & Co.
Marshall Field, Jr.	Marshall Field & Co.
Charles T. Fisher, Jr.	Nat. Bank of Detroit
Ralph E. Flanders	U.S. Senator from Vermont
Henry Fleisher	CIO
Robert V. Fleming	Riggs Nat. Bank
Lamar Fleming, Jr.	Anderson, Clayton & Co.
Fred F. Florence *	Republic Nat. Bank of Dallas
R. G. Follis	Standard Oil Co. of Calif.
Mrs. Robert Foote	Junior League volunteer
Henry Ford II *	Ford Motor Co.
Kirk Fox	Civic volunteer
Clarence Francis *	General Foods Corp.
James Francis	Pocahontas Coal Co.

Name	*Brief Identification*
Walter Frank	Civic volunteer
John M. Franklin *	U.S. Lines Co.
Y. Frank Freeman	Paramount Studios
Joseph R. Frey	Lake Shore Nat. Bank
Rudolph Friedrich	Dentist
Albert Fritz	Civic volunteer
Franklin C. Fry	United Lutheran Church
Frederic R. Gamble	Civic volunteer
Charles S. Garland	Alexander Brown & Sons
Walter Gelhorn	Columbia Univ.
Elbert W. Gibbs	Druggist
Charles Gilson	Druggist
William B. Gladney	Fidelity Nat. Bank of Baton Rouge
A. J. Gock	Bank of America
Fred Goerlitz	Chicago Retail Merchants Assoc.
Dora Goldstine	Univ. of Chicago
Evarts Graham	Washington Univ. Sch. of Medicine
Gordon Gray	Office of Defense Mobilization
Robert M. Gray	Esso Standard Oil Co.
W. B. Greeley	West Coast Lumberman's Assoc.
Crawford H. Greenewalt *	E. I. duPont de Nemours & Co.
Albert M. Greenfield	Civic volunteer
Alan Gregg	Rockefeller Foundation
Merrill Griswold	Investors Trust
Fred G. Gurley *	Sante Fe Railroad
Reuben G. Gustavson	Univ. of Nebraska
Charles C. Haffner, Jr.	R. R. Donnelley & Sons, Co.
Helen Hall	Henry Street Settlement, New York City
Virgil M. Hancher	State Univ. of Iowa
John Hancock *	Lehman Brothers
John W. Hanes *	Olin Mathieson Chemical Corp.
Marion Harper, Jr.	McCann Erickson, Inc.
Lewis G. Harriman	Manufacturers and Traders Trust Co.
James P. Hart	Univ. of Texas
Franklyn R. Hawkins	Civic volunteer
Randolph S. Hecht	International House, New Orleans
H. J. Heinz II *	H. J. Heinz Co.
W. L. Hemmingway	Mercantile Trust Co.
Mary L. Hemmy	Univ. of Illinois
Leo Henebry	Jeweler
Christian A. Herter	Under Sec. of State
Maynard K. Hine	Indiana Univ.
Mrs. Oveta Culp Hobby	*Houston Post*

Name	Brief Identification
R. L. Hodkley	Davidson Chemical Corp.
Paul G. Hoffman *	Hoffman Specialty Mfg. Co.
James P. Hollers	Civic volunteer
Eugene Holman *	Standard Oil Co. (N.J.)
Frank E. Holman *	Holman, Mickelwait, Black & Perkins
John Holmes	Swift & Co.
George V. Holton	Socony-Mobil Oil Co.
Charles R. Hook *	Armco Steel Corp.
Herbert Hoover, Sr. *	Ex-President of U.S.
(Herbert Hoover, Jr.) †	(Under Sec. of State)
H. M. Horner	United Aircraft Corp.
Mrs. Douglas Horton	Civic volunteer
Arthur A. Houghton, Jr.	Corning Glass Works
Charles Howard	Howard Terminal
H. E. Humphreys, Jr.	U.S. Rubber Co.
H. L. Hunt	Texas oil
Ernest Hyster	Civic volunteer
R. L. Ireland	Pittsburgh-Consolidation Coal Co.
Don P. Johnson	Amer. Forestry Assoc.
Paul C. Johnson	*Prairie Farmer*
Eric Johnston *	Motion Picture Assoc.
Jesse H. Jones	Texas lumberman, banker
Albert N. Jorgensen	Univ. of Conn.
Ernest C. Kanzler	Universal C.I.T. Credit Corp.
A. P. Kaufman	Urban Redevelopment
Francis V. Keesling	Civic volunteer
L. Russell Kelce	Sinclair Coal Co.
Michael T. Kelleher	Marsh & McLennan
K. T. Keller *	Chrysler Corp.
Fred I. Kent	Bankers Trust Co.
Meyer Kestnbaum *	Hart Schaffner & Marx
Lawrence A. Kimpton	Univ. of Chicago
Oscar Kind, Jr.	S. Kind & Sons
J. H. Kindelberger	North Amer. Aviation, Inc.
Robert Kleberg	Texas rancher
John W. Klein	Amer. Med. Assoc.
Allen V. Kline	Amer. Farm Bureau Assoc.
Wathan R. Knabelkamp	Bernheim Distilling Co.
Joseph R. Knowland	*Oakland Tribune*
William F. Knowland	U.S. Senator from California
James Knowlson	Stewart-Warner Corp.
Seymour H. Knox	Council of Univ. of Buffalo
Walter J. Kohler, Jr.	The Vollrath Co.
Daniel E. Koshland	Levi Strauss & Co.

Name	*Brief Identification*
J. F. Krey	Krey Packing Co.
George A. Kuhn	Klein & Kuhn
William Fulton Kurtz	Penn. Co. for Banking & Trusts
Robert T. Lansdale	N.Y. State Dept. of Social Welfare
Roger D. Lapham	Hawaiian S. S. Co.
Sigurd S. Larmon	Young & Rubicam, Inc.
Walter P. Larson	Nat. Assoc. Mutual Savings Banks
Jacob M. Lashly	Lashly, Lashly & Miller
John H. Lathrop	Unitarian leader
J. L. Latimer	Magnolia Co.
Frank J. Lausche	Governor of Ohio
W. S. Lawo, Jr.	Pepsi Cola Metro. Bottling Co., Jersey City
David Lawrence	*U.S. News & World Report*
Fred Lazarus, Jr.*	F. & R. Lazarus Co.
Tom A. Leadley	*The Nebraska Farmer*
Mrs. John G. Lee	League of Women Voters volunteer
Mrs. Robert F. Leonard	League of Women Voters volunteer
William Levett	Owens Glass
Fulton Lewis, Jr.	News commentator
John L. Lewis*	UMW
Eli Lilly	Eli Lilly & Co.
James A. Linen*	*Time*
Henry G. Little	Campbell Ewald Co.
James P. Lockhead	Amer. Trust Co.
Henry Cabot Lodge	U.S. Representative to UN
W. I. Longsworth	Lilly Varnish Co.
Mrs. Oswald Bates Lord	UN
George H. Love*	Pittsburgh-Consolidation Coal Co.
Alan V. Lowenstein	Ricker, Emery & Danzig
Henry Luce*	*Time* Inc.
Earle Ludgin	Earle Ludgin & Co.
Alfred J. Lundberg	Key System Transit Lines
Franklin J. Lunding	Jewel Tea Co.
Mrs. Moses H. Lurie	League of Women Voters volunteer
Charles J. Lynn	Eli Lilly & Co.
A. E. Lyon	Railway Labor Executives Assoc.
Leverett Lyon	Assoc. of Commerce and Industry
Harry Lyons	Med. College of Virginia
J. Wesley McAfee	Union Pacific Co. of Mo.
Mrs. Thomas F. McAllister	Civic volunteer
R. E. McArdle	U.S. Dept. of Agriculture
Hughston M. McBain*	Marshall Field & Co.
Thomas B. McCabe*	Scott Paper Co.

Name	*Brief Identification*
John L. McCaffery*	International Harvester
Harold C. McClellan	Old Colony Paint & Chemical Co.
John McCloy*	Chase Manhattan Bank
L. F. McCollum*	Continental Oil Co.
Paul McCord	Industrial realtor
E. J. McCormick	Amer. Med. Assoc.
Donald McDonald	Taxpayers Federation of Mass.
W. A. McDonnell	First Nat. Bank, St. Louis
Powell B. McHaney	General Amer. Life Insurance Co.
Keith S. McHugh	N.Y. Telephone Co.
James Francis McIntyre	Archbishop of Los Angeles
Paul B. McKee	Pacific Power & Light Co.
Carey McWilliams	*The Nation*
William L. Marcy	Statler Hotels
William C. Martin	Methodist Bishop
George Mason	Nash-Kelvinator Corp.
Phillip R. Mather	Nat. Assoc. for Social Hygiene
Oscar G. Mayer	Oscar Mayer & Co.
George Meany*	AFL
Joseph T. Meek	Ill. Federation of Retail Assoc.
Richard K. Mellon*	Mellon Nat. Bank & Trust Co.
Eugene Meyer*	*Washington Post*
Mrs. Eugene Meyer	*Washington Post*
Henry H. Meyer	H. H. Meyer Packing Co.
Justin Miller	McClean, Salisbury, Petty & McClean
R. L. Minkler	General Petroleum Corp.
Broadus Mitchell	Rutgers Univ.
Don G. Mitchell	Sylvania Electric Products
George G. Montgomery*	Castle & Cooke, Ltd.
Ben Moreell*	Jones & Laughlin Steel
James L. Morrill	Univ. of Minnesota
deLesseps S. Morrison	Mayor of New Orleans
Frank Moudry	Druggist
Harvey S. Mudd	Mining
W. C. Mullendore*	Southern Calif. Edison Co.
Clint W. Murchison*	Texas oil
Fred Murray	U. S. Steel Corp.
William I. Myers	N.Y. State College of Agriculture
Albert J. Nesbitt	John J. Nesbitt, Inc.
George A. Newbury	Manufacturers & Trade Trust Co.
Thomas S. Nichols	Olin Mathieson Chemical Corp.
Aksel Nielsen	Title Guaranty Co.
Cornelius C. Noble	Noble's Independent Meat Co.
Ray A. Olpin	Univ. of Utah

Name	*Brief Identification*
Edmund Orgill	Orgill Brothers & Co.
Alex F. Osborn	Batten, Barton, Durstine & Osborn, Inc.
Charles A. Owen	Imperial Coal Corp.
H. Bruce Palmer	Mutual Benefit Life Insurance Co.
James L. Palmer	Marshall Field & Co.
Graham Patterson	*Farm Journal*
T. C. Patterson	Amer. Farm Bureau
W. A. Patterson*	United Air Lines
James Patton	Nat. Farmers Union
Mundy I. Peale	Republic Aviation Corp.
Westbrook Pegler	Columnist
T. S. Petersen*	Standard Oil Co. of Calif.
Neil Petree	Barker Brothers Corp.
Holman T. Pettibone	Chicago Title & Trust Co.
Howard J. Pew	Sun Oil Co.
J. A. Phillips	Amer. Inst. of Accountants
Percy T. Phillips	Dentist
Michael Phipps	Civic volunteer
Paul Pigott	Kenworth Motor Truck Co.
Phil Pillsbury	Pillsbury Mills
Henning W. Prentice, Jr.	Armstrong Cork Co.
Gwilym A. Price*	Westinghouse Electric Corp.
Theodore K. Quinn	Druggist
Clarence B. Randall*	Inland Steel Co.
R. A. Rath	The Rath Packing Co.
Philip D. Reed*	General Electric Co.
Everett D. Reese	The Park Nat. Bank of Newark
Stanley Resor*	J. Walter Thompson Co.
Walter P. Reuther*	UAW-CIO
David Reynolds	Reynolds Metal Co.
Elizabeth P. Rice	Harvard Sch. of Public Health
E. A. Roberts	Fidelity Mutual Life Insurance Co.
Owen J. Roberts	Montgomery, McCracken, Walker & Rhoads
W. A. Roberts	Allis Chalmers Mfg. Co.
Reuben B. Robertson, Jr.	Champion Paper & Fibre Co.
(Nelson Rockefeller)†	(Rockefeller Center, Inc.)
Eleanor Roosevelt	Columnist
Elmo Roper	Public opinion analyst
Arthur G. Rotch	Permanent Charity Fund
Mrs. Oscar M. Ruebhausen	League of Women Voters volunteer
William J. Rushton	Protective Life Insurance Co.
Donald J. Russell*	Southern Pacific Railroad Co.

Name	*Brief Identification*
Mrs. Henry Potter Russell	Civic volunteer
Edward L. Ryerson*	Inland Steel Co.
Leverett Saltonstall	U.S. Senator from Massachusetts
R. E. Salvati	Island Creek Coal Co.
Paul D. Sanders	*The Southern Planter*
David Sarnoff*	Radio Corp. of America
Arnold A. Schiffman	Schiffman Jewelers
Leo J. Schoeny	Dentist
Charles I. Schottland	U.S. Dept. of Health, Education & Welfare
Robert W. Selig	Fox Inter-Mountain Theatres, Inc.
Louis B. Seltzer	*Cleveland Press*
Gideon D. Seymour	*Minneapolis Star & Tribune*
Carrol M. Shanks*	Prudential Insurance Co. of America
Mrs. Thelma Shaw	Civic volunteer
James E. Shelton	Security First Nat. Bank of Los Angeles
Ethan A. H. Shepley	Washington Univ.
Henry Knox Sherrill*	Presiding Bishop of Massachusetts
Boris Shishkin	AFL
Allan Shivers	Governor of Texas
George N. Shuster	Hunter College
George A. Sloan	U.S. Steel Corp.
C. R. Smith*	Amer. Air Lines
Hermon Dunlap Smith	Marsh & McLennan
Norman Smith	Merrill, Lynch, Pearce, Fenner & Smith
George E. Sokolsky	Columnist
Carl Spaatz*	*Newsweek*
Frank E. Spain	Civic volunteer
Joseph P. Spang, Jr.*	Gillette Co.
Francis Joseph Spellman*	Archbishop of New York
Kenneth A. Spencer	Spencer Chemical Co.
Herman Steinkraus*	Bridgeport Brass
Mrs. Waldo E. Stephens	League of Women Voters volunteer
Mervyn H. Sterne	Sterne, Ager & Leach
Joseph Stetler	Amer. Med. Assoc.
Adlai Stevenson*	Stevenson, Rifkind & Wirtz
Wade Stevenson	Eastman Machine Co.
Irvin Stewart	Univ. of W. Va.
John Stewart	Quaker Oats Co.
W. Paul Stillman	Nat. State Bank, Newark
Roger W. Straus	Amer. Smelting & Refining Co.
M. R. Sullivan	Pacific Tel. & Tel. Co.

Name	*Brief Identification*
Arthur Hays Sulzberger*	*New York Times*
Harold H. Swift	Swift & Co.
Gerard Swope	General Electric Co.
Gardiner Symonds	Tenn. Gas Transmission Co.
Jay Taylor	Nat. Live Stock & Meat Board
Reese H. Taylor*	Union Oil Co. of Calif.
Charles Thomas	Monsanto Chemical Co.
Norman Thomas	Socialist
John W. Tramburg	Wisc. State Dept. of Public Welfare
John B. Tripeny	Civic volunteer
Juan T. Trippe*	Pan American World Airways
Harry S. Truman*	Ex-President of U.S.
Solon B. Turman	Lykes Brothers Steamship Co.
Erwin C. Uihlein	Schlitz Brewing Co.
Harold Vagtborg	Southwest Research Inst.
Roy van Bomel	Nat. Dairy Products Corp.
William G. Vollmer	Texas & Pacific Railway Co.
George M. Wallace	Security First Nat. Bank of Los Angeles
Earl Warren	Governor of California
Thomas Watson, Jr.*	IBM Corp.
Charles H. Watts	Beneficial Management Corp.
James B. Webber, Jr.*	The J. L. Hudson Co.
Sinclair Weeks	Secretary of Commerce
Sidney J. Weinberg*	Goldman, Sachs & Co.
Ernest T. Weir*	Nat. Steel Corp.
Robert Welch	James O. Welch Co.
Mrs. Theodore Wendell	Civic volunteer
Henry W. Wendt	Buffalo Forge Co.
Charles L. Wheeler	Pope & Talbot, Inc.
Walter H. Wheeler, Jr.	Pitney-Bowes, Inc.
Mrs. Robert White	Civic volunteer
Frederic Whitman*	The Western Pacific Railroad Co.
George Whitney*	J. P. Morgan Co.
John Hay Whitney*	Financier
Arthur V. Wiebel	Tennessee Coal & Iron Co.
Brayton Wilbur	Wilbur-Ellis Co.
Clyde Williams	Battelle Memorial Inst.
J. D. Williams	Univ. of Miss.
Walter Williams*	Continental, Inc.
Charles E. Wilson*	General Electric Co.
Mrs. Horace E. Wilson	Junior League volunteer
Mrs. J. Thomas Wilson	Junior League volunteer
Robert E. Wilson*	Standard Oil Co. (Ind.)

Name	*Brief Identification*
Mrs. Robert W. Wilson	Civic volunteer
Thomas E. Wilson	Wilson & Co.
Edward Wimmer	Druggist
G. N. Winder	Nat. Live Stock & Meat Board
P. G. Winnett	Bullock's
Mrs. Ellen Winston	N.C. State Board of Public Welfare
John H. Winters	Texas Dept. of Public Welfare
J. Theodore Wolfe	Consolidated Gas, Electric Light & Power Co., Baltimore
R. E. Wood*	Sears Roebuck & Co.
R. W. Woodruff*	Coca Cola Co.
Ben H. Wooten	First Nat. Bank, Dallas
Henry M. Wriston*	Brown Univ.
Howard I. Young	Amer. Zinc, Lead & Smelting Co.
James W. Young	J. Walter Thompson Co.
Robert Young	N.Y. Central Railroad
Benjamin E. Youngdahl	George Warren Brown Sch. of Social Work
J. D. Zellerbach*	Crown-Zellerbach Paper Co.

This foregoing array of names, then, provided the beginning list of persons presumed to be top national leaders by persons who were in positions enabling them to judge their activities. A great many of the leaders mentioned were businessmen, but among others were teachers, social workers, state governors, lawyers, and club women. In other words, the list was a cross-section of American civic life, and it is not set down here as a list to be construed as the names of those who run the nation. (Someone is always seeking to provide us with a list of names of persons who run the nation, the community, or this or that association. Some of my work concerning community power structures has been construed by some merely to be such an endeavor. I am always interested in limited and specified listings of top leaders in any area of power under study, but the lists are used only as a research device to get data on policy development. Configurations of activities of leaders in policy development must always be described as a process. Individual names in a listing, as such, have little meaning from a social science point of view.) Here it should be said, again, that all names mentioned in this writing are those gathered according to a strict social science method. At any point at which I have described the interrelations of persons acting on policy matters, I have used pseudonyms with an "X" middle initial. The individual choices of men in nominating top leaders at all levels of the study—community, region, state, or nation—will be kept strictly confidential. Only consensus listings are included in the materials discussed. Further, the book is not a muckraking venture, and every precaution has been taken to protect the privacy of opinion and to present the facts of controversial policy considerations in a context of social process involving the activities of many.

As the study began, I was acquainted with few of the names of leaders given to me. As I began interviewing those persons presumed to be leaders, short catch phrases were given to me by some about others. I cannot claim any firm acquaintance with most of the men who were helpful in the study. My contacts with all were necessarily brief, and my study interest was sometimes of minor and passing interest to those interviewed. Some, however, were vitally interested in the subject; most were interested in thinking of the names of leaders; most also had very definite opinions about this or that leader. Most wanted to give me the best picture they could of the policy-making process as they saw it and to identify leaders for me.

As names were given to me by national leaders, I put them on cards with brief notations given to me by others and filed them. The notes taken in the early stages of research provided a way of becoming familiar with various men and a means of observing their actions as they were reported publicly or by their contemporaries. In other words, the notes helped to structure the data. Some of the earliest observations in thumbnail form will be listed here. Some of the notations changed during the course of study, but those listed indicate a beginning way of seeing others through the eyes of others.

Stanley C. Allyn, a valuable outfielder in the big league of business. . . . "Barney" Baruch, not now, but has been very influential . . . Steve Bechtel, a potent force on the West coast, and most lately a big help to the Republican administration as a member of the group that worked on the transcontinental roads project. . . . Laird Bell, a quiet force, and civic leader of impeccable integrity. . . . James B. Black, a hard-hitting utilities man . . . Charles R. Blyth, one of *the* financial men on the West coast, a part of the "Wall Street" of that area. . . . Ernie Breech, the man to watch at Ford . . . Harold Boeschenstein, a power house. . . . Edward E. Brown, a banker who was a big Democrat. . . . Ralph Budd, part of the Chicago scheme of things. . . . Vannevar Bush, a scientist well liked. . . . Lucius Clay, one of the war heroes taken into the canning industry. . . . William Clayton, a cotton broker who made the grade as a national leader under the Democrats, pretty well out of national things now. . . . L. L. Colbert, risen star at Chrysler. . . . John S. Coleman, a part of the Detroit team. . . . James B. Conant, a college president made good. . . . George Coppers, National Biscuit comer. . . . John Cowles, a thinker . . . Cleo F. Craig, the operator at Bell Telephone . . . Frederick C. Crawford, Middlewest power. . . . Harlow H. Curtice, as everyone knows, General Motors . . . R. R. Deupree, Procter and Gamble civic enterpriser at the national level . . . Charles Dickey, House of Morgan . . . Joseph Dodge, Detroit banker who moves well in government circles . . . James Doolittle, war hero, oil dealer. . . . Milton Eisenhower, a thinker for his brother. . . . Ben Fairless, a retired power who keeps moving . . .

Fred Florence, a banker's banker. . . . Clarence Francis, Mr. Public Affairs, a committeeman . . . John M. Franklin, shipper, solid tender to business. . . . Crawford H. Greenewalt, DuPont. . . . John Hancock, of the important Lehman Brothers team. . . . John W. Hanes, a southern businessman who has done well in New York. . . . H. J. Heinz II, pickles, a civic enterpriser. . . . Paul G. Hoffman, business liberal. . . . Herbert Hoover, Sr., patron saint of many Republicans. . . . Herbert Hoover, Jr., a son of whom his father is proud. . . . Eric Johnston, busy. . . . K. T. Keller, a builder of Chrysler. . . . Meyer Kestnbaum, a thinker, now mover in politics. . . . Fred Lazarus, developer of a business to something bigger. . . . John L. Lewis, a tired worker in the labor vineyard. . . . James A. Linen, a comer for Henry Luce. . . . George H. Love, important in the coal-steel complex. . . .

Hughston M. McBain, in the driver's seat at Marshall Field's. . . . John L. McCaffery, soft-spoken leader at International Harvester. . . . John McCloy, a Wall Street banker who knows his way around. . . . Richard K. Mellon, scion of family millions, an active worker with money. . . . Eugene Meyer, liberal publisher. . . . Ben Moreell, Navy background in steel, knows the ropes in Washington. . . . W. C. Mullendore, a writer of personal pamphlets, right wing Republican in utilities. . . . T. S. Petersen, link in the West coast network. . . .

Gwilym A. Price, "You can be *sure* if it's Westinghouse". . . . Clarence Randall, writer of books, political actor. . . . Stanley Resor, public relations man on a big scale in the immediate past. . . . Edward L. Ryerson, retired from steel, active in civic affairs. . . . David Sarnoff, scientist businessman. . . . Carrol M. Shanks, insurance money . . . Henry Knox Sherrill, Protestant representative . . .

Carl Spaatz, war hero turned publisher. . . . Joseph P. Spang, "Look Sharp! Feel Sharp! Be Sharp!". . . . Francis J. Spellman, Catholic representative . . . Herman Steinkraus, lower New England metal man. . . . Adlai Stevenson, if worse came to worse for some, an acceptable Democrat. . . . Harry Truman, gone to Independence but not forgotten. . . . Thomas Watson, Jr., "THINK," an illustrious son . . . Sidney J. Weinberg, knowledge of men . . . Ernest T. Weir, was big steel . . . George Whitney, House of Morgan. . . . John Hay Whitney, old family members can still make good in spite of money. . . . Charles E. Wilson, a man with the designation "Electric," a man who will not retire. . . . Robert E. Wilson, thinker in the oil industry. . . . R. E. Wood, long a part of the big league operation in Sears. . . . R. W. Woodruff, the pause that refreshes. . . .

Other figures come to mind upon whom I took no notes, but whom I remember even though the names have escaped me:

The foreman on the assembly line at the International Harvester plant in Indianapolis . . . . the woman tying the end-threads of hose in a North Carolina hosiery mill that turned out 20,000 pairs of nylon hose a day . . . . the guards in the Chase Manhattan Bank . . . . the Detroit chauffeurs who drove from one auto plant to another in company cars . . . . scores of secretaries . . . . the elevator operator in one of the metropolitan daily newspapers . . . . the operator of a crap game table in Nevada who took off his eye shade and took time out to explain how he participated in community affairs.

All are a minute part of the big picture of power. Yet I heard their names but once, recognized that they were not leaders, and hurried on.

But I saw more than a conglomeration of people in the process of making a national study. I began to see that individuals acting in groups to get things done are thereby able to utilize patterns of power with considerable sureness in moving men, goods, and services.

Thirty association secretaries, mostly in New York, Washington, and Chicago, where more than half the national associations were located, were interviewed in the early stages of the study to underscore and complement the materials gathered by mailed questionnaires.

In the course of these interviews and in later interviews with men considered to be top policy makers in the nation, I came to believe that many associations highly rated as powers in political circles are not indeed as powerful as deemed. Some of the smaller, less publicly known associations, committees, and fluid power cliques may operate more successfully in moving legislation, for example, than the large, publicly known, and sometimes feared molders of public opinion. Depending on the matter under consideration and the situation, committee and board organizations like the Committee for

Economic Development, the Industrial Conference Board, or the Business Advisory Council of the Department of Commerce were extremely important although relatively small policy-making organizations. Along with a sprinkling of foreign policy associations and educational bodies, they represent top groupings of national leadership.

After concluding the more extensive study, I feel that the membership lists of the National Industrial Conference, the Committee for Economic Development, and the Business Advisory Council provide good starting points for anyone interested in a quick and partial rundown of national leadership. These boards are highly selective in recruiting members and they represent a stable cross-section of top business leadership. They are made up of persons who have access to each other and who have channels to persons in other power networks of civic, professional, political, and religious leadership.

It became apparent during the process of interviewing association secretaries and lay leaders in associations that there is a generalized pattern of action in the national organizations. In some degree each of them is dedicated to a "grass roots" approach to organization. Some of them go further down to the grass roots than others but a general reliance on getting the organization's story across to as many people as possible and particularly to association members seems to be a pattern. Each, of course, differs in some degree in its general scheme of organization. For example, the Investment Bankers Association reaches down only to top level men within local investment banking houses. The organization pyramids up to an executive committee through a series of operating committees appointed by the self-perpetuating executive committee. Policy within the association is pretty well formulated, on a formal basis, by the central executive committee. Operating committees within the organization are advisory.

The Farm Bureau, on the other hand, attempts to organize down to the individual farmers living in townships and counties. Policy for the association, on the formal level, is initiated at the township committee level and is carried through to the county, the state, and finally to the national organization. Through a long series of meetings, on the various levels, policy is finally formulated on the national level in annual meetings and is published for consideration and approval by all sub-units. A corps of technical organizers operating through regional jurisdictions is in the continual process of educating the members of the Farm Bureau on general policy. Of all the associations visited, the Farm Bureau seemed to be the most highly and efficiently organized. Some of the others apparently have a rather tenuous relationship with their local affiliates.

In one way or another all of the associations visited have lobbying or legislative pressure functions. The general technique of such operations seems to boil down to having paid professional secretaries in Washington or in the state capitals who approach legislators and legislative committees directly or utilize the services of lay members of their associations or from communities in general within states or in the nation at large.

The listing of powerful individuals on national executive committees and boards of directors is a common practice, and it would appear upon observation that some of the men named on the executive committees of the associations would be top power figures in their own right. Persons named on this level of organization would not necessarily be out front on active work for the association, but their names, at least, on a letterhead seem to carry meaning for the association secretaries.

There is considerable evidence to indicate that interaction between associations on a formal level is not very tightly knit. Some attempts by the Farm Bureau and the National Association of Manufacturers have been made to coordinate national policy interests in Washington. The National Association of Manufacturers has a unit in New York which is titled The Association of National Organizations. Rather than to spend too much time in trying to "bring along" other associations, the general tendency within any association seems to be to key activities around its own specific interests. Internal harmony seems to be the keynote, although this is not always easy to achieve.

A generalized process of the development of any particular public policy would appear to me to go somewhat like this: If the needs of a particular industry are such that public law or administrative policy of the government is damaging to the industry involved or if the industry cannot get what it wants, it does several things. The top executive shuttles back and forth across the country, as do some of his staff who are in touch with other men in other industries and within their own industry. There is much talking together at luncheons, private parties, conferences, trade meetings, recreational outings, the citadels of finance, and other types of get-togethers in which a line is constructed on what should be done. Innumerable committees are gathered together to make studies of policy.

A current case in point is that of the question of free trade versus high tariffs. As this study got under way, there was much informal discussion of this matter, because a few of the top industrial leaders have come out in favor of free trade. The men running large department stores also tend to be in favor of free trade. Large industries that have overseas plants favor free trade. On the other hand, there are many persons in the business world who do not favor free trade and consequently there was and is considerable controversy about the matter.

Clarence Randall of the Inland Steel Company in Chicago has been a spokesman for large industry over the past several years. According to his peers he is a thinker; he writes books. President Eisenhower was asked by a group of businessmen

to appoint him to a large national committee that after months
of study made a report on the question of free trade versus
high tariffs. In the months of study, many informal discussions
had been going on; there were meetings between individual
members of various industries, and there were discussions
within the formal national organizations related to the questions involved. Hearings were arranged before Congressional
committees. In the final report Mr. Randall's commission came
out with some policy pronouncements which represent much
compromise. Individual industries and business leaders can
choose the parts of the compromise that fit their own needs,
and any policies developed subsequently have been guided, to
some extent, by judgments made during this process of study
and discussion. During its work, the Randall Commission was
a functional part of the Executive Staff of the White House,
and its offices were in the old Department of State building.

National associations apparently have two or three functions that they perform during the process of policy development. First of all, they act as coordinating devices for gathering and distributing information among their members. They
hold conferences at which papers are given and men are able
to exchange their ideas informally. Another type of association of a group of industries may be a purely technical organization which gathers facts and which, in turn, can be used by
the conference type of organization. A third type of national
organization, within a single industry, may be that of a pure
lobby which puts pressure on Washington when things need
to be done. In a concrete situation, such as getting tidelands
oil for individual companies or states, the whole gamut of
national leaders may not have been primarily interested in
the process, but there is a lot of live and let live in the whole
activity. The large electric companies gave a lot of moral aid
and support via a states rights "line" to the oil people and, I
am told, when their turn came, the oil interests gave support
to the electric people in their bid for taking over the building

and operation of dams. Other industries also have been involved in the log-rolling process along the free enterprise front so that when their turns come they can purchase some of the government factories with the aid and assent of peer industrial groupings.

While the whole process of public policy development sometimes seem obscure because of its bigness and complexity, it became increasingly obvious to me, as persons were interviewed city to city, that the country may not be as big as one sometimes thinks it is. It is complex, but it is not complex beyond the understanding of those who apparently know the lines of communication in connection with given policies. It can be generally comprehended and, when necessary, specifically so.

There is a general network of individuals who stand behind and sometimes aloof from the formal associations but who use and are used by the associations in policy-making. There are definite relationships between such leaders, and the present study has empirically borne out this thesis. This does not say nor imply, however, that I believe we have government by oligarchic conspiracy.

The total, informal, top level network of power status leaders has been estimated by various informants as being between 100 and 300 men. I believe that about 200 men in some 13 cities easily constitute a working nucleus of a network of recognized national leaders, many of whom are given as top names by the associations.

The customary assumption, as we have pointed out, that certain national associations and their lobbies at Washington are mighty strongholds of power may have to be modified. Some national leaders—not a majority—look upon the associations and their secretaries with hostility or contempt. The secretaries are seen as "paid employees" who often go off on tangents. Certainly, none of the associations always obtains all of its objectives.

National leaders tell me they have a wide acquaintance among other leaders. Some men are recognized as top policy makers, others as second- and third-rate figures of importance through informal discussions with the higher-ups, still others as front men for specific interests. The acquaintanceship is not confined to persons who serve on the same corporate boards or belong to the same political party or happen to have similar amounts of money in the bank. Friendships, committee work, clubs and recreational associations, customer relations, and financial matters all tend to intertwine definable action patterns. Policy development thus is a prime social function that defies confinement entirely within formally organized political or associational groupings.

Many of the associations utilize the technique of bringing in the little fellow—the corner druggist, the hardware dealer, or the small-town banker—to promote their interests before government officials or committees. The technique is effective when these individuals are backed by the big men; most politicians know who is behind the willing but carefully coached witness on a particular matter. Any community organizer, Community Chest director, or real-estate board executive uses similar methods. The choice of a person to present a case before any authoritative body is usually well thought out in advance. Deliberations are not published in the newspapers; the final direction of policy may be. Behind the whole process, of course, are innumerable clearances.

The national associations are, admittedly, excellent clearing houses. The main offices are located (sometimes beautifully) in the larger of the national cities but their affiliates are dotted across the map. Most often they represent an important community link to the nation.

Whether an organization is a dinner club or a large pressure organization housed in marble splendor in the nation's capital, within it is a corps of paid employees, a secretariat which, by and large, keeps the organization intact. The association secretaries have power, but a power limited in the various ways that professionals are limited by lay leaders in our society. A professional considered worth his salt or considered good at his job never takes credit for the development of any associational policy, even when that policy might be traced directly to his own analysis of the situation.

I am sometimes indignantly asked, when I address professional groups, "Do you really believe that top leaders control policy development? What about the secretariat?" Or I am asked, "Do you seriously believe that policy originates only within the top layers of national leadership? What about the under-secretaries of policy-making groups?" My whole answer, of course, requires a book in the telling. Partial answers to the questions may be underscored here.

I believe that top levels of leadership do control policy development. They do so by the weight and display of prestige which they are given in their primary organizations, particularly in the larger corporate groups. The professionals within associations strive daily to build up this or that man into a prominent lay leader. To give validity to the status claims of one or another of the individuals within a given policy-making group, consistent work is required. In terms of accepted organization patterning, professional people are subordinate to the lay leaders, particularly to board members of their organizations.

I do not deny that when confronted with problems of policy, many lay leaders are relatively inept or even stupid compared to some brilliant secretaries. I further recognize the wishes of some professional people to be higher in the power status scale than they often find themselves. But, be all this as it may, the role of the professional in most instances is subordinate to that of one or more lay leaders. What I am saying applies to many professional politicians as well as association secretaries.

To say that one's role is subordinate to another's does not mean, of course, that the secondary role is unimportant in a functioning social system. The lowliest caseworker in a civic welfare agency is important to the functioning of the general welfare. The secretary of an industrial association may be almost indispensable to the maximum functioning of his organization, but within the framework of custom, the professional serves the interests of laymen in the policy-making process. The dominant theory of making things go in our society is the trickle-down one. If matters of policy bubble up, as I think vast numbers of policies do, they must be distilled upon reaching the top levels of policy, first, perhaps, by the watchful secretariat, but finally by the lay leaders who top the professionals.

A small number of professionals, college professors, churchmen, writers, and consultants do break into the top structure of national policy-making. Harvard's President Conant and Dean David are among these. But by and large, as one Chicago industrialist said to me, "College professors are not making policy in the country today."

Many association secretaries are not displeased with their lot. If they head one of the larger associations they can often speak with a great deal of authority, authority rubbed off on them by the men whom they may have built up and integrated into the organization scheme they represent. There is a process involved whereby professionals use certain laymen to achieve the ends and goals of their organization, which become their own ends, and in other instances they willingly are used by the top men. It is a process of using top leaders and being used. Community Chest secretaries, for example, have long been acquainted with these dynamics of behavior.

On occasion, when a professional picks a policy maker of some stature to help him in shaping organization policies, the policy maker runs too hard with the ball, and the job can be frustrating. But most often the policy goals of the professional and the lay leader coalesce, and their relationship is one of measured reciprocity.

The importance of the role of the professional organizer is well known in political circles, where organizations must be built rapidly. "Adlai Stevenson," said a *Time* writer, in July, 1956, "[has come] to trust in professional political managers instead of the amateurs who surrounded him in 1952. And his new-found faith in professionals has become the key to Stevenson's drive for the 1956 Democratic nomination.... At Stevenson's headquarters in the heart of the Chicago Loop, Jim Finnegan directs a staff that includes high level volunteers and 18 paid employees."

The secretariat in any organized group is extremely important and in some degree it shapes policy, but the key to its activities must be sought in an analysis of the policy goals of those top men who, like Stevenson's "high level volunteers," hire them—or fire them, when their policy notions do not fit the policy considerations of their status superiors. Policy is made by a combination of efforts.

As I moved from one association to another and began to interview their top leaders, it seemed evident that the associations were a vital part of the process of national policy development. They acted as coordinating groups. They sopped up information, analyzed and distributed it. They cajoled and pressured Congress, state legislatures, and news editors. They were repositories of infinite varieties of data. They were clearing houses for those who wished to match their policy views with others. They functioned as points of reference for many citizens who had no views, but who looked for guidance as issues broke into the news.

More specifically in relation to the present study, they also proved to be valuable sources for national top leadership nominations; and as specific issues and matters of public policy were brought into focus, as will be seen as we discuss housing and textile policies in subsequent chapters, the associations were an omnipresent help. None were as powerful as they would sometimes try to lead one to believe. All had power with specified groups. All claimed some grass roots legitimacy, although often the grass roots of which they spoke consisted of a constituency of top leaders in industrial communities across the nation.

3 STARTING WITH THE COMMUNITY

WHAT are the relations between communities, and how are they linked together to form the nation? Who are some of the key persons in the linking process? Detroit makes automobiles; Chicago packs meat. How are the two related? And do auto makers have any kind of relationship with the meat packers—personal or otherwise?

With such questions in mind and in an effort to get the names and follow up the links in the national chain of power, I went to Detroit in 1953. From Detroit, I moved on to other cities with the same questions in mind.

As I moved about in the city of Detroit interviewing persons who were presumed to be power figures, I was quickly apprised of the fact that this metropolitan community, like so many others, is composed of a cluster of pyramids of influence and authority, no one of which overshadows all the others; there are chains of command, deference and obedience to authority that are topped by a small group of decision makers. They influence the actions of men below them in a geometric progression and are related to each other in various interlocking ways and to certain major and basic functions of the community as a whole and in most instances of the nation at large.

Since there were then approximately three and a half million

people in the Detroit metropolitan area, when I heard some
of the top Detroit leaders say, "Mr. John Coleman is one of a
half dozen men who really make Detroit move" or "Mr.
Ernest Kanzler is a prime mover," I was tempted to incredu-
lity. How could a half dozen men make Detroit move? Why
was Mr. Kanzler designated as a prime mover, while someone
else was not? To thousands living in the Detroit area it was
quite likely that the names mentioned had little meaning and
for millions across the nation this may also have been true,
but for those living in Detroit who knew how things got
moved, the names were meaningful. These were persons who
had achieved distinction in the business community—making
office machinery (Coleman, Burroughs Corporation) or, on
the other hand, extending credit to millions who buy autos
(Kanzler, Universal Credit Corporation).

Other companies represented peaks of industrial and commercial magnitude and might. Ford, Chrysler, and General
Motors companies, the big three, could not be missed. If I
said that Henry Ford II was a Detroit prime mover, I would
have been readily believed in Detroit and elsewhere. Obviously, the product involved and the name were well known.
Less well known, perhaps, but a potent force in Detroit life
was the J. L. Hudson Department Store, another peak organization. Still other companies that were looked upon as key
organizations in community life included the Detroit Edison
Company (electric power), the Nash-Kelvinator Company,
and two leading banks, the Detroit Bank and the National
Bank of Detroit. In each of the companies mentioned there
were men who became recognized within their organizations
as powerful figures either by virtue of the offices they held or
by the services they performed. Top teams of management,
representing the apex of corporate power, also became recognized in the community as basic power groups. Thus, I heard
the statement in Detroit, "If the Big Three [motor com-
panies], the Hudson Company, a couple of the banks, and

one or two other operating companies sit around a table, things are bound to happen!" The statement was too pat and simple, but it had truth in it. A part of its truth lay in the fact that so many in Detroit believed it. They believed it, in part, because on occasion these forces did get together, through representatives, and civic actions of vast ramifications flowed from such meetings.

Some of the men on the top rung of leadership, said to be power leaders in the area, were: Prentiss Brown, L. L. Colbert, John Coleman, Harlow Curtice, Joseph Dodge, Charles Fisher, Henry Ford II, Ernest Kanzler, George Mason, and James Webber, Jr. These men were important in the corporate enterprises they directed and managed. They were relatively independent in their judgments. They were known as policy makers and opinion leaders. They were dependent upon one another in their formulations of judgment and opinion and they were buttressed by scores of men of equal and lesser rank in the community who were also integral parts of Detroit's power structure. In my interviews, men concerned with power arrangements were informally classified by other leaders as high or low in a power scale determined, in part, by each person's distance from the councils of the top leaders.

Those who knew the men mentioned recognized immediately that some were considered to be of greater influence than others, even though the total group represented top level community influence. It also was observed that the men differed in their interests; that they were of different ages; that some had achieved their position in community affairs through working their way up, while others had inherited positions; that at least three of the men were related to one another by blood or marriage and that their names had been repeatedly linked together on civic ventures; that some were more approachable than others; and that all of them belonged to at least one club in common. None could say that this was a

particularly tightly knit group, if a group at all, but none
who knew Detroit leadership would have denied the place
held by these men, who had become symbols of industrial,
commercial, social, and, in some instances, political achievement. They represented a direct influence in the lives of at
least a half million men of the labor force of Detroit and
they made decisions that indirectly influenced the habits of
men around the world.

When asked to name a top civic enterpriser, community-
minded people had some difficulty in making this distinction,
but one of the most thoughtful and modest young men in the
Detroit group was mentioned often enough to give him honor-
able mention. James Webber, Jr., was named as a key figure
in urban happenings as well as being a top figure in the J. L.
Hudson Department Store. His company had long been noted
for excellent public relations in the commercial area. Mr.
Webber had helped to guide the company through the greatest expansion in its history and at the same time had taken a
greater part than most others in community affairs. His outstanding characteristic in civic work seemed to lie in his willingness and ability to do a great deal of work without appearing pressured. He was a person upon whom many depended
and of whom it was said, "He is a great guy, doing a swell
job" (in the estimation of his colleagues). The luncheon
cliché actually seemed to fit Webber as a whole truth. His
major civic interest at the moment was hospital and health
facility development.

No Detroit story would be complete without mention of
the Ford family and its chief member, Mr. Webber's cousin,
Henry Ford II. It was conceded by most that "young Henry"
was admirably suited for the various social tasks and positions
ascribed to him. Inheriting the business left to him by his
grandfather and father, Mr. Ford also took a position in Detroit
vacated by the state leaders of the bygone lumber era. The
Ford family of Detroit has some of the aura of the Dodges and

others who led the city in its earliest history. Henry Ford I was considered a family man and the first of a now illustrious family. Even the Ford company chauffeurs spoke with solicitous interest of the comings and goings of the family.

Coupled with the fact that he owns and operates a large scale family business was another fact, well publicized, that Mr. Ford has achieved distinction as a public figure, especially oriented to leadership in public relations.

The will to do and the achievement, plus family recognition, represent an almost unbeatable combination of leadership characteristics in a community power scale in American urban society, and such a combination has made Mr. Ford a leader at the policy level in his nationally important home bailiwick. Few thought of him as extremely imaginative personally, but he was considered a good organization man filling an important role in a society in which personalities are generalized and symbolized.

The generalized power pattern found in Detroit consisted of a relatively stable group of men who knew each other well and who called upon one another time and again to effect plans that required top level decision. The plans, of course, in many cases may have originated at the lower echelons of leadership. As in other communities, the great bulk of day to day work proceeds along established lines according to habit and custom, but each year new problems arise that require a recasting of existing patterns of community action. When something big is on the fire, those persons designated as decision makers are called upon to play an initiating role, in keeping with their particular interests in civic life, but most men in the decision-making structure have a wide range of interests and a wide circle of friends and acquaintances who keep them abreast of most large scale developments. Thus there is an informal network of clearances set up in the upper levels of leadership. The role of the individual decision maker involves a symbolic function as well as physical participation in civic operations.

The symbolic function served by a decision maker is that of lending the prestige of his primary badge of office and accomplishment to civic, political, or cultural activities. Those who are aware of the achievements of a man in a primary activity are prone to impute organization skills, wisdom, and prowess to him and to choose him for secondary activities. If a successful business leader is willing to take responsibility for decisions affecting the common weal, the populace aware of civic ventures is prone to believe that its projects are in good hands.

In the course of events and time the community leader who engages in civic activities gains skill and proficiency in any type of civic work that appeals to him. He learns cost figures. He becomes acquainted with ranking members of the bureaucratic organizations who man the civic services, and he learns how to judge and place men from his own company and others in proper roles for any civic development. In all of this process there is a growing recognition of his services, and he becomes a person whose judgments can be trusted. In the informal delegations of civic responsibilities and in the designation of persons upon whom one can call for advice concerning specific activities, the experienced leader becomes a symbol of civic integrity.

In all communities studied, such leaders as those whose characteristics are outlined above were called upon repeatedly for their services. Besides being symbolic in community affairs, most of them, in the upper brackets of leadership, also had resources of manpower and finances at their immediate disposal in their companies, and the cash contributions they could make were extremely valuable and necessary to any activity requiring the efforts and monetary contributions of large numbers of people.

Men at the top leadership level are usually very busy persons. Many are expert in delegating responsibilities and manage to keep their desks fairly clear of paper, but even so they meet heavy demands for decisions in their primary enterprises. Consequently, the time that they can devote to the actual working operations of civic affairs is limited. Decision-making in social meetings more nearly fits their daily routines and is less time-consuming, however important. Most top leaders are sooner or later granted the freedom of opinion-giving without being required to sit in on every matter under consideration.

Since the decision makers are freed to perform their specialized function and role, it becomes necessary to call upon a second echelon of civic workers to symbolize leadership and command the work required to make things go. Detroit did this, of course, and the fact can be illustrated briefly by the activities of the famous charitable organization, the United Foundation, which served to spur similar developments across the nation.

Beset by multiple charitable campaigns during the years, the leaders in Detroit became aware of the fact that coordination of their social services needed the attention of Detroit's top leadership to bring order into the whole situation. Consequently, Henry Ford, Charles Wilson, Harlow Curtice, and several others of leadership caliber were brought into a working committee to represent the policy leaders in an endeavor that eventually became the United Foundation, a fund-raising organization founded on the same principles that have traditionally, if theoretically but not in practice, guided the Community Chest movement. The symbolic role carried by these men was potent enough to pull many lesser figures in the Detroit pattern of power into line and assure the success of Detroit's Torch Light campaign.

In this period of minor crisis the top leaders made it plain that their wishes lay in the direction indicated. They enrolled the support of a vast array of talent from lower echelons of

Detroit leadership, and the ensuing campaign was a success. Since the initial dates, however, the leading roles in the United campaigns have been carried by second-string men on the Detroit scene. The top leaders still gave their names, support, advice, and an occasional speech to the coordinated charitable endeavor, but most of their civic energies were spent elsewhere. Secondary men connected with the larger industries were potent figures in their own right. Some of them were "comers," groomed to replace older men; others were members of top teams of the larger concerns. In either case they spoke and acted with good authority. Ernest Breech, top manager at Ford, and Burrough's Edward Littlejohn were the type of leaders who could be weighed in the balance with the top men of their organizations. Scores of other men blurred any hard and fast line that might have been drawn between the half dozen very top leaders and other civic powers and workers. Yet, in our study, fine distinctions were made in evaluations of Detroit's influence stratification. A man's power position was determined, in part, by the independence of his judgment, and if he needed to clear any matters with a superior in his organization he was rated slightly downward in peer evaluations.

Second-string industrial and commercial personnel coalesced with top rank small scale business leaders to goad civic action in a maze of detail. An impressive array of civic organizations, service clubs, and semi-permanent committees on which top leaders were present or represented kept a balance in power relations in Detroit that would have made envious an urban boss of a bygone era. The subtle, and not necessarily devious, social interaction between civic and social club members made for a tightly integrated system of power at a policy level of community life.

Used to handling big scale operations in their own enterprises, the Detroit men of decision were likely to be more interested in civic matters of large magnitude. Most recently

the development of Detroit's growing and magnificent Civic
Center, a show piece for the world, has engrossed much of
the leadership time allotted to community ventures. Nearly
three quarters of a billion dollars had been earmarked for the
building of a veterans' memorial building, a city-county building, and a Henry and Edsel Ford auditorium. The last building
was underwritten by a private gift of one million dollars from
the Ford family and a million and a half dollars subscribed by
Ford dealers across the country. Other redevelopment plans
for Detroit included expressway construction, a convention
and exhibits building, housing, expansion of port facilities,
parks, playfields, parking areas, libraries, schools, and water
supply. No item of this set of activities was without sponsorship by the men of influence who through innumerable conferences, private conversations, committee meetings, and popular appeal put their stamp of approval on these diverse, yet
coordinated, undertakings.

The gross plan of redevelopment and civic improvement
was popularly known as the Cobo Plan. Albert E. Cobo, dynamic mayor of the "dynamic city," symbolized the out
front person in remaking downtown Detroit. Mayor Cobo,
an ex-salesman for the Burroughs Company, had given his
community a business-minded administration. His own past
connections with the business community made him sympathetic to suggestions from civic-minded business leaders,
and he was trusted by the scores of businessmen upon whom
he called for advice and who called him to state their points
of view. The fact that his past business experience had been
accumulated as a self-made man in a subordinate position in a
large company, but not by any means the largest, gave him
somewhat an even footing with leaders of labor and large sections of middle range business and professional people—persons
called upon to man the working committees of the larger civic
programs.

Mayor Cobo thus served as a symbol for the general public

in the improvement boom. He was a person to whom one could refer when the plan came to mind, when a spokesman was needed for an explanation of the plan, or when the plan auspices had to be cited. Because of the many political ramifications of the building program it was logical and expedient for the titular head of the community to be the open sponsor. Mayor Cobo did not work alone as a leader symbol in the middle range. He worked with men at his own level of leadership and with those above him and below him in power status. The whole working arrangement of decision-making and execution brought into play every facet of the local power structure.

At the local level of politics the downtown improvement association informally and financially supported those city councilmen who went along with the Cobo Plan (as well as any other plan that had top policy consensus) and withheld support from those who did not. The various civic clubs through the participation of their leaders were in favor of the plan, and thus it moved. Labor leaders were also drawn into a working relationship with industrial and commercial leaders at the policy committee level.

The role of the Detroit labor leader in civic development appeared to be a kind of outside-inside affair. A realistic recognition of the industrial potency of labor leaders and a modified attitude toward them existed on the part of many of the large employers. One of the top auto men said to this interviewer, half in jest and half in earnest, "Speaking of policy making, when you see Walter Reuther, find out what *his* policy is toward us—what he is going to do to us in the next wage round!" Other leaders in the industrial picture discounted the power of labor, pointing to the fact that labor "spends a fortune on electing candidates and never gets more than 39 or 40 per cent of the vote." A minority simply said, "Labor? Phwee!"

Regardless of the range of expressed attitudes toward them,

which tended toward the negative, there was good evidence of the formal role played by labor leaders in almost any major community project. A part of the technique of making projects move was to enlist a cross-section support of various power elements in the community at large, and labor in Detroit was too large and potent an element to ignore. There was good evidence that labor leaders were excluded from many of the informal sessions related to the initiation of many projects. They were not acceptable in certain circles at any and all times, but when projects reached the stage in which committees were formalized and the membership made public, labor was represented.

Two policy considerations that had long been of major interest and concern to Detroit leadership reached beyond community borders. The tangible proposition of the development of the St. Lawrence Seaway and the more general idea of freer trade with other nations of the world found widespread acceptance among Detroit leaders. Both issues had called into play the organizing skills of a vast number of Detroit citizens who recognized the strategic importance of the issues in the economic life of their world city. The Seaway plan had but recently been lifted out of the category of the controversial. The free trade issue was far from settled at that time. We shall briefly discuss here only the live issue of free trade and some of the informal aspects of promoting free trade, since the waterway promotion patterns of action were of a similar character.

A small group of professional men in the Detroit Chamber of Commerce privately asserted that they first began to see the desirability of a broadened international trade policy for their community. An intensive and prolonged study of the facts, innumerable discussions between themselves, discussions at their national trade association meetings, writing and rewriting of mimeographed memoranda, and many private discussions with selected members of the Chamber board had preceded any public statements on the matter. As the idea took hold in Detroit, other leaders in distant cities across the nation were engaged in a similar searching of the same question.

As in the community, there were leaders at the national level who had become known to one another and interacted with one another on many matters of public importance; eventually, as on any other matter of national significance, a cross-section national committee was formed first to study and then promote on a national scale the idea espoused by the group. This process usually included a few top leaders from the Detroit area, and in the case of the trade issue a Committee for Trade Policy, Inc., was set up with officers in the national capital. The Detroit representatives included Ernest Breech, of Ford; Prentiss Brown, Detroit Edison; Lester Colbert, Chrysler Corporation; Edward Littlejohn, Burroughs Corporation, and Walter Reuther, CIO, with other national leaders of like stature drawn from most of the major cities.

Because of the unsettled nature of the trade question, the national committee was bi-partisan in its composition and cautiously partisan in its operation. Most of its best work had been done in promoting an informal strategy of enlisting high caliber men in its study and clearance. The enlistment of the interest of Henry Ford II at the informal policy level of committee affairs had undoubtedly helped sell the committee in Detroit, if not around the country.

Mr. Ford's position in this matter was to "hold himself aloof from the committee's day to day work, but to come in at times to speak on behalf of a freer trade policy." Some of his public statements have been well publicized. Those who agreed with what he said have applauded him. Others said, "When Henry Ford talks about making automobiles he makes sense; when he talks about this free trade thing, you just know people are putting words in his mouth!" Some of the larger chemical company officials and the watchmakers felt very unhappy with Mr. Ford's statements. Nevertheless, he made them, and they were attentively listened to by a great many people.

To make national policy effective, at some point an issue must be picked up politically by one of the major parties and by the leading candidate of the particular party. The influence of Detroit on the policy of trade was put in this way (para-phrased) by a Detroit spokesman:

Many of us here liked the Republican candidate in the last presidential election long before he was a candidate. He was in-vited to Detroit after he came back from Europe, not by the auto makers, but by some of us who know the whole town pretty well. We entertained General Eisenhower and liked what he said at an informal luncheon and at informal receptions.

When he was slated to be a candidate, some of us went to Chicago to do what we could for him, even though we were not official delegates of the convention.

Later Mr. Eisenhower came to Detroit as an official candidate and he was taken in tow by the public politicians and he made a good speech on Cadillac Square.

After he was elected I called him and asked to see him in rela-tion to the freer trade proposition, and five of our men from Detroit went to Washington and met with the President in the Cabinet Room to discuss an insertion of policy in his first speech to Congress. The rest is history.

How much influence these actions have had on the current of history may be problematical, but we shall see when we come to a discussion of textile policy that the events described may have had a marked bearing on the textile case. The point here is that specific men with definite interests from important cities like Detroit do act in similar ways to influence policy beyond the boundaries of their particular communities. The role in defining national issues of the recognized leaders, com-munity by community, cannot be discounted.

There were those in Detroit who said that the top leadership had been so concerned with the big issues of free trade and civic center development and the like that they did not see many of the pressing problems of a community character that had been left untackled. If this were so, and undoubtedly it was so, one remedy would appear to have been at hand: Form more committees and use the names mentioned!

If one wishes to accomplish any good purpose in the city of Detroit, he would go about organizing for its success much in the same way he would in Tulsa, Toledo, or Tupelo. He would talk up his idea with those technically qualified to judge the merits or demerits of his project. He would interest those persons in the community who have spent their professional lives organizing top leaders for broad range and large scale tasks. Sooner or later, and more often later than sooner, he would need cross-section, top level sponsorship for his idea. If he could interest any of the top leaders in spearheading his idea, the ultimate success of the project would be more nearly assured than otherwise, but overnight accomplishment would not be an automatic certainty. Many of the top leaders have had bees in their bonnets for years before their pet projects had become realities. The men of power in Detroit are powerful indeed, but they are not superhuman.

Prior to going to Detroit to get nominations for the top leadership structure of that city, I had polled the Chambers of Commerce and Community Chests in cities of over 100,000 population in the nation for leadership nominations from their cities. I had also sent the list of names that I had received from the national associations to each individual on that list, asking one simple question, "How many of these leaders do you know personally?" I was of the opinion, and still am, that if the leaders were unknown to each other, their working relationship could not be very close. I found through the polling processes that nearly 200 persons on a combined list of slightly less than 500 knew each other.

By combining these knowledge choices with the leader

nominees of the urban Chests and Chambers of Commerce, I was prepared to interview leaders, as I had interviewed Detroit leaders, in Dayton, Toledo, Chicago, Denver, Salt Lake City, Seattle, Portland, San Francisco, Dallas, Houston, New Orleans, Birmingham, Atlanta, Washington, D.C., Philadelphia, New York, and Boston. Twenty small towns on a sample basis between these major urban centers were also visited and three leaders in each were interviewed for their views on national policy development.

The leaders interviewed on the cross-country tour were asked to look at the refined list I had compiled for their use and were asked to think of the list in terms of national policy-making figures. They were asked to comment on the names and to rate the names in a 1, 2, 3 scale. They were also asked to outline their thoughts on national policy development and to give examples of policy matters in which they were interested. The first trip was a pilot, exploratory venture and was not intended to prove or disprove the notion of a power structure at the national level.

If the trip proved anything at all, and I believe it was a very crucial test run, it did prove that there is a good knowledge of national leadership segments across the country. It was also apparent that men could rate each other in some kind of status scale and it seemed further apparent that the top-rated people seemed more related to each other than those down-rated by all others.

The names followed by an asterisk in the longer 1953 list, Chapter 2, pp. 17-28, are those of a nuclear group of policy makers and power leaders who were named most frequently on my first cross-country research tour in 1953 and who were considered to be persons who should know the most about the processes of developing national policy. This later list does not include the names of ranking national elected or appointed politicians. At least they were not elected or appointed to office, to my knowledge, at the time the names were given to me. (I felt during the early stages of research that public politicians should be left off the list since many of them obviously would be concerned with the development of national policy. I later added political names when I was ready to explore specific policy-making procedures, and they were then rated by other national leaders.) After the first interviewing trip, it was apparent that a long list of 300 names was a cumbersome research device. The interviews showed that about one third of that number were considered definitely to be top leaders by all informants. Therefore from that time forward, although various combinations of cumulative lists were used, no more than 100 names were ever presented to those interviewed.

To those who know well the names starred in the Chapter 2 list it will be apparent that in three or four instances persons were identified with a single company or corporation. For example, Edward Ryerson was a chairman of the board of Inland Steel, in which capacity Clarence Randall succeeded him, and Henry Ford and Ernest Breech were in the same company. But very largely the list was a cross-section of individuals who acted in their own right concerning their attitudes and opinions. Some were considered first raters, others were considered second and third raters, but all were considered powers and policy makers at the national level of decision.

The list, like the longer one earlier gathered from associations, cannot be construed as a listing of the men who run the country. Such a concept is far too naïve, but the men named were said to be at the center of things, and their activities and opinions were said to carry considerable weight in any course of direction taken by the nation as a whole. A few of these persons denied that they had any influence whatsoever in the development of national policy. It is in the American tradition that such denial be made. Others may have thought they had much more influence than their peers actually allowed. The influence of each varied according to time and in relation to any particular policy that may have been under discussion. Some were leaders on the way up. Others were on the way out. As the study progressed, some leaders named before retired, died, or withdrew entirely from active participation in policy development. Consequently, such a listing, as a whole, may have been good for a few weeks or months, and then needed to be revised. On the whole, however, it served as a fairly stable guide or point of reference in observing leadership action patterns. A yearly poll helped keep lists up to date.

Regardless of the shifting nature of the lists of policy-making lay leaders, the patterns of policy development remained relatively stable, and such patterning will be the subject of exposition in some later chapters.

If one were to have added to the list a few names of ranking, elected and appointed politicians, a sprinkling of news editors and columnists, and a few organization secretaries and lobbyists, the core structure of power at the national level would have been more nearly complete. The names of politicians might have included those of most of the cabinet members, four or five administrators, two or three Supreme Court justices, three or four state governors, a couple of representatives to the United Nations, the President, and, according to my informants, at least the following Senators and Representatives (1955 poll):

SENATORS	REPRESENTATIVES
Clinton P. Anderson	Leo E. Allen
John W. Bricker	Leslie C. Arends
Styles Bridges	Graham A. Barden
Harry F. Byrd	Clarence J. Brown
Clifford P. Case	Clarence Cannon
Paul H. Douglas	Emanuel Celler
Ralph E. Flanders	W. Sterling Cole

SENATORS	REPRESENTATIVES
Walter F. George	Jere Cooper
Lister Hill	Clifford R. Hope
Hubert H. Humphrey	Walter H. Judd
Irving M. Ives	George Mahon
Lyndon B. Johnson	Joseph W. Martin, Jr.
Estes Kefauver	John W. McCormack
Robert S. Kerr	Sam Rayburn
William F. Knowland	James P. Richards
Herbert H. Lehman	Hugh D. Scott, Jr.
Joseph R. McCarthy	Howard W. Smith
John L. McClellan	John Taber
Eugene D. Millikin	Carl Vinson
Richard B. Russell	Francis E. Walter
Leverett Saltonstall	
John Sparkman	
Stuart Symington	

Regardless of whether or not the leaders interviewed agreed with them, the following columnists in 1955 were considered most influential: Joseph and Stewart Alsop, Roscoe Drummond, David Lawrence, Fulton Lewis, Jr., Walter Lippmann, and Drew Pearson. Ed Murrow was universally commended for his telecasts. And according to most, if national associations could have been, for example, in as capable hands as those of Allen V. Kline, who until a few years ago headed the American Farm Bureau, or H. R. Northrup, of the National Retail Lumber Dealers, the country would have been made safer in a policy sense.

Through interviews with a broad sample of the persons named in the first cross-country tour and with others, the present general study was carried another step forward. The patterns of top leadership in the large metropolitan community of Detroit did not appear to be radically different from those earlier observed in Atlanta, the community, it may be recalled, in which Mr. Baffin spoke of his ties with Mr. Ford.

The top circle of leadership, underpinned by corporate sub-ordinates, association secretaries, and various community followers and interacting with each other through innumerable committee formations, is a standard pattern of policy-making behavior found in the nation, city by city.

Because the present study has been dedicated to the field method of investigation, much of its substance lies in describing the ways of study, and consequently, before turning to a discussion of leadership views and opinions, I wish to speak further about fact-gathering.

4 LISTENING AND LOOKING FOR THE FACTS

A S I have listened to men of power talk, I
have found that it is more productive of
information to limit the number of questions asked. Two or
three basic questions, with a few subordinate and easily answered questions, spaced at ten or fifteen minute intervals,
tend to hold an interview to specifics rather than allow it to
run to generalities. I have learned that if a man really has given
thought to a topic, he can give good answers to questions in
a very brief time. By spacing basic questions over short intervals of time, fifteen or twenty minutes may be allowed at the
end of an hour's interview in which one can be more relaxed
and give the person being interviewed an opportunity to
reveal his own interests. Or, as importantly, the interviewer
may have the opportunity of picking up some of the questions
that may have occurred to him during the interview. Residual
questions, raised but unanswered in previous interviews with
other persons, also may be asked. The last, flexible period of
the interview might be characterized as an open-ended portion; that is, questions asked at that point are not specific to
the point of seeking a yes or no answer. Such free periods
have seemed extremely productive.

Each interview in the period I was getting leadership information was begun by making a brief explanatory statement about the purpose of the study. I indicated that the find-

ings would be published. The man would be handed a list of names of persons who were considered to be influential policy makers in the nation. With a small notebook in hand, I would begin the interview by asking the man to judge the men on the list to determine their relative power and influence. The rating of influence was done on a 1, 2, 3 scale, the number one rating applied to a person considered to be a "top rate policy maker," followed by second and third raters.

The men interviewed had very little difficulty with the first question, which asked them whom they knew. Most of them recognized on the list many of their friends and associates, and they had no trouble in giving their private ratings. The ratings given by each differed, but there was a good correlation of opinion concerning who they were and how influential those with top ratings were.

As the interviewee went down the list of names, I made notes on his comments. He was assured that his individual judgments would not be identified in this writing, but I reserved the right to discuss composite findings. Presently I shall give examples of parts of interviews. At those points where an individual judgment was expressed by the person interviewed, as previously suggested, I used pseudonyms or otherwise disguised the findings. The men interviewed apparently expected me to take notes, but occasionally they would ask me to accept a specific remark off the record. I have, of course, honored such confidence.

After putting the first question and its related sub-questions, I would listen. Occasionally I might ask for fuller explanation or make a suggestion to draw a man out. As the interview progressed, I would ask specifically about the interviewee's interests in the development of national policy and would press for information on what he had actually done toward implementing the policy or policies of interest to him. During the latter part of the interview, I would ask questions that might help clarify statements the man might have made earlier, and, importantly, obtain data from a free flow of ideas that may have been stimulated by previous questions. At this point, too, I might have in reserve one or two questions that I designated as roll-up ones. Let me illustrate the latter type of question.

As I moved from one person to another, I would pick up terms or words that seemed to be in fairly common usage, but which did not have immediate meaning to me. (For example, as people would look over the list of names, they might say of Meyer Kestnbaum, of Hart Schaffner & Marx, John Cowles, of the *Minneapolis Star Tribune,* or any of several other people on the list, "There is a real thinker!" This was said often enough that I felt I should inquire of a few people concerning the "thinker" concept. I found that a thinker is a person whose judgments have been right more times than wrong, and often he has been in accord with the opinions and judgments of the speaker.) Consequently, in the next few interviews, during the free period I might ask what the term meant to the person being interviewed. After several such queries my curiosity might be satisfied, and I would drop the question in favor of another.

This process of questioning was cumulative. One accumulates questions as well as data through interviewing, questions that cannot be anticipated at the beginning of study. They may not be important enough to try to get information about them from everyone seen, and a few answers may satisfy the research requirement of objectifying findings by getting answers from others rather than coming to purely subjective conclusions.

The statement was made to me early in the study, "If you can get to thirty percent of the influential Senators and twenty percent of the House members, you've got it made!" The statement was intriguingly simple, and I asked the man to name names to clarify his meaning. He named a few influential members of both houses of Congress, but upon further investigation I found that the names he had used were those of leaders of important Congressional committees who everyone agreed were important representatives whose attitudes on major pieces of legislation quite naturally were very important. Many people confer with them to give them their opinions.

I also learned that in the very definite division of labor in Congress, certain members become quite expert on this or that policy matter, and consequently they are frequently referred to about the matters in which they are experienced. One could hardly read conniving and conspiracy into this kind of arrangement, so I spent little time in following the matter of percentages of influential Congressional members further. I did remain interested in specific Congressmen, however, in relation to specific matters of policy development and I believe that Congress represents a functionally integrated social system with an internal power system just like any other institutionalized group.

Also, in the early stages of the study I was interested in getting opinions on policy control exercised by America's so-called sixty families. After a dozen or so inquiries, the answers were so uniform that I dropped the question. Sixty families do not constitute a control structure in American life. Some active members of socially prominent and wealthy families are a part of the over-all national power structure, but as a group or class they act within the bounds of behavior of the general citizenry.

I do not believe there were many questions that occurred to me that I might have asked but did not. A few were, I felt, too personal to be asked. On occasion, I heard things from some about others that seemed to be on a kind of common gossip level. As in community life, personal idiosyncrasies and shortcomings have a way of being passed around the circuit at the top leadership level. I avoided repeating the personal gossip I heard. I did not attempt to trace the power complex of crime and juvenile delinquency—matters upon which many political reputations, both positive and negative, have been made in recent years. There is, I believe, a sociological study to be made in this area, but it was beyond the scope and resources of the present effort.

In the beginning states of study, I was interested tangentially in asking about the relation of top business executives to policy development in the field of public welfare. There was so little interest on the part of those whom I asked and the questions related to such policy had been delegated to someone so far down the line in the corporate hierarchies, that I dropped it.

On the whole, the main purpose of study was to get answers to questions on patterns of power in our society rather than to get isolated, keyhole, or side opinions, and I believe the men interviewed understood this. If my questions were clearly put, very, very few were evasive, defensive, or hesitant to talk.

I have come to realize that people who are secure in their positions, the top policy makers, are less than shy in their pronouncements. They are persons who deal with and talk with other people all the time; they are easily engaged in conversation. They engage in policy and power considerations as a part of their routine work, and they are not hesitant to speak their minds. Not all speak their thoughts publicly, to be sure, but many of them have written and spoken publicly of their observations on matters of public policy. Such conversations as I had with the latter apparently constituted a kind of stock-in-trade shop talk.

The interviews usually lasted for an hour, but a few of them ran two hours. Some of the men would state ahead of the interview that they could give thirty or forty minutes of time, but once they began talking they would consume two hours. After my basic questions were answered, I was perfectly willing to listen for a longer period of time, but, because I usually had other interviews scheduled, my limit was two hours. Since some of the men interviewed were worth considerable money per hour to their companies, I could always understand any limitation of time a man would invoke, and, although I could afford to linger if the conversation was stimulating, I, too, had a limit.

It was not always possible to write letters ahead of time to all of the people I wished to interview. Sometimes while I was in a city I would be told that I really should see so-and-so. In such cases I would try to reach the man by phone, or if the office were nearby, I would go directly to his place of business and try to arrange time for an interview with his private secretary. Without an exception that I can recall, the secretaries were most helpful.

Harry Truman's secretary was one of the very helpful ones. I was on a cross-country trip seeing a random sample of decision makers. In studying a map on the plane between Tulsa and Kansas City I noticed that Independence, Missouri, was quite close to Kansas City. Mr. Truman was not in my one third sample on this particular trip, but I mused over the notion that it might be interesting to interview him, anyway.

Upon arrival in Kansas City in the afternoon, I called Mr. Truman's office. After I had stated the purpose of my call, a very pleasant, feminine voice said that Mr. Truman was not in, but that he would be in promptly at nine the next morning. She said she would tell Mr. Truman of my call. The next morning it was apparent that she had told my story to Mr. Truman, for when I telephoned, I was put through directly to him. He agreed to see me immediately.

When Mr. Truman learned of my interest in doing a study of top leadership, and after he had looked at a list of names I gave to him, he said, "I guess I know all of those people." I asked him if he knew and had worked with the Republicans as well as Democrats on the list. He said seriously, "These men, a lot of them, put country ahead of party. Yes, I've worked with most of them on the list." Then with a chuckle he continued, "I've worked against a few of them!"

He talked about some of his experiences in the Senate and felt that the Congressional committees were extremely important in policy development. He cited examples of investigations made by committees he had been on (relating to railway and electric public services) that had helped form public policy "in the interest of the people."

When I inquired about men who get to the President to help him make up his mind on issues, Mr. Truman emphatically replied, "No man can make up the President's mind. He has to come to his own decisions." I wondered about the help he gets from his immediate advisors, and he said, "Of course, the President gets facts and points of view from all kinds of people, but when decisions have to be made, the President alone can make them."

The rest of our interview related to questions that were posed and answered in Mr. Truman's book.

The photographs in an office, as with those in Mr. Baffin's, referred to at the beginning of this book, sometimes told me something. John McCloy, of the Chase Manhattan Bank, had a picture of Conrad Adenhauer, which fact fitted into his interest in international relations, his own postwar experiences, and his views on the settlement of the German question. Plaques and other civic mementos also trace a history of interest and achievement for many men. (Mr. Truman had Averell Harriman's photo on his desk prior to the 1956 Democratic convention.)

I wish to illustrate two or three things by the paragraphs to follow. First, I shall exhibit two examples of the type of sketchy notes I was able to take as an interview progressed. These notes will include my brief impressions as I listened to the person interviewed. The first set of notes will be a reproduction of those made in an interview with a top labor executive whom I shall call George X. Weathers. The second set will be sketchy statements made by another man as he talked about selected names on the list of leaders provided him.

Secondly, I shall give in some detail an illustrative write-up of an interview first recorded on tape from notes and memory. In this recording, I will have deleted some references made by the speaker about other individuals.

And lastly, it may become apparent through these several illustrations that, while the individual interviews can only be considered definitive as case studies in picturing the whole national policy-making process, they are suggestive of the fact that a series of them might shed light on many questions about the process.

The notes to follow were made in the summer of 1954, and I added a few explanatory phrases to them immediately after leaving Weathers. Returning to my hotel room, I dictated on a tape recorder all that I could remember of the interview. The notes given here were my memory joggers.

Negro secretary, attractive girl, says she has sister teaching in Durham College. Says house in front of new office building was once the home of prominent industrialist. New building modern. Old house used as clinic (?). New building has desks, furniture, to match modern building design.

[After introductory remarks with Mr. Weathers, we discussed the names on the policy leadership list.] Does not seem to know too many, or does not say so. Hard to get down to cases. Maybe "global thinker" tag right. Friendly, young looking. Big thinker maybe. Illustrates local talk with two auto makers on Detroit problems. Housing in this connection. Not always about wage negotiations.

Mr. W. talking anti-communism as national policy to be carried forward. Be prepared, at least by stepping up production to meet threats and to meet needs of all kinds. Kind of social work talk on global scale. [This policy question was then current.] Down-dip in Detroit employment important. Foolish not to think of Detroit as a "critical" city in relation to it. Should not try to cover this up with newspaper sweet-talk. ["Sweet-talk" was not Weathers' word but was my own short, summary word for the gist of the conversation.]

Most interested in free trade. Thinks this idea fills out the big picture. Some of the unions do not agree with this. Especially bicycle-making unions, who are hit by imports. He sees how this can be, but feels broader view more important. Gave batch of policy statements and copy of speeches from files.

In this interview labor problems and welfare, anti-communism, and free trade were mentioned as national policy matters. The printed materials given to me by Mr. Weathers listed a great many other policies that were of concern to him, but those mentioned were the ones that came readily to his mind at the time we talked.

The next interview material will illustrate, in tabular form, my notes as one man, Mr. X. Jones, looked over the list of names of potential policy makers. The statements made reflect the ideas of only this informant and cannot be considered a composite view or identification of the men listed. He was asked to rate the men about whom he talked, in a power scale, and to indicate under what circumstances he knew each. Only the latter material is given here. As Mr. Jones talked, I took notes as follows:

MAN KNOWN BY JONES	WAY IN WHICH MAN WAS KNOWN
Harold Boeschenstein	War Production Board
Lucius Clay	Business association, good customer
E. H. Crump	Met occasionally at Kentucky Derby
K. T. Keller	Business relationship with Chrysler tank arsenal
George Sloan	Co-director of U.S. Steel
James B. Black	Director U.S. Steel
William L. Clayton	Customer relationship
John L. Collyer	Worked with him on War Production Board
Benjamin F. Fairless	Associated U.S. Steel
H. J. Heinz II	Business relationships Pittsburgh

Man Known by Jones	Way in Which Man Was Known
Charles R. Hook	Various ways, especially on Department of Commerce Advisory Committee
Ben Moreell	Pittsburgh business community
Fred Murray	Customer relationship
Clarence Randall	Government committee
Carrol M. Shanks	Personal friend
Charles E. Wilson	War Production Board

In the process of hearing in other interviews one man after another tell of his associations with the men named here and with others not known to Mr. Jones, a definite patterning of such relationships became apparent. The most frequent relations between men could be classified as friendship ties, association in trade, civic or governmental committees, prestige club co-memberships, and customer relationships. As I heard talk about various men on my lists of names, even before I met them I knew a good deal about them. Some of the issues or policies in which these men were interested also became quite familiar topics of conversation.

A few of the men with whom I talked kept in their desks, or handy to them, a card index of men of their acquaintance. One, a banker, even had pictures of the men pasted to these identification cards. There seemed to be little question that many of the men knew each other personally. There was little question either concerning the fact that many had a rough evaluation in their minds of others' relative influence in matters of public policy.

One of the first interviews held with a leader on my listing was with Clarence X. Hathaway of American Form Design Corporation, one of the nation's largest industrial firms. My interview with him is given here as an example of processed recording, with an inserted paragraph of slight disagreement, made later by another leader, with one statement made by Mr. Hathaway.

On April 23, 1953, at 8:15 a.m. I called on Mr. Clarence X. Hathaway, Chairman of American Form Design. His offices were on the top floor of the Design Building in Chicago. I was greeted at the elevator entrance of the executive suite, at that hour, by a young Negro male receptionist. This man led me to a private waiting room furnished in modern design. Soon I was asked for my calling card by another male secretary, who asked me, "Is Mr. Hathaway expecting you?"

When I replied in the affirmative, the secretary disappeared and in two or three minutes came back and asked me to follow him. We went down a heavily carpeted hall and at the end of it there was another male Negro standing in front of a door. I was then shown into Mr. Hathaway's office and announced to him by the door secretary.

As I observed Mr. Hathaway I would say that he was a man of about 5′ 11″ in height and in his mature years. The hair at his temples was grey and he looked a little older than the picture that I had seen of him that was taken for the NAM executive board group. He was dressed in a conservative brown suit, with a matching pocket handkerchief. He had a good-humored expression and talked with a twinkle in his eye when illustrating his points.

Mr. Hathaway's status was reflected in his surroundings. His office was spacious and hardwood-paneled. He had a large desk in the center of the room. Like many other executives, he used a two-desk system, for behind his large office desk there was another desk which he used as a work table. His office was not furnished in keeping with the modern furniture of the reception room in which I had waited. It was more conservative, made of dark hardwoods. With the exception of the *Wall Street Journal*, his larger desk was free of other printed materials or work papers.

We began our interview by my stating the purposes of my visit. First, I had a list of names that I had gathered from national associations which I wished Mr. Hathaway to go over to see which people he knew and whether he would take some of them off or add others to the list. Secondly, I wanted to get his opinion on some of the basic issues or policies confronting the nation which he felt were current and requiring decision. Thirdly, I wanted to know what Mr. Hathaway had done in policy-making, stating that I wanted to learn whether there was a hard core of policy makers on the national level similar to that found in local community studies.

Rather than waiting to see my list of names, Mr. Hathaway began talking about policy matters. He said that if I had visited him two or three years before he would have told me that the major issues or policies that needed to be worked on in the country were inflation and ridding ourselves of governmental controls. He felt that the new government in Washington was handling these problems fairly satisfactorily and that businessmen now could turn their attention to work within their own companies. He indicated that he had been quite active previously in working on these two problems. At the present time he is interested in matters of public welfare and the private support of education.

He said that he would like to read a statement he had prepared for a meeting of his board, scheduled immediately after our interview. His secretary came in with a handwritten copy of the statement he was to read to his board. He was recommending to the board of American Form Design that it appropriate between $150,000 and $200,000 for the support of private education. His statement stressed the fact that large gifts from individual families were no longer available in amounts as they had been in times past and that private education was dependent on corporate giving.

He said that he was interested in development of state associations of private colleges for fund-raising. "There is," he went on, "a group of business leaders behind this movement, and the American Form Design Company with a few others is in the vanguard of it." He said that he was on the boards of three colleges, Chicago, M.I.T., and the College of Wooster. He was also interested in the United Negro College Fund and the National Fund for Education. John D. Rockefeller, Frank W. Abrams, Harvey Firestone, Alfred P. Sloan, Irving S. Olds, Richard Mellon and himself, among others, had been instrumental in the development of the United Negro College Fund. He said that the college presidents lined up the men he had mentioned to help the fund-raising venture.

I asked Mr. Hathaway if education was a primary civic interest with him and he indicated that it was. I named a person in Atlanta who also makes education a primary interest and concern and who is also in the upper brackets of the power hierarchy of Atlanta. Mr. Hathaway knew him. At that point I brought out my list of names of persons who represented leadership in some of the major cities of the nation.

After he had discussed various persons on the list, I commented on the fact that Mr. Hathaway knew so many of the names. He said, "As I think I may have said before, I get around the country a lot. A few weeks ago I was in the Dakotas at the opening of some new business interests there. I belong to a lot of different associations and am particularly interested in the work of NAM and the Carnegie Foundation. I am also on boards of different corporations and through these activities I meet an awful lot of people."

I suggested that the interaction between the men Mr. Hathaway knew might make for a uniformity of interest and bring them to agreement on questions of national policy. He replied to this by saying, "There is probably not as much unity as you would expect." "A great part of my job," he continued, "is conciliating conflicting claims in three major areas. Three groups—the stockholders, the consumers, and the workers—basically have conflicting claims. I am continually having to put our company straight in relation to these various claims and mediating between these groups. The interests of my company often differ from the interests of another company, not necessarily a competitor, and in certain issues we could never come to agreement. Let me take an item that is not primarily in our business bailiwick. According to the way I think, certain electronic industries should be greatly expanded at the present time. To contract too severely all plant building operations would be cutting too deeply. You have to take every situation and size it up as it comes."

I asked Mr. Hathaway about the role of national associations. He did not answer directly, but said that in his opinion NAM is the most potent national association. It "almost single-handed carried the day in saving the Taft-Hartley Act after Truman won in the 1948 election." "By working behind the scenes, that is, organizing business interests and getting them down to Washington to speak up, NAM was able to do something effective for business. There are always a lot of little associations springing up, and professional association executives who want to make a good thing out of pitting little business men against big business, but the real job of NAM is to show little business that their interests are in accord with those of so-called big business."

Mr. Hathaway said, "With the rise of the managerial type of organization, things have changed. Fellows like myself have come up from the ranks and we recognize that you cannot treat consumers and labor and stockholders with a high hand. The 'public-be-damned' attitude on the part of business is completely dead, in my opinion." I suggested that John D. Rockefeller had started a public relations program for Standard Oil that may have set a pattern. He replied, "Yes, but he got started pretty late. I think we do a much better job now, and the national associations are very helpful." Mr. Hathaway also said that "sometimes NAM itself gets pretty far out in left field. It may send out broadsides on this or that issue but it, again, is not as effective when it does this as when it works behind the scenes organizing people in the business community to put the pressure on where pressure is most effective." (Somewhat different points of view concerning the role of national associations were expressed by different leaders. Another leader, in discussing and weighing his various associational connections, had this to say: "I am greatly interested in the work of the United States Chamber of Commerce. I feel that the U.S. Chamber is a lot closer to the grass roots than many of the larger industrial associations, and even it may not be too close sometimes. But if you really want to know what people think on any given issue, I'd say go to the Chamber fellows. I know that Clarence Hathaway would not agree with me on this, because he is a great champion of the NAM. I think, though, that the NAM is pretty well tied to the industrial people and presents a rather one-sided view. In our company we are not only interested in industrial matters, but we have nearly 3,000 retail outlets to consider. Therefore, we keep a lively interest in the Chamber of Commerce.")

In speaking of Chicago affairs and other leaders of Chicago, Mr. Hathaway said that the industrial group, in his opinion, would be the top opinion leaders of the community. Other groups in Chicago may do many things "on a purely local basis," but the industrial group would carry the ball on major national issues.

He went on to say that in the process of hammering out policy and putting it into effect most industrialists would look first to their own corporate group; in his own situation he would look to American Form Design and would get in touch with some of Design's subsidiaries in other parts of the country. He would look to the chairmen of the boards or presidents of various company subsidiaries and rely on some of their opinions on major national issues. As any project moves along, such as the one in private education, these men would reach out to others, and, as in the community, there is a group within the national leadership that is always called on. One has to exercise some discretion in choosing men according to the project under consideration, because interests of the various men differ.

At this time, we had reached a point a little better than three quarters through the interview, and I asked a question which was indirectly related to the topics he had been discussing but which could not be considered a basic study question, since it dealt with social status considerations. It was the type of question I reserved, as the study progressed, for the free period of the interview. I asked Mr. Hathaway if he was familiar with Lundberg's book on sixty ruling families in America. He said, "Yes, I know about the book but I think this sixty families business is bunk. Some of the charitable associations like to get the names of some of those families on their boards because they can get contributions out of them, but these families often do not have much influence elsewhere. The exception to this is the man who does things; then he can be considered a leader. Money has meaning, but most of the fellows who are actually doing the job are like me."

Before leaving the office I asked Mr. Hathaway for a biographical statement of himself which he asked his secretary to give me. He also gave me a copy of the annual report of American Design.

With this interview material, as with other data gathered in the study, news clippings related to it were filed for future reference and to aid in filling out the whole picture. It was always interesting to hear of a policy in the making, as in American Form Design's growing interest in gifts to private education, sometimes months before statements about it appeared in the press, and then watch the process of its public unfoldment. Most often, matters related to policy shifts were announced, without debate and as if firmly established. In those cases where some debate arose, it often appeared that those who argued, argued with themselves.

Standing alone, Mr. Hathaway only represents a person who has an interest in education, but Mr. Hathaway does not stand alone in the education venture described. He has the apparatus of his corporation with which to bolster his interest. The corporation itself reaches into hundreds of communities around the nation and world. As a leader Mr. Hathaway is in contact with leaders of other large corporate groups, and, in turn, these persons are in touch with a multitude of college presidents and educators in the top position of the structures of educational institutions. These individuals are also capable of moving associational groupings such as the NAM and the various educational associations.

By moving from one man to another and by listening to what they say, I began to get glimpses of and insights into a whole set of relationships, but isolated statements come first. I shall now move to a series of statements that provide a fuller background for a later ordering of data.

AS I re-read the journal of my interviews with leaders, I find that they speak very eloquently for themselves. Therefore, with as little as possible deletion of data or editing of it to fit hindsight, but with the notion of stripping out repetitious material and including only typical interview case records, this chapter is presented.

It was from materials such as these that finally I began to draw some major conclusions concerning the structuring of national power. No single interview is given here completely, nor does any single man quoted have a complete picture of the whole process of policy development or power-wielding. Some confess to know little about such matters. Some speak with authoritative conviction and know relatively little. Others speak with clear knowledge. Most talked with little prompting.

The first excerpts of material presented have been included to illustrate further the degree of knowledge these national leaders, in large cities across the nation, had of each other. Their choices of other leaders can be gathered from their remarks. In the case illustrations to follow these nine, I have limited the statements related to leadership nominations. In each case presented I have given a pseudonym to the speaker, disguised his city, and given a fictional name to his business or profession. Profane, spiteful, or hurtful statements about individuals have been disguised or deleted.

Mr. Norwall Chose Other Leaders

Dan X. Norwall. Banker. (Number One)[1]

Dan Norwall, a grey-haired man seated at the top executive desk in a very neat, pastel-colored office in the National Bank of Rail Junction, served as its president. Around the molding of the ceiling, carved in bleached hardwood in gold letters, were the words, "Work is an open door." Mr. Norwall told me that he started in life on a 55-acre farm in the West and that for many years Rail Junction had been very good for him. He showed me a plaque that was given to him very recently by his employees.

He added certain names to the list that I presented to him, including the following: Fred Murray of Dallas; James A. Elkins, president of the Chamber of Commerce and lawyer in Houston; Humphrey Lee, president of SMU; Heinz Baker of Houston; Dan Moody, ex-governor of Texas, Austin.

Mr. Norwall said the best way to develop national policy is to get around personally and to get directly to people like the Secretary of the Treasury and others to express your view. He said that a certain amount of work in the banking field, of course, is done through the American Banking Association and through the clearing houses. But in his own bank he said he had a crack economist who kept in touch with all that's going on in the banking field.

He talked at considerable length about H. L. Hunt. He said, "H. L. Hunt is the richest man in the world, and that takes in all of the nabobs and potentates around it." He said that Mr. Hunt had not put himself forward a great deal but was a "modest and retiring man. He is the type that speaks softly but carries a big stick and uses it when necessary." He spoke of Mr. Hunt's developing of Northern oil fields in which there were a billion barrels of oil valued at $2.60 a barrel at current market prices. He said that Mr. Hunt probably had a billion dollars in liquid assets, such a large sum of money that he himself could hardly comprehend it.

1. The rating placed after the pseudonym of each leader represents the final rating given to the man by other leaders in the study. "Number ones" are top leaders; second and third raters are down the power status scale, but even so, may be quite influential. We are dealing here with status considerations of a top structure in the nation.

Mr. Powers Selected Leaders by Levels of Influence

Don X. Powers.   Industrialist.   (Number One)

Looking over the names listed, Mr. Powers said, "The levels of these men vary, as you well know. Take, for example, Jordan X. Crow. He would be a top rate industrial person in the automotive field. Compare him with a man like Ford and you would find that Ford represents an entirely different level. Ford would of course top Crow." He said that he saw many names that he would put a great deal of trust in. For example, he felt that he would trust anything that General Wood might say. If he wanted to know something in Chicago or something about what is going on in the nation he would probably get in touch in one way or another with General Wood. From this and other statements made by Mr. Powers it was apparent that he put the greatest emphasis on interpersonal relations and had formed in his mind a pattern of personal contact. He said that he would use the associations on occasion, but he did not feel they are as potent as the personal contact idea.

Mr. Rinklind Kept Tab on the Leaders

R. X. Rinklind.   West Coast Banker.   (Number One)

Mr. Rinklind said that he had had considerable interest in national leadership over a number of years, and as a matter of fact he had been keeping a card index of names of leaders from the beginning of his business experience, telling where a man is from and some of the pertinent facts about him. Mr. Rinklind went over his own list of names and gave some of them to me to jot down, including: Harry J. Bauer (several of the names given to me by Mr. Rinklind were names contained on our list and I have not repeated them here); Don Belding; Dr. James W. Fifield, Jr.; Conrad Hilton; Justin Dart; Walt Disney; Dr. Lee DuBridge; Dr. Hubert Eaton; Dr. Ruth Milliken; Leonard K. Firestone; Allan Hancock; Paul H. Helms; Howard Hughes; Louis B. Mayer; McIntyre Faries; John A. McCone; Ed. W. Pauley; Alden G. Roach; W. S. Rosekrans; Spyros P. Skouras; Dr. Robert Gordon Sproul; E. H. Stuart; I. C. R. Atkin; Henry C. Alexander.

He said the interests of his bank were geographically wide-

spread and that they had to know the operations of many community industries and political organizations. While his bank was
one of the largest banks in the world it did not cater primarily to
large-scale industry but was more interested in straight-out banking operations in communities and in encouraging and fostering
small-scale industry. He said that he could best express himself
by going down the list of names, which he had me read out to him,
and telling me whether or not a man was any good. If he said
they were okay, or all right, they were Number One's, if he said
they were no good I could drop them into second or third place
or clear out of the picture if I wanted to. His list of names consequently was marked that way.

Mr. Batesaw Did Not Wish to Rate Others

G. X. Batesaw.   Banker.   (Number One)
  Mr. Batesaw was an example of the old-family person in his
town. He was a graduate of Groton and Yale and told me that I
might find materials about him in *Who's Who*. He did not wish
to rate people on a 1-2-3 scale but he said that he would go over
them, give me his opinion about some of the top people, and I
could rate the others myself. He went down the list and made
comments on the men such as: "This man speaks for himself."
"I went to school with this man at Yale." "This fellow is 100%."
"McKee is *the* man up in his region." "Mudd is a top fellow."
"X. Gimly is self-advertising." "Ryerson is highly thought of and I
think of him highly myself." "Symonds is a go-getter." "Robert
Fleming speaks for himself." "X. Grady is a person that I will let
you draw your own conclusions on." "Walter X. Johnson of San
Francisco is a top man in the city in a business sense but he does
not mix much in the life of the city." (The implication was that
he did not mix much in social life.) "Keesling is ill." "X. Killion is
a successful Democratic politician which puts him down now."
Of other men he said that they were very able, that they had
strong characteristics, they were good men, etc. He spoke of Mr.
X. O'Toole of San Francisco as a very good man but not a very
big one. He said that O'Toole had headed an association of employers who were trying to head off strikes. The association was

not very successful and consequently Mr. O'Toole had rather dropped out of things.

He believed that the national policies that need to be worked on were those of balancing the budget and reducing taxes. He felt that President Eisenhower coined a good phrase when he spoke of "the honest dollar" rather than "the hard dollar." He felt that the hard-dollar phrase had some notion of depression and that we should not talk ourselves into another depression.

Mr. O'Toole Downrated Himself

James X. O'Toole. Lawyer. (Third Rater)

He did not feel at all sure of himself in marking the list of names and he asked if he could look them over and send them to me. I consented to this. He said that he doubted that he should be on the list with some of the other men that I have from his city.

Mr. Daringware Thumbnail–Sketched an Array of Leaders

Kilby X. Daringware. Industrialist. (Number One)

Mr. Daringware made many comments on the names on the list. Of Bechtel he said he was a "builder of ideas as well as things." Of Black he said that he was the public service type of big businessman who has many connections in Washington and that many people looked to him for conservative business viewpoints. Blyth was a conservative banker and was known better nationally than locally because of the business connections he had; he was in a class in the banking business with Dillon and Read. When Daringware came to the name of Terrence X. Colow of New Orleans he said that Colow's influence was not too great because he was too long in government, from 1941 until two or three years ago. He now had to prove himself as a part of the business community rather than as a Washington bureaucrat. He knew Fred Crawford as a contact within NAM. When he came to the name of Hugh Roy Cullen he said that he had had dinner with him a couple of nights ago, knew him very well, and thought he was a top leader.

Joe X. Glencoe of Chicago was an aggressive salesman-showman who carried on an extensive public relations program. He held big luncheons and other get-togethers at his home and in the clubs of Chicago. He invited top men from the West coast, all of which helped his competitive, nationwide business to hold its own. Holton was a little like Pete X. Lodestrom. Holton was an attorney for the Spode Oil Company and chairman of the board but he was a secondary man. Daringware thought that Humphries was a young fellow but coming along. He thought that Mc-Collum was one of the upper oil executives as president of the Continental Oil Company but he was not particularly active in national affairs. Daringware agreed with others that McKee was a leading businessman in his territory. He said that X. Joiner of the Fellen Oil Company in Los Angeles was a little like Colow in New Orleans—he had been active in government too long but was probably making a good president of a subsidiary company of a big oil company. Mudd he thought of as one of the richest and most prominent men in the Los Angeles business community. He did not believe that X. Hall was respected because of his radical "right" point of view. He thought that Reuther was only effective in labor circles.

Symonds was a promoter and had made a lot of progress in a few years. He was probably moving up into the big time. Griswold was an outstanding investment trust banker who held a lot of Standard Oil stocks. Haas was an outstanding banker in San Francisco. Koster was an old businessman who ran his business as it was run 100 years ago. Lapham made a spectacular success when he broke the 1934 strike in San Francisco, but he had not done much since. Boyson ran "a big, low grade department store comparable to Macy's in New York." X. O'Toole was "just a paid manager for some of the local associations." Mailliard was an outstanding civic leader, one of Governor Warren's early supporters. He had been police commissioner, and inherited an interest in a firm that dated back to 1850.

Montgomery was a senior top-flight businessman. Stanton was an economic royalist, a bit too old for action. Pigott inherited a large foundry and was a member of the Standard Oil board. X. Courtwright was on the Industrial Conference Board but that was about all. Russell was just interested in business. Gregoff was a much publicized man. X. George of the Greater Air Lines was a great entertainer, like Glencoe, and the speaker saw a lot of him. Whitman had made a name for himself by developing the California Zephyr. Zellerbach had inherited his business and had a great interest in civic affairs.

Mr. Grover Was a Rapid Talker

Zachary X. Grover.   Industrialist.   (Number One)

Mr. Grover was a man apparently in his late fifties or early sixties, rather stocky with lots of hair and a florid complexion. In going over the list of names that I had with me he made rapid-fire remarks. He stated that he knew Randolph Burgess very well. He felt that someone from the National City Bank of New York should be on the list. He felt that the U.S. Chamber of Commerce, NAM, and the National Community Chest Councils were three of the outstanding associations in the country. He indicated that Mr. Swope was a personal friend of his. He felt that most of the men on the Business Advisory Committee of the Department of Commerce should be included on our list. He also felt that Mr. Proctor of the Commerce Committee should be on the list. He felt that I should see G. Keith Funston, head of the New York City Stock Exchange. Fred Lazarus was important. He said that Thomas Watson, Sr., of IBM should be included, although he was a senior member for any list. He named a fellow in agriculture in California, Kemp. He thought I could get some good information from Arch Booth, executive director of the Chamber of Commerce in Washington, D.C. He indicated that I could use his name in approaching any of these men. [I never used this method.] Another person named was George Sloan, Blue Ridge Mutual Fund, New York City. He said, "Spang was with the meat packing people in Chicago. He switched over to razor blades, and this created some discussion in the industrial field." In going over the list of names he checked off names of persons whom he knew well and with whom he had worked in times past. He said he knew most of them and had served on various corporate boards and committees with most of them. Mr. Grover talked very rapidly, and some of the things he said about the men on the list I did not catch.

Before I left Mr. Grover's office he gave me a copy of a speech that he had delivered to a workshop at a large university a few days before. He talked a good deal about his civic interests and indicated an interest in education particularly. One of his own major interests was Red Cross work.

After we had finished the interview, he called his personal secretary and asked that a Mr. X. Bailey, a public relations man, come into his office. When Mr. Bailey came in, he asked him to show me around the main offices of the plant and he further asked that I be shown a motion picture that had been made of company operations. It was a 30-minute film and I sat with only Mr. Bailey in an auditorium that would hold perhaps 5,000 people.

Mr. Farewell's Remarks Briefly Underscored Others

John X. Farewell. Broker. (Second Rater)

Mr. Farewell said that the size of his city (42 square miles) allows people to get to know each other much more easily than in other cities. He felt that men like X. Sedley of the Eastern Company, who was a close advisor to many cabinet members, Lockhead of the banking interests, T. S. Petersen, Montgomery and Zellerbach, along with A. Crawford Greenewalt, were among the most influential men on the national level. He limited his national choices to a few. He felt that power-wielding in the nation is really a process of linking leaders who are influential in their own communities with leaders in other communities and that being a solid citizen in one's own community is the first essential of national leadership.

Mr. Grayson Thought 100 Top Leaders Too Many

Thomas X. Grayson. Editor. (Second Rater)

Mr. Grayson was an executive editor of a Northern newspaper. He knew a considerable number of men on the list and checked them off rather quickly since he had to catch a plane. I had about 30 minutes with him. He said that his ideas on policy could be summarized in saying that he was a liberal Republican. He believed that our national policy in relation to other nations of the world should be spelled out in a policy of lower tariffs and free foreign trade. He felt that we had been very inept in our international relations and that only a liberal Republican way of doing things could save us from a disastrous conflict.

As he looked over the names (then 300) he asked how many of them I thought would come up as very top names in the development of national policy. I estimated that perhaps 100, or approximately ⅓, might be considered No. 1 leaders. He expressed great surprise at this, because he said he felt that the men who are real policy leaders in the nation were in much smaller number. He was interested in hearing how the study came out and whether or not I came to the same conclusions later.

Not all of the men interviewed were familiar with as large a proportion of the national leadership network as these. Some showed embarrassment at being asked to name top policy leaders of whom they had heard, perhaps, but whom they did not know personally. Most, however, were local leaders and apparently secure in the vital positions they occupied. Some were familiar with the power groupings within the business or the profession in which they operated, and therefore chose only to talk about the people in these groupings. Some said they knew many leaders across the nation, but they did not do anything about the formation of policy either in their businesses or in the public interest. The next excerpts are taken from materials gathered from such men.

Mr. Burns Was a Big Man Locally, a Little Man Nationally

Joseph X. Burns.   Local Manufacturer.   (Third Rater)

Mr. Burns was the head of a large fertilizer company in his city. He ran a good-sized business, but he indicated very quickly that he did not know many people on the national level. It became increasingly apparent that he was completely out of his depth as he looked at the various names on the list. He could not understand how I had got his name, and the interview was somewhat uncomfortable. He felt that he should have known a lot of the people who were listed but the fact was that he did not. I learned something from Mr. Burns about the fertilizer industry. But on the questions related to the development of national policy he could not help me. Mr. Burns did indicate, however, that in his local civic work he had briefly met some of the people on the list, but he would say, "I have met this fellow, but he would not know me." The great glided into town once in a while and Mr. Burns shook hands with them.

Mr. Glassman Knew Men in Only His Field of Endeavor

N. X. Glassman. Department Store Operator. (Second Rater)

Mr. Glassman said that the National Association of Retail Dry Goods Merchants and the American Retail Federation were the best lobbies for his business, the oldest and largest department store in his city. He said, however, that he did not participate in national association affairs, because "I figure that only those who are not doing so well or those who are looking for a job go to those meetings. The men of real influence in the field do not go." There were four stores, according to Mr. Glassman, that were really prime movers in a power way and at the same time were real merchandising establishments in the country. They were the Lazarus stores in Columbus, Hudson's in Detroit, Marshall Field's in Chicago, and Rich's in Atlanta. They all meant a great deal to the people in their communities and had influence through their leaders in national affairs.

He was concerned that he did not know a great many people on the national list. He said, "I guess that shows what a local yokel I am."

He thought the national associations and businessmen were all mixed up in taking the stand that government should be out of everything. He gave as an example the postal fight. He believed that every other government service is free and that no one should expect the post office to pay its whole way. He believed that the excess profits tax had hurt small business but that the NAM stand was premature. He felt that the budget must be balanced. He thought that Eisenhower was not doing anything but carrying out Truman's policies.

He showed me plans for an extension of his present store facilities, but he believed that there would be a slight "shakedown" in the economy and he was waiting to see what would happen. He was very interested in various city plans for industrial expansion in his community and showed me some of the materials related to this.

He spoke of knowing Dick Rich in Atlanta personally; he was well acquainted with the uncle of Dick Rich, Walter Rich, and visited them often. He said that Frank Neeley of Rich's had seen the uptrend in business back in the late thirties and was largely responsible for Rich's expansion before World War II; the company in Atlanta has quadrupled its original size. Before I left, he came back to his attitude toward Eisenhower as President to say that during the war he had been in the army and had seen how wasteful that proposition was; he was fully convinced that no general should ever run the country.

Mr. Dodds Stayed Put

Nick X. Dodds.   Mining Operator.   (Second Rater)

Mr. Dodds said that he did not get around the country a great deal but that he had voluminous correspondence with many of the men on the list. His primary interest was in financing mining industries in some of the Western states. His own interests in national policy boiled down to certain policies in conservation of mining resources, exploration of such resources, mining laws, tariff, health and safety factors in the mining industry, governmental controls, and labor relations. He said that in any of these policies he relied considerably on various associations and he gave the names of some of them. He said that for technical and professional advice he got in touch with Edward H. Robie, secretary of the American Institute of Mining and Metallurgical Engineers, in New York. He also thought that the American Mining Congress was a very effective policy development organization and lobby and that on a visit to Washington I should get in touch with the executive vice president, Julian D. Conover.

He said that he felt that in national leadership one would probably find those in the manufacturing industries having the strongest influence. He felt that the use of basic committees to make reports and report their findings to various leaders was the most effective. He said that most of the reports were usually summarized in resolutions that were either carried to Congressional hearings or taken directly to a man in government who might be able to do something. He felt that most men were influential because of the positions they held and consequently one found leadership in the larger corporate enterprises. He felt that our list was weak in the area of banking, particularly Eastern banking.

Mr. Dodds said that he felt he was most effective when he worked directly with individual men. He told me that I could get a biographical statement on him in *Who's Who*.

Mr. Burr Just Sat

Henry X. Burr. Department Store Owner. (Third Rater)

Mr. Burr was the owner of one of the largest department stores in the Middle West. He came from an old local family and knew a good many of the people on our list of names. When I asked him what he did about national policy he said, "I just sit in my store and gripe!" He felt that he really ought to do more about some of these things than he did but he relied on the American Retail Federation in Washington to be effective for him.

He said that he took his place in Community Chest drives and in local charities, but he did not participate in national affairs and he did not see how his name got on our list. He was a Yale graduate whose father thought he was a radical on tariff ideas. He was now for free trade. Although Henry Ford was not from his city, he knew him quite well and went along with Ford's ideas on tariffs.

Mr. Winkler Was a Civic Leader and Business Spokesman

Jerry X. Winkler. Commercial Enterpriser. (Second Rater)

Mr. Winkler was said to be a spokesman (called by some a front man) for many of the larger interests in his city. During the war he had been active in Washington, D. C., and had worked under Donald Nelson. He said that he knew Sidney Weinberg before he went to Washington, and he was a fraternity brother of Paul Hoffman. With these connections and because of the fact that he had worked up in a wood products industry in Bee Town, he was asked to head the OPA program in the state. He had been on the Hoover board, and he met many men when he was a student at Stanford University. Traveling and making acquaintances had got him where he was, he believed. He had been in his present position for fifteen years. He was active in the local Chamber of Commerce and many civic affairs. His philosophy was that of "putting into the community more than you take out." He was on the state Chamber of Commerce board and he was a past president. There, he said, he got to know the governor and the lieutenant governor and it "gave him an in" in state politics. He had been very active in getting freeways for his town and had appeared before many Senate sub-committees. He said that one of the problems of leadership was trying to get younger men to replace the older ones. Every time they had a meeting, they tried to pick a group of men who could put over any issue, and the question always arose whether they could bring in young men. Usually they felt that they could not but on occasion they brought in one or two "to train them up."

Mr. Springer Had Been Overseas

Ed X. Springer.   Manufacturer.   (Second Rater)

Mr. Springer worked in an open area office on the top floor of the Cosmetics Products Company. On the walls were pictures of the nine foreign operations of the company. Mr. Springer impressed me as congenial and interested in public relations. He was middle-aged, gray-haired, rather short and stocky.

As he went over the list of names I supplied him, he kept saying, "This is a man one sees around the track." He continued to use the phrase and I asked him what it meant. He said, "You see these fellows around the track all the time. You can think of it as a race track if you want to. They are owners, touts, and fellows that have the inside of the track, so to speak. You can enlarge on that if you want to." Mr. Springer added several names to the list.

In talking about the men, he said that a good way to illustrate picking leaders is a story of the selection of a NAM committee to do some work for the Department of Commerce in Europe. The Secretary of the Department of Commerce had called him and asked him to go to Europe for a 14-day period to do something about economic aid. Later, when he was going to a dinner in a Midwest city he saw an auto manufacturer. He called to him and asked him if he could see him for a few minutes following the dinner, and the man agreed. When he saw his friend later he asked him if he could use one of his men, a top-ranking officer in the auto company, to accompany him on the European junket.

The auto man said that he would agree to release his subordinate for whatever use Springer could make of him, but he felt that Springer had picked the wrong man. The auto company had a foreign representative in Paris who knew his way around in European defense and economic planning, and he felt that this man was the one that should be used. He insisted, however, that Springer could use the first if he still wanted him. Springer chose the Paris representative. He said that they spent fourteen days in Paris. "We really worked the auto maker's representative and we worked ourselves too. We only had one night free in Paris!" He said that there were twelve top-flight men involved in this process and that they picked men under them to do the job. Someone asked him later how he had been able to get such high-powered men on the particular committee. He answered that he did not pick twelve but picked one good one who in turn picked the others. (I later learned that a national leader who rates above Springer had a hand in picking Springer, who in turn picked others.)

Speaking of recruiting men for government assignments, Springer said that one way he got men to work on top-flight projects was to call them on the phone and ask them how they thought the President was doing. He said invariably they answered, "Oh, fine, fine!" He then asked them whether or not they thought it was a good idea for a top-flight businessman to go down and help out and they heartily agreed. He then put the bee on them for a job, and although they might complain about the fact of being tagged they invariably went along with him.

Mr. Springer indicated that his company engaged in a large volume of international trade, and I asked him whether he worked through Washington on these matters. He said, "No, not necessarily. The fellows in Washington promise you all kinds of support and help on these things, but we feel that it is better to go directly to operating men in the country involved. We recently had some criticism in our board of directors about going directly to France because of the unstable political position of France. Some of us argued that France will be there for a hundred years, and we invested in pumping up an operation there. This is good business because we put American dollars in there that were needed very badly and it all comes back to us anyway. We do not go around shaking in our boots about unstable countries. One of them may freeze up for a while but sooner or later they thaw out and we get our money out. Brazil is a good example of this. At one point about five years ago our funds and other operations were frozen, but this last year they were unfrozen and we are on an even footing in Brazil again. We figure that we can move into a place and move out just as quickly."

He said that the company paid some attention to the consumption of its products, but it is mainly interested in having an even production rate. He was highly critical of the violent fluctuations in the production curve of some of the textile firms in the South. He felt that the textile industry needs to be stabilized and that if the textile manufacturers would add adequate research departments they could probably do something about this problem.

In going over names, Mr. Springer said that some of the old families no longer count in the question of power- and decision-making. The men on my list who had come into managerial positions in the larger corporations seemed to be the fellows who were "around the track." He felt that any man could move from one industry to another, as he had done, and that it might be good for industry in general for this to happen.

Before I left Mr. Springer's office, he gave me a copy of a speech that he had made of which he was very proud. He also provided me with a biographical sketch.

The materials in the next cases to be presented illustrate the ways in which some of the top policy makers spoke repeatedly of the process of "getting things done." In these paragraphs they speak of organizing to effect policy; opinions and attitudes toward government; business requirements and policy; and the general processes of policy development. On the whole, they agree in what they say.

Mr. Jones Spoke of the Policy Development Process

Ed X. Jones.   Mining Operator.   (Second Rater)

Mr. Jones appeared to be a young man firmly in charge of a mining empire. Mr. Jones went over the list of names with me and picked out the persons who were known to him. Mr. Jones' choices and remarks are listed in Chapter 4 to illustrate a point there.

When he came to the name of a well-known political boss on the list he laughed and said, "Sometimes you have to go along with these local politicians. This fellow is an astute businessman. He has a monopoly on the sale of strategic commodities in his town. In order to get a contract from him, you have to take him to the race track and make his bets for him, and not at the $2 window, either! I took him to the Kentucky Derby last spring. It's common knowledge among those in the know that whoever is sitting in his box at the races is making his bets and trying to get something out of the old boy!"

He said that he had made it a rule to get to know as many people as he could personally and that his various jobs both within his own industry and in Washington had made a wide acquaintance possible. He felt that the trade associations are good unifying devices. He said in his business he had between 3700 and 3800 individual customers. Whenever he went to a city he tried to see as many of them as he possibly could. Of course, he was not able to get around to all of them, but he made it a point to see not only the big customers but the small customers.

Mr. Jones handled matters of public welfare and development of policy in welfare himself. Any man in the company, of course, was free to engage in any civic activities that he wished and was encouraged to, but there was no delegation of such responsibilities.

Mr. Jones felt that labor had got too big for its own good in the past few years and he felt that industry should take a tough policy in relation to labor matters. He cited as an example of this his own stand in relation to some members of the CIO in his plant who were working on a summer shift of 40 men. He said that during the summer 40 men were necessary for the job because it was very hot work and the shifts had to be constantly relieved. Traditionally, this shift was cut down in the winter, but a couple of years ago the union decided that the 40 men should be held through the winter. Mr. Jones felt that this was a clear violation of the union contract and insisted on reducing the labor force. Consequently, the union struck, but in the end the Labor Relations Board upheld the company and the "featherbedders" were not rehired. He went to the newspapers and the public with his story, and he considered it a great victory for management in the industry. He said that the whole deal cost the company $6 million in loss of production but the victory was worth it.

Mr. Jones felt that "some men are too much in the newspapers." He felt that publicity for leaders was sometimes harmful and often misleading. He said that a man whom he knew, considered in some circles to be quite a leader, might be a case in point. This fellow earned $40,000 a year in a family-dominated industry. The business was going badly, so the stockholders took over and replaced the management. The man was then reduced to a $15,000 a year income. Mr. Jones indicated that when such a person lost his position he had lost most of his influence.

Mr. Jones said that he had been studying the question of the complexity of organization, particularly in business, and he felt that the larger industries were almost required to have some man in the state capital and in Washington who could have an ear in matters that were being discussed. The main thing that these persons did, according to Mr. Jones, was to get to know a lot of people, whether by playing golf or drinking cocktails with them, and their influence grew with their widening circle of acquaintances.

During the war Mr. Jones and seven other men drawn from various companies in his industry went to Washington. As far as he was concerned, "We made policy for the industry while we were there." He indicated that most of the policies that were laid down during that period were freely discussed with topnotch men in the industry. At the end of the war most of the seven men, whom he got to know quite well, had been stepped up in the positions they went back to. Only one of the seven fell from grace, and he was a fellow who got the Washington bug of political power, "Potomac fever."

Mr. Jones said that he believed that the speeches that men made on the top level of leadership were very important, and he tried to keep posted on what other men were speaking about in public, but that in order really to get the dope on what a man was thinking, he would rely on a friend to tell him what was in the air.

He felt that the old families did not mean anything in connection with power in American society because they did not work and consequently they were not moving anything. He thought it was better for a man to have to work for a living because he would take more interest in the industry.

Mr. Jay Had Opinions on Policy Matters

B. X. Jay. Banker. (Second Rater)

Mr. Jay was a banker in a metropolitan Southern city. He was an older, heavy-set man, seated at an old rolltop desk. He said, "Some of the men on this list like to think they are more nationally recognized than they are. Some of them think they are leaders when they are not." In going over the list of men Mr. Jay indicated that he knew most of them in a general business way or through some civic or philanthropic enterprise.

He did not think of himself as being generally concerned with matters of public policy, except that he felt in general that eventually there should be an abolition of the excess profits tax. He said that the President was right in coming out for keeping the excess profits tax for one year, and he felt that the national office of the National Association of Manufacturers had been "hasty and ill-advised in pushing for the repeal of that tax this year." He felt that there were too many "hired hands and paid secretaries" running the national associations, and sometimes they got themselves out on a limb. In general he felt that most leaders were influenced by a man with ideas, and he illustrated this by saying that when a man like Lister Hill from Alabama comes forward with the proposition of building hospitals all over the country, people get behind him. He said, "You are bound to listen to a man who has made some kind of contribution and who thinks the way you do."

Mr. Jay indicated that he had considerable interest in state politics at one time. He told a story of some of the men in his city who got together and felt that they could put over an income tax measure in the state. They decided that they would concentrate their efforts on the rural counties, and they spent a good deal of money trying to get their proposition across. He felt that they were completely naïve politically. In the areas where they spent relatively little money, such as in the large cities of the state, the measure carried overwhelmingly on a popular vote, but in the counties where they had spent a great deal of money, the accusation that "big men" were behind the measure defeated it. He felt that they would have been better off by not having been so public in their manipulations.

He said that his city was overrun with a lot of men who came in from national organizations of industry because of the location of the metropolis. He cited Ed X. Jones, in one of the larger industries, as an example. He felt fellows like Jones used the community as a stepping stone to bigger jobs and were not really interested in the town itself. Because of the size of the industry that Jones headed, he was a powerful individual, but he did not do as much for the city as Mr. Jay felt he should. Jay felt that a lot of the corporation executives were not as interested in the affairs of their individual companies as men had been in the past. Jay felt that this was a bad thing for industry generally and that the managers might not be as interested in the welfare of their companies as they would be if they were stockholders.

Mr. Brinkler Knew His Way Around

Harold X. Brinkler.   Newspaper Publisher.   (Number One)

Mr. Brinkler went over the list of names and was not too communicative as he did so. He did say that since the newspapers are such a widespread source of information, they are naturally interested in all phases of public policy. He said that much of his information was based on what he read not only in his own newspaper but in competing ones. He felt that conferences between leaders to discuss the pros and cons of all questions were perhaps the most effective means of development of public policy. He said, "Usually, you listen out a group of people in whom you have confidence, you get opinions from within the organization to which these people may belong and also outside, and then you make up your own mind." He said that during the discussion of tidelands oil he was one of the leaders in bringing out that the state had owned the lands for 100 years and it was only just and logical that they should be turned back to the states. He said that on a matter of specific interest in policy, for example, cutting down expenditures in the air industry, he would call fellows like Kindelberger and others and needle them by saying that too many planes were being built and that we could not balance the budget in this way. Then he would call some public officials in Washington to see what they had to say and formulate his editorial policy.

Mr. Untervurst Explained How Things Get Done

Harley X. Untervurst. Food Processor. (Second Rater)

Mr. Untervurst was the head of a food-processing industry. He said that his interests were rather widespread. He was now in the United Nations cultural association and he was actively engaged as chairman of his state's agricultural development committee. He gives a motto to all his employees, "Drive straight ahead with a positive mental attitude." He believed that one of the biggest problems of industry was keeping the morale of workers high. He thought the businessmen of today were "a new breed of cats." He said that he often told his employees that they were fortunate if they were young and involved in the struggle to make a living. He felt that the happiest years of a man's life are those in which he struggles to make a living. He recognized that some of his employees might not understand him too well, because they thought that "he has already got his" and "it is all good and well for him to talk about struggle now."

He said that he knew Eisenhower very well and that Eisenhower would probably be remembered as winning more battles by negotiation than by frontal attack. His own company was particularly interested in crop restrictions, because he said the country now had more grain than it knew what to do with.

On the matter of developing any kind of national policy, Mr. Untervurst said that the process to him was very simple. First, you got a committee of top men to agree on what you wanted to get done. Second, you hired people like yourself (pointing to me), professors, to research a problem and get all the facts on the matter. Then the top men could restudy the thing after the facts were gotten together and could figure out what they wanted to do with the facts. They could figure whether they wanted to take them into account or disregard them. Then, third, you got to the people who could really move any matter that you wanted to get moved.

Mr. Untervurst said that he wanted to contribute the rest of his life to doing things, out of gratitude for what the country had done for him. In this he likened himself to Mr. Eisenhower.

Mr. Byton Added a Word on Informal Contacts

Bill X. Byton. Banker. (Third Rater)

Byton told a story of a defense tool company that wanted to come into his city, Blanton. He said that the Blanton banking interests and the political administration were all friendly to the new company's interests, and particularly to a man named X. Barton, who was its representative. But a Mr. Staymon of the West coast came into Blanton and said that he wanted to build a rival production company and freeze Barton out. He said to the bankers, "What would you say if I said the Secretary of War said that there would be no contracts for the Barton Company?" The Blanton men had already purchased a 75,000-acre tract of land upon which to put Barton's company. Finally, however, under the circumstances the first company was frozen out and Staymon came into town. A neighboring city got the defense tool company and Blanton got Staymon. It cost the neighboring city 4½ million dollars for roads, water, sewer lines, etc. It only cost Blanton $75,000 to put their company into operation. Mr. Byton said that in all situations, friendships such as the Blanton men's with Mr. Barton may count a great deal, but when the chips are down you have to move in accordance with the dictates of your particular interests in a particular situation.

Mr. Smythe Outlined Some Business Requirements and Policy Processes

Gaylord X. Smythe. Utilities. (Third Rater)

In discussing the policies that concerned the Pipeline Company, the industrial production man, Boyd X. Benton, said that one of their major concerns was the cost of money. Any regulation that might come before the federal power commission in relation to money or any other matter was usually handled by lawyers who were in the company's employ or could be called upon by the company and by Mr. Smythe and others gotten together to go into the matter. He said that his company was formed in the early 1930's and had expanded tremendously until now they had oil lines that extended clear up into Maine and had a network over most of the Eastern part of the U. S. The operation grew up under Mr. Smythe. He said that they borrowed about 60 million dollars a year, and consequently they had a very real need for cheap money.

They used the technique of installing some of their men in government positions on annual leave, as do men in other industries. Sometimes the men of their companies sit across the desk from those of competitors. They get to know each other, and certain things are worked out harmoniously. He said that Mr. Smythe was a good friend of Dean David of Harvard, where Smythe was educated, and that through him Smythe knew a great many men around the country.

Mr. Benton said that naturally his company was interested in all kinds of public policy and the workings of various levels of government. He used as an example the building of an oil transmission line across the Mississippi between the states of Arkansas and Tennessee. He said that one of the towns projected a new toll bridge, and the pipe transmission people wanted to hang four lines on the suspensions of the bridge. The engineers told the local people that the weight would be too heavy, and consequently the company dickered with the local and state governments involved to help build the bridge. The company put around $5 million into the project, and eventually the bridge became a free bridge rather than a toll bridge because of the company's contribution. He said that of course there were many legal and political matters that the company had to go into because of its needs. He also said that they had to condemn and purchase lands all across the country, and this meant tremendous work for their legal staff and in relation to local and state politicians.

The company used a great deal of institutional advertising and public relations materials in which it discussed national policies.

When I finally got to see Mr. Smythe, he impressed me as the type of executive who drives himself at top speed. He had an airplane ticket in his pocket which he had to use within the next hour and he went over the list of names with me quite rapidly. He said that he was interested in the study and that he wished that he had more time to talk with me.

Mr. Peckman Diagnosed Potomac Fever, Among Other Things

Gordon X. Peckman.   Manufacturer.   (Number One)

Mr. Gordon Peckman was a tall, balding man who appeared to be in his middle or late sixties. He was dressed in a gray suit of conservative cut and had on highly polished black shoes. His offices were modern.

I was met very pleasantly by Mr. Peckman, and immediately after stating my purpose I went into the list of names with him. As Mr. Peckman went over the list of names, it was apparent that, like so many other leaders, he knew most of the men on the list. When he came to the name of one banker, he indicated that this man was now working in Washington. His way of stating this indicated disapproval. I asked him why it was that when a person took a job in Washington he seemed to be somewhat in disfavor with some of the policy-making leadership. He said, "A lot of these fellows, when they go to Washington, get Potomac fever." I asked him what he meant by Potomac fever, and he said, "Well, when those fellows go to Washington they have to temper all of their actions. When you are working in a corporation you can go directly and get things done without a lot of red tape. When you get to Washington you have to carry water on both shoulders and temper everything you do in accordance with a bunch of conflicting interests. If you don't do this, you don't stay. Sometimes when a man goes to Washington he drops out of industry altogether."

Mr. Peckman was interrupted by the telephone, and turning from it he indicated that he was glad to have a junior member of his corporation on a committee that he had been talking about. He said that his own calendar was booked up for several days in advance always and that it was a good thing to have some younger person within his corporation to help him out on some of the civic activities. He said, "You have to understand that industrialists are a selfish group. In any matter we like to have somebody from our company represented on any committee of top importance."

When I asked Mr. Peckman to name some of his connections with men of the dominant urban centers in the country, he went over the list of some of the larger cities. He said, "You have to remember that as far as I am concerned almost any city in the country is important because we have outlets in almost any city you would name. There has been a shift in recent years away from many of the larger centers. For example, New York used to be tremendously important in banking, but in these days other centers do a lot of their own financing. Although the bulk of the banking still goes to New York, you cannot get away from the importance of such large banking institutions as those in Chicago or the Bank of America in California. Because of the farflung interests of business —for example, our company does business around the world—you find a tie-up between people in almost any community you could name. Businessmen are gamblers at heart, and they will go anywhere in the world where they can make money. For example, they go into Venezuela to get oil, or into Mexico, and sometimes they get burned. As you know, Mexico expropriated their oil properties, and the men who took the gamble down there found themselves in pretty bad straits. The picture is not altogether one-sided. If I were a Mexican citizen, I believe that I would not like to have my own country's oil resources expropriated by foreigners. You would not get my friend over at Tide Oil to agree with me on this, but businessmen take such chances when they move out on the world scene."

Mr. McCloud Raised Political Money

I. X. McCloud.   Industrialist.   (Number One)

Mr. McCloud was a slender man perhaps 5'6" tall. He had iron-gray hair. His movements were rather quick and nervous, and he talked quickly. He responded almost instantly to questions asked of him but did not relax and ramble on as some informants.

I asked Mr. McCloud how he had got interested in welfare activities. He said, "I guess I have became a kind of specialist in money-raising. I am now in the process of raising several hundred thousand dollars for an educational TV program, and I was in a meeting this morning with a man whom you have on your list, trying to get this job accomplished. I also helped raise considerable money for the Republican party before the last campaign. When anything comes along that they want money raised for, it seems that I get called upon." He then went on to say that different men had different interests, and in his case his own money-raising interest was something that had been recognized. He continued his discussion of political money-raising by saying, "I was finance chairman for the GOP in the Chicago area, and in that position I and other men here raised a substantial sum for Mr. Eisenhower." I asked him if he knew the President well, and he said, "I would not say that I know him extremely well. I have met him several times and I introduced him about three weeks ago to some people that were gathered in Washington in relation to the United Fund campaign. In view of the fact that we raised so much money for Mr. Eisenhower's campaign here in town, I suppose that I could go to him and get something if I wanted to and if it were necessary." He went on to say that he did not consider himself a politician in a partisan sense of the word but that he had been as interested in seeing the Truman administration thrown out of office as many businessmen.

When I asked Mr. McCloud how he knew the men that he knew, he said that besides his own corporate connections he had been interested in social work boards for many years. He had been a member of small agency boards in his city and had also been connected with some church activities. He was active on the Community Chests and Councils board and had been active in the Carnegie Peace Foundation. He said, "You can get a lot of this material on my activities out of *Who's Who*." He went on to say that activities of this nature put him in contact with a great many people, and consequently he knew many of the men on the list.

I asked Mr. McCloud how the group of national leaders came into being, from the point of view of recruitment. He said that "position has a lot to do with it. The fact that I hold the position that I do in my company almost automatically puts me on some of the boards we have been talking about. When you come to younger men, you will find me a kind of nut on this subject. I feel that older men in industry should retire at a reasonable age to make way for the younger men. The method of recruiting the younger men is to watch them as they work and put them on something of a civic nature and see how they work out."

In continuing to talk about leadership in his city, Mr. McCloud said that there was a stable group of persons that seemed to have a hand in everything that came along. He felt that several of the men from his area on my list represented the type of top leadership that we were seeking in the study. He said that he would make one exception to this, and that was the name of a politician on the list. He said that he knew Mr. X. Doughty, but most of the time he had been on opposite sides with him. Therefore, he could not say that he knew him well.

Speaking of the national associations, Mr. McCloud said, "We probably could get along without them. On the other hand, they do draw people together to some extent and they get certain things done by a meeting of the minds. Most of the time, however, I think that it would be just as important for men from individual industries to go directly to Washington or anywhere else to get things accomplished that they might want."

Before leaving Mr. McCloud, I asked him to name a national policy or national issue in which he was particularly interested, and he said that it was hard to choose between international defense effort and getting a hold on the money situation in our country. He said that we needed a strict domestic money control, including taxation and inflation, and some kind of balance was needed. He felt that handling this matter would require more than the efforts of various national associations but would include them. He said, "Some of the men we have been talking about would be important as opinion makers in getting the national associations to move, but you would have to involve the interest of an awful lot of people to get our present situation under control."

Mr. Quinton Was an Organization Man

O. X. Quinton.   Bankers Organization.   (Third Rater)

Mr. Quinton outlined in great detail the type of educational program carried on by the Organized Bankers. The association had written a textbook in economics published by one of the larger publishing houses, which it tried to get in all colleges and universities. It also had a program of internships of professors who went to New York, thirty or forty of them each year, to get a firsthand look at the operations of its financial institutions. When asked for leaders in the association of bankers, Mr. Quinton said, "Just look for the leaders in the National Association of Securities Dealers, New York Stock Exchange, the American Securities Exchange, which used to be the Curb Exchange, and the Association of Stock Exchange Firms. All of these people are closely allied with us, and they either look to us for certain types of leadership or we look to them. Of course, we do not advertise the fact that we get together with these larger associations because we would not want the public to think that a bunch of bankers were getting together to decide on policy for the country. It is only natural in our meetings that some of the top men from these various associations get together and exchange ideas on what is good for the banks and what is good for the country."

The board of Mr. Quinton's association had representatives from the various banking interests. Since his board represented a policy group for his whole association, he felt that a good deal of national policy was discussed within this group.

Mr. Quinton felt that the members of his organization worked more closely with the National Association of Manufacturers than with any other group in relation to national legislation. He felt that New York, Chicago, Detroit, San Francisco, and possibly Philadelphia would be the outstanding cities in relation to banking matters.

I asked him whether he knew an investment banker in Atlanta, Allen X. Guppy, who was one of the top leaders in the Atlanta community. I had previously learned from Mr. Guppy that he was active in the affairs of the Organized Bankers Association and had gone to Washington for them as a community representative. Mr. Quinton said, "Yes, I know Guppy quite well. I usually think of his brother, Marcus, as the person in that firm with whom we work most closely. I remember that Allen Guppy was chairman of our legislative committee a few years ago, and as I recall he did go to Washington on various occasions. We use many of our people that way because we like to have men from local communities approach our representatives on matters of legislation.

Allen Guppy represents a substantial banking house, but you would not say that he is in the same league with some of the New York organizations, and therefore he is more effective with some of the senators and representatives. I have not been in contact with Allen for some time, but, as I say, we do have some dealings with Marcus from time to time." (The fact that Mr. Quinton looked upon Allen Guppy as a grass roots person was of particular interest to me, because to the national people Allen Guppy apparently was one of the little fellows, but in the local community of Atlanta he was a big wheel.)

Mr. Tidman Was Troubled by a Detail of Policy

Walter X. Tidman.   Manager.   (Third Rater)

Mr. Tidman said that the main national policy that concerned him at the present time was that of the naval stores which continued to sell luxury items in the P.X.'s. He said that in order to combat this policy of the Navy you had to get to the men who had the policy decision in their hands, and usually you got to them through men that you knew. This same process applied to getting to Congressmen or any others that might have something to do with the policy.

He felt that the American Retail Federation and the American Dry Goods Association were particularly important to his business, in sending out trade information. Mr. Tidman ran a very large department store in his city, but it was considered by other business leaders in the area second rate in the type of goods it sold.

Mr. Mintz Wanted a Constitutional Amendment

George X. Mintz.   Lawyer.   (Second Rater)

Mr. Mintz had recently got a lot of national publicity because he was the man behind the Bricker Amendment, designed to limit the President's power to make treaties. He showed me a gold medal and a citation given to him recently by the American Bar Association at its annual meeting. He had a great deal of literature concerning the amendment, with which he loaded me down. He said that some men thought of him as being a kind of nut on the subject of this amendment.

He thought that Philip Reed had the clearest mind in the United

States. He said that he knew Eisenhower well and Secretary Dulles and had talked to them on the subject of the amendment. He said that he got started on this subject in February, 1948, when he picked up an article written by a New York lawyer in an American political science journal. He said that after he got started trying to get his ideas across, Senator Bricker picked up the subject, and without his knowledge or anyone else's put Resolution No. 130 into the Congressional hopper. Some people felt that this was a bad move and that some other Senator should have introduced it. Bricker got 58 Senators to sign a petition to get the matter on the floor. Hearings were held before the Judiciary Committee, which was filled with Democrats, and nothing was done about it in the early stages. Mr. Mintz had spent $25,000 to $30,000 of his own money trying to organize people around the country into a "non-political, non-religious committee" to get their ideas across.

Mr. Swartz Did Not Believe in the Frontal Attack

Manuel X. Swartz.   Banker.   (Third Rater)

Mr. Swartz was an older man who was in an investment banking business. Like many of these men, he had a relatively small office. I understand that at one time Mr. Swartz had a large banking enterprise that failed back in the late '20's or early '30's, and for some time he was *persona non grata* with a lot of people around his community. He had, however, recouped his fortunes and now he was looked upon as kind of an elder statesman.

Mr. Swartz indicated a wide acquaintance and he spoke often of general public policy matters. He thought that one got to know many men over the years, on boards, in association work, civic work and in open politics. You read what they speak or what they write, and you have confidence in what a man is and what he stands for, he said. He thought that the associations were sounding boards to coordinate opinion, and they could do a better job of interpretation.

He said that you got to know men who were in the same business, and they went before committees and talked informally with officials. He would rather rely on this method than on a $50,000 a year man to lobby for him. "The frontal attack is no good, anyway!" He believed that the names that I had represented a well-balanced list. Undoubtedly there were others, but he felt that this was a good sample.

He used the executive vice-presidents in his organization for civic work, but he said that some of it he could not avoid. He said frankly that he was a policy maker himself and not a front man.

Mr. Ring Worked with Industrial Associations

S. X. Ring. Oil Producer. (Number One)

Mr. Ring outlined the functions and operations of three of the national associations that were extremely important to the oil industry. The first was the National Petroleum Council, which he said was of tremendous authority and prestige in the industry and published no materials that could be considered controversial. It was a long-range planning outfit that had a very definite hand in the formation of government policy. He said the Secretary of the Interior often gave problems to the Council and asked it to go into them. When a problem was given to the Council, it went to an agenda committee to see whether it was a legitimate problem for study. This group was interested in long-range availability of petroleum, which was one of the most important questions before the country according to Mr. Ring.

Another association that was considered important by Mr. Ring was the American Petroleum Institute, which was the usual trade association dominated by major companies. He said that each year 5,000 people gathered in Chicago for a "wing-ding." Papers were read at this meeting, which was a general conference and talk session. The group set up various standards for the industry and had a research function. It went into such matters as the smoke problem in the burning of oil and the improvement of technical proficiency in the industry. It had no lobby function, and it avoided all controversial issues.

A third group, the Independent Petroleum Association of America, engaged in any kind of controversial issue that might come before the industry. It had lobbies in Tulsa and Washington mainly, but it was active anywhere else it was needed. It represented the crude oil production industry of the United States. It handled questions related to the imports of foreign oil. Its general counsel and spokesman was Russell P. Brown, whose offices were in Washington, from where he informed members of various issues that might be before the Congress.

In discussing the question of how his company handled welfare matters, Mr. Ring said, "Welfare matters are pushed down to the treasurer in Houston." "Denver uses the marketing manager there." He went on to say that there was no company policy in this matter, but "we don't spill out our guts on public relations and that kind of thing that is involved in the welfare field." He went on to say that there were only three people in the public relations department, two of whom were clerks. He felt that I should also talk to Mr. X. Dee on my next trip to the city, since he considered him one of the very top leaders in the oil industry.

Mr. Hall Hammered Out Opinions

Estes X. Hall.   Industrialist.   (Number One)

A hard-bitten, tough talker, Mr. Hall thought national associations were poor because they had no authority to enforce decisions. He thought Eisenhower was doing a very poor job, because he had not changed things completely, such as getting rid of Social Security. He was anti-war as he was anti much of everything else. He was full of the clichés of the press. Eager to talk, he got excited and thumped his desk. He talked at great length about private control of electric power, in which he had a vital interest, and he said that the lobbyist in Washington was just a hired hand.

He did not think in regional terms but national and international terms. He said a handful of men really counted, but some of them were so eager to please and not to stir up trouble that they were their own worst enemies. He thought the American businessman was the guardian of all that is good and true in the country. He said that fifty men in his community called the shots, and policy was the key in the community and nation. Public relations was a lot of boloney, for there was no science or technique to it. He thought that churches and contributions to welfare projects should be used to preach the way of American life. He believed that the Methodist Liberty League was a very vital organization. He got so wound up in his talking that I spent two hours with him when he had told me I could have only 45 minutes.

His feeling about general policy was related to drastically reducing taxes and decentralizing the government, and he believed that all businessmen would be able to agree on this platform. Everything should be a company or industry proposition, including such things as rural electrification and flood control and irrigation.

Hall spoke very favorably of the Bohemian Grove group that met in California every year. He said that although over the entrance to the Bohemian Club there was a quotation, "Weaving spiders come not here," there was a good deal of informal policy made in this association. He said that he got to know Herbert Hoover in this connection and that he started work with Hoover in the food administration of World War I. He felt that business had a duty not only to operate business but to maintain it. He thought that many businessmen had let the country slide gradually into socialism, and he saw no way out. He felt that big business should be opinion leaders, putting forward their opinions in all kinds of situations and really leading the country.

He was absolutely convinced that the federal government should get out of all power operations in the electric industry. He felt, along with others, he said, that the power facilities should be completely taken over by private companies. Their plan, which had been rather widely publicized, was first of all to purchase all the power generated by the public dams and other utilities and resell it to industry. To such questions as what would they do about continuing reclamation and irrigation services, their answers were not clear. They felt that perhaps it should be a government function to carry on these services, but anything related to electricity should be carried on by the private companies. They were now working hard on Secretary McKay to make their policy ideas effective. In general, he said, anything that government could do, private industry could do better. When the question was asked whether private companies could finance such large operations as the Bonneville Dam, for example, he felt that this could be done.

In spite of Mr. Hall's attitudes toward the efficacy of control by big business, he did indicate some awareness of the need for a public relations program. He told the story of opening up a new plant in a Western state. Before they went into the community, they were aware of the fact that many of the people in that region were opposed to their operations. Consequently they held a big get-together for people all over the county to which they were going. They served hot dogs and drinks free, and had many of their technical men there to explain what kind of operation they were going to have. He thought this was a great success, for it brought the people in on their project and eliminated any adverse criticism that they might have had for coming in. He said that in that state there was a history of "socialistic control" and that the legislatures there sometimes made studies of nationalizing certain industries. He and other men in the industry were always alert to any of these movements, and got up to the region as fast as they could to change legislative committees' attitudes.

Mr. Allison Did Not Beat Around the Bush

Fred X. Allison.   Utilities.   (Number One)

Mr. Allison told me of the electric companies' trying to get control of the distribution of power from public facilities, a story essentially the same as other utilities leaders'. He said that all of these things were purely political and that they had to use all the means at their disposal to get men into public office to do the things that they wanted them to do. There was no reason to beat around the bush about this, according to Mr. Allison. You utilized personal friendships, money, trade organizations, public or private studies and inquiries, or any other means that came to hand to effect your purpose. He thought that relationships with state organizations and state legislatures were particularly important because of the stress that was now being placed on turning functions of federal government back to private hands and to states.

Having determined empirically that there were leaders in the great cities of the nation who knew each other and who knew a good deal about each other, power structure questions still remained. "Do these men ever work together to accomplish common goals?" "If these men are an executive committee for the nation, do they act like one?" "If they act together, how do they act?"

During my trips across country, I had reached a tentative conclusion that it would be difficult, if not impossible, to find any one issue or public policy in which a majority of the top leaders I had been interviewing would be interested. It was plain that interests of these men ran along business lines (their own), along regional lines—e.g., Texas men were interested in tidelands oil, and everyone from Nebraska west was interested either in water or electric power—or in some cases interest lines crossed, as in free trade vs. tariffs. Speaking of the relatedness of national leaders, Clint Murchison of Texas said, "I think you are going to find that bankers know bankers, scholars know scholars, utility men know utility men, and politicians know everybody." I found this to be true, of course, but I also found more.

I found that although communities serve as a home base for many national leaders, I could not stop with merely studying community relationships, saying that a basis of knowledge of national power processes was thereby established. Even a long series of comparative studies would not have been sufficient. There were other elements in the equation. Besides community relationships, relationships of leaders in industry and in government at state and national levels needed to be established.

Faced with the necessity of limiting the scope of research because of restricted resources, I followed a line of investigation that finally took into account power structures not only in selected national communities, but in two states and two industries. As it turned out, the economy package of research appears to me to have produced as valid results as the larger project had intended.

In a few words before concluding this section of the book, let me clarify the three levels of study: community, state, and industry. The community is the obvious place that I might begin to look for top national leaders. Several studies had made it quite clear to me that top leaders could be identified as members of community power structures. The statements of such leaders, as indicated in this chapter, led me to believe that community leaders were acquainted with other leaders in communities at some distance from them. It was also apparent that some leaders in community affairs were purely local in their thinking. For example, some thought only in terms of getting a new school or new streets, or of stopping this or that local movement, but rarely, if ever, did they think in terms of policy matters that affected the state or nation. Other leaders in the community, such as Mr. Baffin in Atlanta, thought in national and even international terms. Still others thought and acted on matters of state policy. Regardless of the geographic dimension, a very large number never thought of policy matters except in terms of the industry or business they were most closely connected with.

In a study of leadership patterns, any one of these levels or areas of civic life might be of real interest in itself, but a study of any one of them alone which infers national patterns of leadership from a single source would be misleading. Each area operates as an entity and is functionally related to each other area. Thus, the research problem was to study one of each of these areas and to find relationships between them.

My initial community and association studies had provided a basis for inquiry into interrelationships between city leaders. Could a state be studied in similar fashion? Would a study of a national industry be rewarding to provide clues to national policy formation? Did the national associations act as catalyst forces between various groups of national leaders? Each of these questions had to be answered in turn.

At this stage in my quest, I was asked to do a state study of leadership in South Carolina by a Northern corporation interested in industrial development in that state. The request provided the opportunity (the funds) to look at another facet of a traditionally recognized power apparatus. I gladly undertook the state study, with the notion that it would add to the background of national study. Such has proved to be the case.

Part II

LEVELS OF LEADERSHIP

6 POLICY MAKERS: A STATE MODEL

THIS is a summary of a study tracing out configurations of power networks, blocs, or groups in a Southern state, South Carolina.[1]

To what extent is it possible to define and prove that a group of persons, relatively small in number, really does develop and execute policies at the state level? If it is possible, to what extent does such a group of policy-makers decide and act on a state level in accordance with the wishes and desires of community top leaders?

1. This study followed a test or pilot study of North Carolina power leaders. Both studies were vitally useful in the national study, but only the more complete South Carolina materials have been given here. The study of two states out of 48 may at first sight seem a small proportion. On the contrary, it is a sufficient number to illustrate the national policy I chose to prove the national structure, namely, a textile policy related to Japanese imports. Had I chosen the nation's Hell's Canyon policy matter, perhaps six or eight states would have sufficed to perform the same research function. Had it been a policy in the auto industry complex, three or four states might have been a sufficient number. In other words, the policy chosen for study limits the geographic area to that in which power is functional to the solution of political conflict. This, then, is a basic delineation of the research model.

The counties included in the study (1955) were: Aiken, Allendale, Anderson, Bamberg, Barnwell, Beaufort, Berkeley, Calhoun, Charleston, Chesterfield, Colleton, Darlington, Dillon, Dorchester, Florence, Georgetown, Greenville, Greenwood, Hampton, Horry, Jasper, Marion, Marlboro, Richland, Spartanburg, and Williamsburg.

The task of the study was, then, twofold: to define community power structures and to discover connections between community power figures and their role in the development of policy at the state level.

At a later stage of study, state model studies of North and South Carolina were used to test the national leadership model.

As in other community studies, power was defined in terms of men acting in relation to policy considerations. In order to trace power relations, I had to ascertain what issues or policies provide a basis of action for groups and individuals involved in power. In a preliminary survey, or in the first stages of investigation, with others I visited three sections of South Carolina and informally interviewed persons presumed to be leaders in their localities.[2] Since some communities were quite small and located in rural counties, each leader was asked for the names of other persons in his county who might be considered powerful and influential in the professions, business and industry, banking, agriculture, and politics. The initial interviewees were also asked to give their views on community and state policies or issues that most affected their locality.

The persons named as top leaders, county by county, were listed and subsequently were systematically questioned to show personal relationships, if they existed, between them. A broad sample of those known to each other was sent questionnaires, then interviewed and, on occasion, re-interviewed to establish deference relationships and power patternings at the state level. The method of study thus developed was both quantitative and qualitative.

Three sections of the state were chosen for exploratory interviews, because it is well recognized that South Carolina has three distinct social, physical, and climate areas, namely, the Blue Ridge area (relatively small); the Piedmont plateau; and

2. E.g., Chamber of Commerce executives, county officers, and, by chain referral, merchants, professionals, and businessmen.

the coastal plain.[3] Only one of the Blue Ridge counties, Greenville, was included in the study.[4]

It was also recognized at the beginning of the study that the Blue Ridge and Piedmont sections of the state had undergone a rapid industrial expansion within the past two or three decades, and it was felt that this fact alone might provide a basis of comparison of power leaders there with those in parts of the state that had been, and were still, predominantly rural in character.

In the Piedmont area of South Carolina, the clusters of towns and cities along the arteries of north-south travel were filled with traffic, shoppers, and a general busyness. Outskirt hot dog stands, beer taverns, trailer sales yards, frozen custard stands, dog hospitals, industries, rail sidings, giant textile mills, and blinking neons told the world that the Piedmont cities and towns were bustling.

As I dropped from the rolling Piedmont plateau to the coastal plains and terraces, the land flattened to table-top evenness. I passed mile upon mile of cotton, corn, and tobacco, broken by green squares and rows of pine timber growing from the sandy loam. The towns became smaller and further apart, and in place of the jumble of business establishments at the edge of each town, I was more likely to see a fringe of modest, F.H.A. financed new houses belonging to lower-middle income people, and as I proceeded closer to town, the shaded lawns of big white houses belonging to in-town farmers and prosperous local merchants began to appear. A few small road signs heralded a town, and in several coastal communities, conspicuous by their size, billboards proclaimed "Blankville Welcomes Industry" and elaborated on Blankville's advantages.

3. South Carolina Research, Planning and Development Board, "Resources of South Carolina" (Columbia, January, 1955), p. 10.
4. For the purposes of this study, Greenville County will be included in the grouping of Piedmont counties.

The town centers with their chainstore signs looked like Main Street anywhere. It was easier to park, usually, in these towns, and I was often waited on by store proprietors who said, when I left, "Sure do thank you! Come back and see us!" The town leaders usually had more time to talk to their neighbors, visiting researchers, and strangers.

Since houses were so clearly visible along the country roads, it was easy to distinguish social stratification of the people by their living arrangements. The traditional "big house" of the larger land owners stood in contrast to and away from the tenant houses and those of the smaller renters and freeholders. The yard of the big house was more likely to have been landscaped with shrubbery and magnolia, water-oak, live-oak, or palmetto trees, depending on the area. The tobacco processing and curing sheds and barns, pens for livestock, and machine shelters tended to be placed at some distance from the big house and nearer the tenant houses. As I approached the coast and drove south, I noticed Spanish moss hanging from the live-oaks, in tranquil beauty.

In many places I saw uninhabited tenant houses, of the two- and three-room, unpainted, batten strip type, rotting away. If they had not completely fallen or been burned and not replaced, gaunt, bare chimneys bore physical testimony to social change.

New tenant houses were larger, freshly white-painted; and in a great number of the yards, beds of petunias, zinnias, coxcombs, purple-pink thrift and other easy-to-grow flowers provided colorful borders. There were, of course, many tenant houses whose occupants still allowed cotton or corn to grow almost to the door, and what little yard there might have been was still vigorously and regularly swept with a broom of branches lest any grass grow. The number of flower-bordered yards, nevertheless, was increasing.

As I drove along the roads I was impressed by the number of power machines I saw in the fields. In 1920 there were 1,304 tractors in the state. By 1950, the figure had increased to 30,329 or a positive change of 2,225.8 per cent! [5]

Over the highways, by rail, and by air, South Carolina products were carried to national and world markets. Counties which ranked high in agricultural production figures in the first 100 counties of the United States were Marlboro, twenty-eighth in cotton harvested; Horry, fifth in tobacco; and Spartanburg, seventh in bushels of peaches harvested. Cabbage in Charleston and sweet potatoes in Horry were ranked twenty-second and seventh respectively.[6]

From the manufacturing plants mainly along the highways of the Piedmont came 41 percent of all printed cotton woven goods (1948),[7] and the total value of all manufactured products in all industries in 1952 was $2,226,000,000.[8]

In ten years, 1943-53, capital invested in manufacturing had increased 118 percent, with 126 percent increase in value of products.[9] During eight years previous to the same period, 1060 new industrial plants representing a total investment of $563 million had come into the state, and existing plants had announced plans for expansions costing $360 million, making a growth of more than $923 million.[10]

With this upsurge in business prosperity, cash income from cattle and dairying in the state had increased from one sixth of the total farm income in 1942 to nearly one fourth of the total in 1952, amounting to $81 million. Forest products, the second largest source of income of the state, were manufactured in plants worth more than $200 million, supported by $500 million in standing timber on 12 million acres. Thirty to forty

5. South Carolina Research, Planning and Development Board, "General Statistics on South Carolina," Pamphlet 12 (Columbia, 1953), p. 28.

6. *Ibid.*, p. 4.

7. South Carolina Research, Planning and Development Board, "South Carolina on the March" (Columbia, 1953), p. 7.

8. "General Statistics," p. 7.

9. *Ibid.*, p. 6.

10. *The State*, Columbia, June 17, 1955.

million seedlings were being planted each year to preserve this valuable resource.[11]

South Carolina was, of course, caught up in the exhilaration of the nation's business boom of 1955, and according to forecasts then, its prosperity was to continue through the year.

New school buildings by the score ($83 million worth were being erected, in part to offset the effects of the Supreme Court ruling on segregation) and new churches ($70 million worth in the past decade) dotted the landscape.[12]

The beach areas along the coast in the summer of 1955 were crowded to capacity. In one town, motorists with out-of-state license plates were systematically stopped by a policeman who introduced the out-of-state guests to a bevy of ladies, who in turn plied them with doughnuts and coffee furnished by a local civic club—all wishing the travelers a pleasant stay. On the outskirts of the same community a sign had been erected by aggressive leaders advising southbound motorists to save mileage on their way to Florida by going through a nearby town on the same highway and thus missing the crowded highways around Charleston. The Charleston leaders protested the sign, but apparently the community did nothing; someone, no one knows who, finally tore the sign down at night. The tourist flow of gasoline, money, and good will was worth considerable struggle in this section.

But the statistics cited, as so often happens, did not tell the whole story of the state and its people, just as fleeting glimpses of the green above the topsoil tell little of what lies beneath.

As I drove along the back roads, other sights indicated that other statistics might balance those put out by anxious and eager Chamber of Commerce leaders. At the tiny crossroads stores that, since the Civil War days, have sprung up everywhere and have remained an institution, some men sat and passed the time of day even during planting and harvesting

11. "South Carolina on the March," p. 7.
12. *Ibid.*, pp. 12, 13.

seasons. Some sat on their porches at home. They were the men who were not counted in the percentages in over-all gains in employment. Some leaders were prone to say of some of these men, "They won't work no matter what you give them. They much prefer to sit." But other leaders, probably a majority, admit that machines have displaced many men and will continue to displace them and that after they are displaced they may sit awhile before moving to communities that offer employment. A few hold-out farmers refuse to mechanize. One said, "A tobacco harvester costs $1800, a cotton harvester $2300. You can do a heap of hirin' for that kind of money." But most of the farmers said, "The machines are here to stay, and more are coming." The ones who had gone to agricultural college cited figures of competition between themselves and the industrial farms of Texas and California and felt that they were hard put in the race for survival.

The larger farmers, and even some of the smaller ones, were a part of the leadership system in their counties and adjacent towns, and the thoughtful ones asked themselves what they could do with this surplus labor around them. They answered themselves by saying that there needed to be a balance between agriculture and industry. This then became a policy goal.

"The state is good. The state is sound." The figures out of Columbia said so. But something else was needed to make it better. "Blankville welcomes industry!"

In order to attract industry, most counties in South Carolina used as selling points, an ample supply of manpower (with emphasis on numbers of white workers available), modest tax levy, freedom from county debt (where possible), stability of government, adequacy of electrical and water supply, the willingness to subsidize entering industry by land purchase and building construction, labor docility, and a liberal supply of friendly interest toward business.

Industrial development, as a policy matter, was concerned with more than labor. It was further related to taxation, finance, power (energy) development, water control, and the political processes inherent in such matters. As a research instrument, it was a door opener at all levels of civic action.

In the initial interviews, county by county, 271 persons were named as policy makers or top leaders in their counties. Although those who named top leaders were asked to name leaders from various categories, the question was open-ended, that is, I allowed for additional information, and any person named as being outstanding in power and influence in the county was added to the list. The number of such leaders varied by counties, but not radically. There was a tendency for a smaller number to be named in the large, well-organized, highly industrialized communities. The very top people of the large corporate hierarchies were considered very powerful by persons who in a small community might be at the very top of the power policy pyramid themselves. The whole power structures of the larger industrial centers of South Carolina were of considerable size and complexity, composed of pyramids and interlacings of relationships at the top of the various structures. The power structures of cities like Spartanburg, Greenville, Anderson, and Columbia, however, did not appear to differ greatly from those found in a more intensive study of a very large metropolitan city in another state in the Southeast.[13] The very top power status figures were easily isolated and identified by their civic compatriots. They were relatively few, but the interlacing of their activities with like-powered individuals exerting pressure and influence on formal and informal community groups gave them a large measure of personal power.

In the smaller communities, civic power tended to be somewhat more readily visible than in the larger cities. The corner druggist, dry goods merchant, and leading grocer would be

13. Floyd Hunter, *Community Power Structure; A Study of Decision Makers* (Chapel Hill, 1953).

teamed on many issues with the banker, lawyer, and cotton ginner, among others. The presidency of the Lions Club or the local Chamber of Commerce would have more meaning in terms of power recognition in the small community. Nevertheless, there were power cliques and structures in the smallest hamlets that had a great deal to say in "what will go and what will not." Many of the 271 county leaders resided in the larger population centers of their counties.

The persons named on a questionnaire used in the counties were asked to check the names of all other persons on the listing known personally to them and to give qualitative data on patterns of interaction.

If the old maxim of policy development is true, "It's who you know that counts," then persons in leadership positions in local communities should have known leaders elsewhere. At least, this was the reasoning behind the construction of the questionnaire. If answers showed that very few knew very few others, county by county, then another method would have been indicated for getting at a patterning of power.

As it turned out, there was a definite grouping of people who said they knew others on the list personally and who in turn were known by the persons of whom they claimed knowledge. It was also found that most of the leaders had interacted with others on matters of social policy.

Out of 181 responses, three persons were drawn from each county—persons who were most widely known by others on the questionnaire. These 78 names were cross-indexed to determine the extent of mutual acquaintance. Grids made for the persons who said they knew few other people revealed that few other people knew them, but some of the low vote group were known to enough of the more widely recognized people that the whole pattern seemed to be that of a tight circuit of persons across the entire state.

This was a finding that I had guessed might be true, but I had some doubt as to how complete the circuit might be. I felt at the beginning of the study that there might be isolated rural counties where little connection could be made between local top leaders and leaders from other parts of the state. This, of course, did not prove to be the case.

An analysis of the 73 of the 78 top leaders in the poll who gave data shows that more lawyers were known to each other and by others in other occupations than any other occupational group (See Table 1).

TABLE 1

TOP COUNTY LEADERS OF SOUTH CAROLINA WELL KNOWN TO
73 COUNTY LEADERS, BY OCCUPATIONS, 1955

Occupation	Numbers Known
Attorneys	35
Businessmen	10
Industrialists	9
Professions other than law	7
Farmers	5
Bankers	4
Politicians (vocational)	2
Retired	1
Total	73

Almost half, or 35, of the top rankers were attorneys, and of that number, 18 were state senators (each county has one member in the state Senate).

The leading persons, other than the senator-lawyers of the attorney group, included the most recent ex-governor, the present governor and lieutenant governor, both United States Senators, and members of the House of Representatives in the state and nation. Obviously, these persons were well known in terms of political prominence. Some of the other leaders were well known because of occupational connections with state-wide organizations such as the Farm Bureau, state Bankers Association, Cotton Ginners Association, Textile Manufacturers Association, state Chamber of Commerce, Masonic orders, and the Democratic party executive group. A few were apparently known merely by the fact that they held important corporate or other occupational positions and had got around the state and made friends. At least no official organization ties could be made to and from them, but, informally, they were named as leaders.

What now is about to be said about power relations in South Carolina should be modified before we begin. The power of which we shall speak is devoted to putting into operation the policy considerations of industrial development outlined earlier. It is not the kind of power with which one person could directly tell another to go and the second goes without second thought or protest. There was no one man nor group of men in the state, not even the reputed political boss and those with whom he supposedly dealt, who could command and gain immediate response. But there was a group of men within the larger group mentioned in this writing, who strove mightily, consistently, and with dedicated purpose to effect changes in the ways of action of hundreds and thousands within the state and abroad.

Many of the top policy makers at the state level of affairs might have been surprised to be called such, even though on reflection they might have admitted to having some power as individuals and to having had some part in an organization or two that had policy goals in which they were interested. As individuals, most men felt relatively powerless, and most were, relatively speaking. But in organized combination a few men could often accomplish works that could only have been designated as the products of wielded social power.

In "satisfied" counties people said that nothing was being done to alter or change conditions toward a better way of life. In one county it was said that "Ten years ago five funerals were needed to hasten progress. During the past ten years we have had three of those funerals, and things are looking up." The county had a group of five leading men who had opposed any movement toward industrial development, and the ma-

jority of people and the supporters of the top leaders had been
unwilling to oppose the will of those in power. The power of
conservatism was very real in many places, but the example
cited is extreme.

In most counties, typically, the local policy-determining
group of the power structure consisted of the leading banker,
a lawyer, a farmer-merchant, a large-scale farmer, one or two
merchants, the ranking politician, and, perhaps, a professional
man or two.

In the majority of counties studied, the ranking lawyer was
a combination attorney and state senator. The farmer-merchant
was a person who owned and operated farm properties and in
addition operated a cotton gin and/or a tobacco warehouse,
farm machine business, general merchandise store, or fertilizer
business. The businessman in the group operated any one of
the businesses not run by the farmer-merchant, who in many
cases represented traditional, old-family ties to the land and in
the community in which he operated. The professional men,
doctors, dentists, farm agents, or undertakers, were often relatively prosperous persons who had some interest in real-estate
manipulations and who could be counted on for civic work.
These were not numerous, but they represented a sort of social
respectability in the affairs of policy. The town banker was
usually the same fellow one meets in fiction. Somewhat cautious and exceedingly correct, he showed deference where
deference was due and a firm stand where needed and supported. The professional county politician was a good employee who knew quite well who put him where he was, and
his virtue lay in keeping quiet and doing the job he had been
chosen to do. In most counties, especially coastal counties, his
tenure of office was measured in decades, and at most times,
in elections he was unopposed.

In general, the power figures mentioned were busy each day
making a living. Some of them devoted no time or effort to
doing anything about getting industry to come to their com-

munity. Most, as has been pointed out, would not have opposed such a move, and also some of the inactive persons might quickly have become active if a real and tangible proposition was put to them individually or to the local power group.

In the drifting towns, that is, in those that were not aggressively seeking industry, most matters of general policy were considered settled. The tax rate was fixed, the water supply assured, loan rates were stabilized, the price of "fertilizer" was set at what the traffic would bear, teachers were hired, the courts and county offices were in good hands—almost everything but the weather had been adjusted, over a long period of time, and "even the preacher was supposed to do what he could about the weather." To bestir too much about industry might have appeared suspicious. It might have seemed that a fellow's business was not prospering as it should have been or that the livewire fellow was fixing to elevate himself. Besides, the state was supposed to look after these things. "There's a development board and a state Chamber in Columbia, you know." The development board in Columbia and the state Chamber of Commerce said that such county leaders "need to be educated," and they did what they could to bring enlightenment.

In all counties, including the advanced Piedmont counties, the stability of the settled policies was a continuing matter of concern to existing power structures, but they, like some of the more progressive coastal counties, did more than just sit and wait for a windfall of industry. They formed committees, with the leaders of such committees carefully screened or watched over by the larger industrial interests. They studied any prospective industrial situation, formally and informally. They weeded out propositions that might have been hurtful to the existing pattern of commercial operations. They manned the civic boards and they helped to establish new organizations, civic and commercial, as the need arose or the time appeared propitious. They integrated top-rung leaders of newly established industries into the general fabric of the structure and dropped or froze out dissident elements. They sent lobbyists to Columbia and Washington, and the lobbyists, in turn, called upon the top industrial and business firms to appear at proper times to testify for or against legislation that affected the community, or for that matter, the state. They watched with interest the rise or fall of leaders in the outlying counties and helped bring into the state associational apparatus those leaders in the ascendancy or who had long since "arrived" in a particular locality and who evidenced some disposition to do something for their state. They raised and distributed money for commercial and civic investment. They received, in turn, honors and security of a sort (for power is always on somewhat slippery footing), and they were able to call scores of men by phone and by their first names.

They liked recent state political regimes and they intended to continue supporting those, within the present one, which continued to perform as well or better than their predecessors. They watched with interest the fact that the present young governor had established friendly relations with leading financial and business circles in New York after having been introduced into these circles by one of the leaders of the state Senate. The senator described the process of getting a new corporation established in the state. "I took our young governor by the hand and we went to New York. I introduced him around at the House of Morgan. They liked him. They thought of the state as being in capable hands, and it helped." A leader of the state House of Representatives had a file of material inches thick of the details of getting the whole enterprise under way.

One of the community leaders in Florence, in a burst of insight, said, "Most of us do not know the big men in the national organizations. I do not even know who is the head of one corporation, but when one of their second-string fellows came down here nosing around about plant sites, we entertained him as well as if he had been the head of the company. The man was the head of a division that has an operating capital of about a half billion dollars. That's mighty big money in these parts, and as far as we were concerned, he was a top man."

They watched with interest and had a hand in choosing members of the state executive committee of the state and national Democratic party. They raised and helped distribute party funds. In like manner they were interested in fluctuations in the important committee memberships in the state Senate, and were particularly concerned with understanding the operations of the finance committee of that body.

Some of the leaders may have profited by state contracts and federal largesse piped to them by the appropriate legislator or legislative group, but patronage in the form of the traditional office-holding had little meaning to the top leaders. An opening into the financial or top board or management structure of a large new or an older established corporation was a more modern-dress political reward.

The little fellows in the outlying counties and communities watched these and assorted similar activities and either joined in when they could or imitated, in lesser ways, these patterned actions. Those who joined or imitated were the "hustlers," as C. Wright Mills calls them.

In essence, the scheme of action is none other than establishing policy, primarily, and secondarily delegating authority and responsibility for seeing that ensuing actions conform to that policy. Those who knew the pattern knew upon whom to call for assistance in any situation requiring it.

When, for example, it was firmly established that industrial development was the key policy for the state as a whole, the state government set up the Research, Planning and Development Board to further this policy. The Board itself was composed of a combination of professional and lay persons drawn from the group of top leaders just described. Others who may have had use for the excellent materials and efficient services of the Board or its staff could call upon them at will. The formal and informal processes involved were as old as our form of representative government. Only the issues, policies, and personnel changed. The processes remained relatively stable, varying according to the needs of the hour. Within and between counties there was competition and rivalry in getting industries located here or there. In a very real sense, there was much isolation of one county from another. The state as a whole, the threads of knowledge that some persons had of others, the state association ties, or even the partisan ties in formal government were less strong than they appeared, when confronted with the inertia or active negation of policy by balky community power structures.

The power of the state was held to be supreme in selected fiscal matters, certain matters of education, certain road construction projects and the like, but even on such constitutional and quasi-constitutional matters, action was tempered to fit the needs, requirements, wishes, and demands of the more close-knit community power groupings.

The power of those who headed the larger interests of the state and abroad was persuasive in many matters and powerful indeed when persuasion carried with it a real offer of assistance in locating an enterprise in a particular community; on the contrary, it was a dread power when it could block or withhold such assistance. Facts of this nature were known or guessed at, and the leaders of the larger interests were listened to attentively when they spoke of labor relations and other items of import that might have improved or obscured the chances of a community in attaining its goals.

Since the interest in industrial development in South Carolina was a prime consideration shot through with policy and power considerations, the same men who were interested in a broad program of industrial expansion were generally found to be interested in a multiplicity of other power problems. These same men were top leaders, prime movers, opinion leaders, decision makers, or policy makers. Any program of action carried through at the state level of affairs necessarily would have had to take them into account.

Let me illustrate this statement by posing a simple hypothetical situation, and follow it by naming some of the persons one would have found in 1955 at the center of power in the state.

If one were a Northern industrialist seeking a South Carolina location for a medium-sized industry, the chances would have been good that he first would have been able to obtain rather good advice from any one of a number of banking and financial houses in New York. He then might have been advised to obtain more specific data from the state development board. If so advised, he certainly then would need to have talked to a number of political men in the state, and among them would have been James F. Byrnes, Strom Thurmond, Edgar A. Brown, and possibly Olin D. Johnson. He also would have been introduced to Governor George Bell Timmerman, Jr., and possibly to Lieutenant Governor Ernest F. Hollings.

If he had wanted advice and counsel from established industrial and business leaders of the state, he might have been steered to them. He might have seen editor Roger Peace, bankers Hugh C. Lane and Ernest L. King, and utilities man M. C. McMeekin.

If he wished to move into individual communities to make discreet inquiry, he would have done well to be advised to look up the name of the attorney-senator from the county chosen and be briefed on him by senator Edgar Brown or senator Brown's colleague in political command, Sol Blatt, speaker of the House of Representatives and resident, like Brown, of Barnwell County.

Or if he had wished to get in touch directly with top county leaders, he could have contacted and been welcomed by most of them. He would be moving, in any case, toward or into the network of power and decision of the state.

Recognizing that the general pattern of action at the state

level of affairs originates often, informally, with members of the leading associations, anyone wishing to promote an activity in 1955 on a state-wide basis would need to have been aware of at least the following associational connections: South Carolina State Chamber of Commerce, South Carolina Bankers Association, and South Carolina Textile Manufacturers Association.

The general pattern of action in getting a bill through the state legislature usually ran as follows:

1. Informal clearances between some leaders named—particularly between members of the textile group, bankers, state Chamber of Commerce, and selected farm leaders.

2. Informal clearance made with Edgar Brown of state Senate, and Sol Blatt, House leader.

3. A state committee may or may not have been named to study the matter and/or make recommendations.

4. The action ball was often thrown by the manufacturing group to the organized farm groups who fronted for the leading industrialists in a legislature largely made up of rural representatives.

5. The senator-lawyers from the counties were alerted and kept informed of major legislative developments by various formal and informal devices of communication.

6. Hearings, bill introduction, and various maneuvers of legislative action were assigned to legislative wheel-horses.

In this process it was historically and generally understood that a higher priority was given to projects originating in the upland counties, which are the major population and industrial centers.

If I had wished to reveal the state power structure by using measuring devices other than industrial development, I might have taken specific issues or projects, such as right-to-work laws, school laws, or industrial plant location, and traced definite connections between persons mentioned in this report. I might also have proved the network by beginning a new project and utilizing the lines revealed. If I had done so, my prediction would have been that the network must be used in successful prosecution of projects. To ignore it or try to by-pass it would have been to court failure at the outset.

The least common denominator of relationship utilized in this study was personal knowledge. That is, I was not willing to say a relationship existed between two individuals unless the two knew each other. From this point, personal knowledge relationships were of differing intensity—to the point of actual control of one person over another.

The stable local power structures, tying into a narrowed circle of leadership at the state level, provide a base that links with the larger structures of power within the nation. South Carolina's boundaries, in many ways, provide limits for the core of power.

We shall see that some members of the top power structure of South Carolina appear again as specific policy makers when we examine textile policies that affect the nation. The South Carolina study gave a solid base for our analysis of the leadership of the nation, which begins after the following chapter describing yet another type of power structure, a functional and service network of coordinate influence in the housing industry.

7 A POWER STRUCTURE IN THE HOUSING INDUSTRY

BY 1956, three years after I had begun the series of studies comprising the national power structure study, it had become evident that besides the community, state, and national lines of communication on a geographical basis of policy development, there were large networks of functionally related service groups not necessarily geographically oriented—housing, welfare, health, labor, and safety operations, for example, did not seem altogether related to any one geographical area—but the service organizations comprising their activities had definable power relations within them that obviously reached across the nation. An analysis of the housing industry at this stage of study was made possible, which, besides proving the assumption that a power structure in service groups is definable, provided the methodological basis for a later study of the textile industry, which in turn helped to clinch the total study of national power relations.

Since the Federal Housing Act of 1934, housing has become a formal part of national policy development. Before the legislation of that year, housing long had been an informal public issue, but the housing act gave a coordinated direction to housing policy that ultimately had widespread acceptance among certain national leaders, and it has continued to guide general activity devoted to meeting the housing needs of the American people. By insuring the entrepreneur's risk, the Federal

Housing Administration had wedded governmental actions to actions of specific, able men in the housing business. The crux of power in housing matters had revolved, for the twenty years previous to 1956, around adjustments and regulations of acts between governmental agencies of the character of FHA and the Veterans' Administration. The activities of men in the money market had set in motion thousands of builders, contractors, and suppliers to meet, particularly, the housing demands of people in the middle ranges of income.

Outside this core of activity had been sporadic attempts at public housing, slum clearance, and urban redevelopment. It had been admitted by most that in spite of ten million housing starts since 1943, activities like the FHA's had failed to solve the problems of need for housing low income families located in urban and rural areas of deterioration and blight.

The problems of poorly housed low income families everywhere and of universal urban deterioration are well documented in innumerable writings and are of such a technical nature that I could not go into them here except to mention them as a background of policy development. They are, in the main, a part of the policy struggle in housing that has been deferred for many reasons. Wars, rising incomes, fear of socialism (real and assumed), lethargy, social lag, and the struggle for the control of the effective market all have played a part in neutralizing the quantitative gains in general public housing.

Politically, in the policy sense, it has not been necessary fully to face up to the basic issue and the distasteful subject of low incomes over the nation. It has been more politically expedient within the past decade and a half to pretend that there are no low incomes. If the statistical averages showed otherwise, a countering fact has been available, i.e., incomes have been rising steadily. In view of such facts, housing policy makers have been troubled somewhat, but low incomes, per se, are not primarily their policy problem nor considered in de-

veloping a housing industry that can meet effective demand
for houses, which has been in the middle and upper range income groups. Efforts by housing policy makers, therefore,
have been geared to this fact.

Policy considerations of the housing industry, then, had
been guided in two ways: (1) by effective market considerations which had, by and large, been geared to manipulation
of the credit market made available by government agencies
and private financial groups, and (2) by the holding off of
large scale public constructions that might have depressed the
existing private market.

Such considerations, to be made operatively effective, become power considerations. Whether by trial and error or
cold calculation, certain men must decide on courses of action,
formulate policy, and move other men to accept and act upon
it. Power, by definition here, as elsewhere in this writing, is
the ability of some men to move other men, goods, and services
toward socially allowed objectives, or conversely to stop such
movement when it seems undesirable at a given point or time.

What a researcher is told by individuals, piece by piece, is
important in getting a relatively complete picture of a power
structure in operation. It has been observed previously that
comparatively few men in a given power structure see the
operation of it as a whole, nor is an individual fully aware of
all other individuals and factors that may guide his own power
structure. Each individual plays a singular role in regard to
policy-making and power-wielding. Each may see with considerable clarity his own role and his general part in decision-
making in the total policy development and he may see the
roles and parts played by a few others. Some men play down
their power actions. Others inflate them. Some attribute power
to others which the others do not possess. In like manner, some
detract from the real power possessed by others. In all cases
only collective opinions become meaningful for the researcher.

Men in our society resist autocratic power as they resist

monolithic power. No individual can say, as the French Louis did when authorizing the construction of the boulevards of Paris for the movement of troops against Parisian mobs, "It is my will!" and expect his will to be heeded universally.

The wielding of power in American community life has a more subtle kind of purposefulness. It is a combination of powerful individuals willing that things be done or not done and sometimes getting others to believe they thought of the idea in the first place and wanted to do it all along. It presumes a reaching out on the part of powerful individuals for the support of equally powerful persons to accomplish ends. It implies a recognition on the part of certain men of other men as peers in the process of decision and power execution. And, as in all manifestations of power, it demands, no matter how obscured, obedience and deference on the part of the many to the will and purpose of the few.

America has a tradition of equality that makes men believe that power is inherently evil and morally wrong; yet I have not found any individuals in organized groups who cannot point to a few other members and say, "They are the powers that be!"

The question of who wields power is a meaningful one to most, although it may be subject to trivial limitations on the part of any respondent. Scholars quibble abstractly about the meaning of the questions but this quibble revolves around reassurement rather than around the general implication of the term "power." Who, for example, will deny that Harlow Curtice of General Motors (1958) is a powerful man? How to measure his power is another question, one over which the scholars can, perhaps, rightly quarrel. My own way to get a rough measure of Harlow Curtice's power depends on the answers to two questions. First, is he named and recognized as a power by his peers, and secondly, do his actions, coordinated with those of others, move men toward definite and specifiable policy objectives? The first-named step is important in social research, and the measure of power thus is comparative analysis.

It is also apparent that each major, particular power structure is related directly and indirectly, through its personnel, to every other structure. This is not to say that there is a monolithic power structure in the nation moving in willful accord on every national issue, but it may be said with confidence that various groups of power within the nation are interlocked by persons who can and do communicate core policy decisions of a particular power structure to key persons of other structures as occasion demands.

A part, but only a part, of the cementing of the various structures is the ideologies which tend to bind the major national political parties together loosely. "Free private enterprise," "individual initiative," "our free heritage," and like slogans that constitute stock platform phrases may be in the back of an individual's mind when he speaks of a power structure to which he belongs, but uppermost in his mind he holds some policy or set of policies which specifically affects his pocketbook and/or prestige when translated into action. "For the good of the country, yes!" "For the good of my organization, yes, yes!" "For my own good, yes, yes, yes!" All six yesses must be recognized, in the given order, for any power structure to be effective in holding its membership. The housing industry is no exception to the general rule.

Although the construction of houses is an activity as old as the nation, the national housing industry as such is only some twenty years old, brought into being with the FHA, which made large scale home financing and building possible. As the Act has been administered, attacked, and modified, certain individuals have come into prominent view in the process. The process of organization of the housing industry has been, in some degree, a groping one.

As an industry, housing has been characterized by countless thousands of operators in its total activity. The National As-

sociation of Home Builders, for example, claimed a membership of 36,000 individual builders in 1956. Add to such a
figure the members of real-estate boards across the nation, the
lumber dealers, bankers, mortgage lenders, material suppliers,
insurance lenders and brokers and it is sizable indeed.

At first glance it would appear that a power structure within
the industry might have been impossible to locate. It would
seem that the diversity of interests of so many independent
operators would make any kind of coordinated activity impossible. To some extent this was true. And yet, the gigantic
groups of men engaged in the industry narrowed to several
power pyramids. As in any vital structure of power, the personnel at the various apexes of the power pyramids of influence
operated in coordinate relations to each other.

In order to speak meaningfully of the various coordinate
relationships within the housing industry, I need for a moment
to go into the background of the study. I then shall go into
the process of study to reveal elements of the power structure
of housing and to connect these elements with a larger structure of policy-making in the nation.

As has been demonstrated in previous chapters, to make a
study of policy-making in the nation as a whole, by 1956 I had
done several things. I had made a series of studies of local
power structures. They were geographically balanced and
oriented to specifiable areas. It had been demonstrated that
specifiable men within these areas had policy-making relations
with each other on scores of issues or civic projects. It was also
evident that a study in some depth related to a structure of
power that would cut across geographical lines, that involved
issues of national concern, and that might relate to a definable
proportion of the general group of national policy makers
would aid in proving the efficacy of the method of research I
had been using.

Early in 1956, fortuitously, I was presented with the opportunity of determining some of the factors that might or

might not be present in a national structure of power in housing activities. Professor Nick Demerath, an imaginative, free-wheeling research entrepreneur, called and said that a study was being made by the national Commission on Race Relations. A part of the study was to determine why minority groups were so apparently at a disadvantage in acquiring new homes. I was asked by Dr. Demerath to do a detail within the study, i.e., ascertain the limits of the housing power structure. I was not required to get answers to the many questions posed by the Commission, but only to furnish them with a picture of the operations of a policy-making structure within the field of housing.

Utilizing the model of study found workable in earlier power structure studies, I called on the secretaries of housing associations in New York, Washington, and Chicago and got from them listings of leaders, presumed by them to be influential and powerful in the development of housing policy. During the course of these interviews, I asked questions concerning the processes of policy development. I then sent questionnaires to the leaders named, and after ascertaining a general pattern of mutual knowledge I interviewed a comprehensive sample of the leaders most frequently named in the poll and considered to be of top power and influence, according to answers to a question on the poll. In subsequent interviews with the leaders, I was interested in getting a picture of the processes of coordination in policy development, and of the relation of the leaders of the housing industry to the larger, general structure of top leaders in the nation as a whole. The process of study, from its inception, revealed elements of a structure of power.

I began the study by calling upon one of the several housing trade association secretaries in Washington. I was referred, by him, to several other secretaries in that city, and I began to compile a listing of the several housing trade association secretaries in Washington. I also began to compile a listing of associations and leaders in this chain referral process.

As I moved about among the association officials, certain marks of organization status were apparent. The National Association of Home Builders, for example, was housed in a new, multi-storied building of contemporary design. Its executive offices were comparable, although on a somewhat smaller scale, to offices of many leaders in the largest national corporations or to some of the modern labor temples that have been built in the nation's capital and in some of the nation's larger cities. A modest exception to the expensive office locations and designs was the office of Lee Johnson, executive vice-president of the National Housing Conference, an association that had been devoted to keeping the issue of public housing alive, was supported, in part, by labor organizations, and was considered the liberal wing of the industry.

Not all of the associations had surroundings like the Home Builders, nor do visible appurtenances make a complete case for the power of an individual or an association, but I was struck with the fact that there were gradations in the surroundings of various secretaries. They were one sign of the value imputed to an association by its members and to some extent a symbol of the affluence of the association. Let it be said in complete honesty, however, that some of the secretaries and some of the consultants for private housing interests, men who were attorneys or specialized lobbyists for these interests, had very modest offices, and I am convinced that they had much influence. The office of Miles Colean, a consultant for the mortgage bankers' group and considered by many to be the top man in effective work, was a case in point. Like James Rouse, Thomas P. Coogan, Earl Schwulst, Robert Patrick, William A. Clark, and Ferd Kramer, builders and financial operators in the industry, he was considered a thinker, a man of ideas that count.

In response to my initial, general question, "Who are the power leaders, the policy makers in the housing industry?" I was told, "The question is too general. You must understand that the industry is made up of big segments—each of which is important to the whole." The secretaries would follow this statement by indicating that, aside from the obviously important and visible group within the industry, the builders, I had to take into account financial groups (savings and loan associations, savings banks, life insurance companies, mortgage banks, and commercial banks); material suppliers (lumber, glass, bricks etc.); public interest groups (mainly related to public housing); private consultants and attorneys; trade association officials; and government officials, including personnel related to both administration and legislation. Thirteen associations, and 21 secretaries within them, were asked to give information related to policy and power personnel within the industry.[1] "Names," they said, "should be obtained in each of these groupings."

The secretaries were in agreement on a majority of the names, that will be listed presently by categories. In choosing housing leaders, some secretaries would add to the list the names of their board people and of the current president of their organization. Some would disagree with such choices on the part of others, particularly in relation to current presidents, saying, "John So-and-So is a good man, but this year the association has a presidential dud. Not a big man, not the kind of man you are looking for. I certainly would not consider him a top leader." There was, however, knowledge of a core of men, indicating that top leadership within the in-

1. The associations were: The Amer. Committee to Improve Our Neighborhoods (ACTION); Amer. Inst. of Architects; Associated General Contractors of America; Construction and Civic Development Dept., U. S. Chamber of Commerce; Mortgage Bankers Assoc.; Nat. Assoc. of Home Builders; Nat. Assoc. of Real Estate Boards; Nat. Housing Conference; Nat. Retail Lumber Dealers; Nat. Savings and Loan League; Prefabricated Home Mfrs. Inst.; Structural Clay Products Inst.; and the U. S. Savings and Loan League.

dustry had limits and that there was consensus on leaders within the segments of it.

There was no hard and fast, common agreement between association secretaries regarding specific housing policies. That is, there was no evidence that I could see that there was a tight coalition of secretaries moving as a single entity on a majority of housing issues. Each association had several policies in which it was interested. Some of these policies overlapped the interests of others, but each association, according to the interest group it represented, tried to maintain its own identity and policy integrity. The leaders, particularly the professional ones, jealously guarded their association's individuality, and some of them resented the charge, often hurled at them by President Truman, that as a group they were the housing lobby or real-estate lobby. There was, of course, within some associations a value aura related to individual and private enterprise versus public housing, with the private value at this time in the ascendancy.

During the period after Truman's election in 1948, when public versus private housing development was being strongly debated, a luncheon group of secretaries met weekly under the leadership of B. T. Fitzpatrick of the U. S. Chamber of Commerce to exchange views and come to broad, general agreement on how to lick the Truman program. But since Mr. Fitzpatrick's death and with the advent of the present administration in Washington, which is sympathetic to the private groups, there had been little attempt publicly to coordinate closely the various competing trade groups. This does not mean that they did not watch each other with interest, know the leaders of other groups, and gear their activities according to the temper of the times or in accord with the needs of a given situation. More has been said about the activities of various policy groups at a later point, but here it can be said that the so-called housing lobby should be looked at, during relatively normal periods, as a segmented affair, coalescing only under stress. Also, the Republican administration probably had a quieting effect on some.

The general functions of most housing associations and consultants are those of watching what goes on, particularly in Congress, putting proposed legislation in digest form for members or clients, and persuading others to a particular point of view. Some of the lay leaders of the associations say that the secretaries magnify issues and keep some of them alive in order to protect their jobs. They scare their constituencies into continued support. This scare process had been least effective and most transparent during the period of a "business climate" in Washington. "Only Lee Johnson and his labor boys keep public housing alive as an issue. They have some influence, particularly with some Representatives in Congress, but their threat is greatly overrated. You cannot discount them, though. . . ."

The names most frequently cited to me by the association secretaries may now be listed categorically (Table 2). I have indicated by a number after a man's name how widely he was known by a majority of those who answered a questionnaire on the subject. Asterisks after a man's name indicate a judgment, on the part of his peers, of his relative standing as a person "influential in the policy-making power structure of the industry." One asterisk indicates the least weight; three, the most.

It should be noted, too, that the men are categorized according to the general interest of each. For example, Philip Klutznick's name is placed under the Builders category. Mr. Klutznick had built a large, private housing development south of Chicago. His major building activities were relatively quiescent at the time of the housing study. He was active in managing his properties at this time, but he was remembered by his peers as a builder. The categories are thus approximate.

TABLE 2

SELF-RATINGS OF HOUSING LEADERS BY GROUPS, 1956

	Name	Number to Whom Known Personally
1. Builders	Irving Blietz *	11
	Fritz Burns ***	38
	George Gross *	10
	Joseph Haverstick **	20
	Richard Hughes ***	38
	Philip Klutznick ***	33
	William Levitt **	30
	Rodney Lockwood **	32
	Earl W. Smith *	27
	Alexander Sumner *	17
2. Financial Groups		
a. Savings Banks	Harry Held **	23
	Robert Morgan **	24
	Earl Schwulst ***	27
b. Life Insurance Companies	Norman Carpenter *	18
	Paul F. Clark *	4
	L. W. Dawson *	2
	Lou Douglas *	3
	Frederick Ecker *	8
	R. D. Murphy *	6
	Robert Patrick *	18
	Carrol M. Shanks ***	16
	Milford Vieser **	26
c. Mortgage Bankers	John Austin **	18
	William A. Clark *	27
	Thomas P. Coogan ***	35
	Ferd Kramer ***	30
	Aksel Nielsen ***	29
	James Rouse ***	35
d. Savings and Loan Associations	George Bliss **	21
	Oscar Kreutz *	22
	Charles Wellman **	13
e. Commercial Banks	William Marcus *	21
	John Scully **	24
3. Material Suppliers	C. J. Backstrand ***	12
	Leslie Cassidy **	8
	Joseph Grazier *	16
	George T. MacNichol *	11
	Fred Weyerhaeuser *	14

TABLE 2 (continued)

	Name	Number to Whom Known Personally
4. Publicists	Edith Evans *	12
	Ed Gavin *	16
	Andrew Heiskell **	30
	James M. Lange **	17
	Perry Prentice ***	37
5. Private Consultants	Frederick Babcock *	23
	Miles Colean ***	47
	Herbert Colton **	28
	Ernest Fisher *	29
	Raymond Foley *	35
	Seward Mott *	17
	Robinson Newcomb **	22
6. Trade Association Officials	Morton Bodfish **	30
	Harold Braman *	20
	Eugene Conser *	16
	John M. Dickerman ***	40
	H. E. Foreman *	9
	Neal Hardy ***	35
	Lee Johnson **	25
	James Lash *	16
	Samuel Neel ***	32
	H. R. Northrup ***	28
	Al Payne *	12
	Edmund P. Purvis *	18
	Stephen Slipher **	23
	Harry Steidle **	16
	James Steiner *	10
	Douglas Whitlock ***	25
	John C. Williamson **	17
7. Labor	Bert Seidman **	14
	Boris Shishkin ***	17
8. Others	Catherine Bauer *	3
	George Beavers *	2
	Ernest Bohn *	1
	Frank Fernback *	1
	Frank S. Horne **	16
	Andrew Means *	1
	Msgr. John J. O'Grady **	14
9. Government Officials a. HHFA	A. M. Cole ***	48
	Annabelle Heath *	17
	M. Carter McFarland *	14

TABLE 2 (continued)

	Name	Number to Whom Known Personally
b. FHA	Norman Mason ***	42
	Charles Sigety *	15
c. Urban Renewal Administration	James Follin *	33
	Richard Steiner *	16
d. Community Facilities Administration	John Hazeltine *	13
e. Public Housing Administration	Charles Slusser *	18
	Warren Vinton **	18
f. Federal Reserve Board	Guy E. Noyes **	16
	Winfield Riefler ***	24
g. FNMA	Stan Baughman *	22
h. Council of Economic Advisors	Arthur Burns ***	17
	Leo Grebler **	19
	R. J. Saulnier **	20
i. Census Bureau	Howard Brunsman *	13
	Wayne F. Dougherty *	16
j. Veterans' Administration	Thomas Sweeney *	26
k. Others	Charles Abrams **	19
	Joseph P. McMurray **	24
	Robert C. Weaver ***	21
10. Congress and Staff		
a. House Banking and Currency Committee	John Barriere *	13
	Orman Fink **	15
	James McEwan *	16
	Robert Poston *	17
b. Senate Banking and Currency Committee	Jack Carter **	18
	Milton Semer *	10
c. Top Congressmen in Housing	Sen. Paul H. Douglas **	20
	Sen. J. W. Fulbright **	12
	Sen. Irving M. Ives **	12
	Sen. H. H. Lehman **	13
	Rep. Wright Patman *	6
	Rep. Albert Rains ***	12
	Sen. John J. Sparkman ***	30
	Rep. Brent Spence *	5
	Rep. J. P. Wolcott ***	27

From returns on the questionnaire, 26 other leaders were suggested, but these names were additions to the original listing on the questionnaire and could not, therefore, be rated like the others. With the exceptions of one or two of the Congressmen, no more names were added when I interviewed a majority of the lay leaders and a sample of the professionals named in the first poll. The leaders named in the categories above were said by most to offer a pretty good cross-section within the power structure of housing.

A complete list of all the persons who have power within the total configurations of activities in the housing industry would have been impossible and meaningless to compile. Men did recognize leaders who became spokesmen and status figures within the industry, leaders whose opinions on matters of general policy were taken into account as the activities of building houses on a mass scale broadened and developed. Knowing what some of the other leaders thought and did does not necessarily mean that one had to agree with them or like them, but their views became a point of reference in a policy-making process. The general goal of the whole group, differentiating it from every other group in American society, was that of producing houses. Individuals within the total group may have differed on how the goal might best be accomplished, but in terms of power, of moving goods and services, there was a meshing of individuals and segmental power structures within the larger whole. The leaders of the smaller pyramids of power in the industry were looked upon as a stable, on-going power structure in themselves. The housing power structure was, in turn, related to a generalized structure of power and policy decision in the nation.

Not all of the categories named here were of equal weight in the eyes of those who viewed the industry as a whole. The builders were an obviously important group, but, as one builder said, "I see these builders in conferences and conventions strutting around like cocks of the walk. They've got the world by the tail—they think. Yet, I think to myself, 'Every one of you birds is dependent on some banker or mortgage lender.' If I were to say what group is most influential and important in the housing industry, I'd have to say the bankers." One also had to recognize the importance of government in underwriting home finance and the importance of the people who kept other men informed of major activities in the field through trade publications; each group was extremely necessary and important to all others. However, the financiers and builders appeared to be key groups in the whole process.

In the governmental category, the administrators of agencies were readily recognized power figures. Some of the understaff named above were extremely important in furnishing data for decisions. By the fact that they gathered data in certain ways and from selected sources, they could deflect or guide certain courses of action. They were important parts of the over-all power structure, but they were not leaders in a status and general policy-making sense. I was told that Leo Grebler was an intelligent economist in the Council of Economic Advisors, and from my observations of him of a few moments' duration I agreed. He helped get facts for Arthur Burns, who "on occasion had the ear of the President." His selection of facts became important. He was in a key position, if not a decisive one, in the policy process. Other persons on the listing were, in this way at least, important functionaries in the whole structure of policy decision.

Because of the bigness of the housing industry and because it had so many small scale operators (a big builder was still considered one who produces a hundred houses; the Bill Levitts and Phil Klutznicks were notable exceptions), the national associations played a much more important role in the development of policy than did some of the associations related to the established, single industries. In the more integrated steel industry, for example, there were very large operators in four or five concentrations. The single units within the steel industry were so large that they had weight individually in a policy-making sense. They also had developed lines of contact with governmental officials and other financial and industrial groupings. Their top leaders said, "I would not go to the associations to get a policy hammered out. I'd go directly to a friend, a cabinet member, the President, or to top Congressmen and get satisfaction."

A builder of one hundred houses or less could not talk like this. He was dependent upon allying with other small scale operators to have his voice heard. The trade associations thus became extremely important to him, and he supported them with a fervor not found in other industrial groupings. An exchange of information, a feeling of belonging to a power organization, and an understanding of the elements of his industry come to a man who engages in organization work.

The small builder was dependent for financing on very large concentrations of capital in the Eastern banks and insurance companies. For a few who knew the intricacies of the system, a way could be found—for example, to the doorsteps of the Chase Manhattan Bank or the Prudential Insurance Company in New Jersey—but most little fellows were not of the notion they could walk into the offices of the leaders of these institutions and be welcomed or get satisfaction. They knew there must be channels, however, and their associations helped them to open them. If their associations were not strong enough to move the larger financial interests directly, the men began to exert pressure on government officials to change rules in their favor. The point here is that in unity of association there was strength.

The professionals in the housing associations had a vital role to play in policy development. They had literally hundreds of committees and subcommittees active in Washington and at the community level. They attended cocktail parties, went golfing, ate in the clubs of the national capital, buttonholed Congressmen, buttered up various government officials, secretaries, and each other, and prepared their key members as witnesses in top level governmental hearings on housing legislation. They produced research facts by the ream and distributed the results of their labors.

They coached lay members of policy commissions that set the line for major trends of housing development. According to the status of the associations to which the professionals belonged, some were accorded more deference than others for their proficiency and efficiency. Some were probably as powerful, if not more powerful, than the majority of individual lay leaders they represented. These did not have to defer to many, but most knew where they earned their bread and gave the proper signs of recognition. All claimed to represent powerful interests (in combination, if not otherwise). This claim gave them status with those in Congress and elsewhere who were impressed with the weight of numbers—whether the numbers were in terms of dollars or men.

As I moved about, hearing the men in the housing industry talk about themselves and their activities, I was again impressed with the fact that national processes of power formulations are not unlike those found in communities. Similar systems of status were operative. Patterns of committee and group action were similar. Personal relations and evaluations of persons of one another were similar.

The status of most of the top leaders in the housing industry was generally a cut below that of the top community and national policy makers. At the community level, a builder might have been an important person in community affairs, but he usually did not have top billing in the over-all policy-making group. The same manifestations of status were present on the national scene.

When asked whether they knew personally 106 men listed as top status, power leaders at the national level, 45 men answered the question. A majority had worked on one or more projects with 86 of the 106 status bearers, who were number-one leaders in the country. (I use the designation "number one" to distinguish top leaders of the larger national power structure from those in the more limited power structure of the housing industry.) It was apparent, however, and significantly, that leaders in housing, considered top leaders in their industry, knew or had worked with more of the number-one national leaders than had those rated downward in the deference scale. The top housing leaders had worked with an average of 10 leaders of the number-one list, while second-rate and third-rate leaders averaged only 3. In other words, top leaders in the housing group tended to work more closely with the number-one national leaders than did lower echelon leaders.

It was further significant that some of the top leaders in the housing industry were second men in companies dominated by men listed in the number-one group of national power figures. For example, John Jewett was a vice president in the insurance company presided over by Carrol Shanks. Among the building suppliers, manufacturers of plastics, glass, metal products, cement and the like, the top men in particular industries made the top billing as national, number-one power leaders, while second- and third-string men within their companies were assigned responsibilities for being acquainted with, and becoming themselves, recognized leaders in the housing industry.

The relation of men in the housing industry with governmental officials differed from that with number-one leaders. The latter helped directly to put the President in the White House. They could go to him as the occasion demanded. This could not be said, with but exceedingly few exceptions, for the top policy makers in housing. Many of them were proud of the fact that they could go directly to Norman Mason or Albert Cole, Presidential administrative appointees, with their problems. None of the men I asked had ever directly got to the President on housing matters. Some, if not most, of the top leaders in housing were aware of indirect channels of

policy development in relation to housing at the federal government level. They knew that unofficially Attorney-General
Herbert Brownell had been given policy authority for watch-
dogging housing policy. They knew that the unofficial policy
of the administration was to keep public housing on the back
burner, as a matter that might be steamed up in the event of a
major threat of downturn in the economy, as a kind of
public works program.[2] They knew that the lending and underwriting powers in government were being held in abey-
ance for similar reasons. They felt often that housing had become a political football. They believed that the present
administrators of the larger housing programs in the federal
establishment were second-rate figures who had no real in at
the White House. "The esteem in which housing is held can
be guessed from the fact that the top administrator in housing has only seen the President twice in four years," said the
editor of one of the national housing periodicals. They were
aware of the fact that Arthur Burns, White House economist,
advised the President officially and that Aksel Nielsen, Denver
banker and friend, advised him unofficially. They recognized
the general policy of avoiding a housing controversy, and
many were in accord with it. They further recognized that
phrases like "slum clearance" and "urban redevelopment" had
been good but relatively empty campaign slogans for the incumbent administration. "The present administration has no
housing policy," said some. "It is trying to pretend that it has.
It wishes to placate some of the radical elements by keeping
public housing alive, while it says it is devoted to a system of
private enterprise." The housing leaders knew their relative
positions in the power structure of the housing industry. They
knew that their power structure related to a larger structure of
power and a policy development.

2. In both 1951 and 1958 this policy direction was proved correct. Housing was being steamed up by the President to meet the recessions in both of
these periods.

Let us now examine some of the policy considerations of the power groups in housing and relate them to activities. When asked, "What are the issues in housing?" 55 leaders in the industry felt that the major issues revolved around ways in which to solve the problems of urban blight, to get more mortgage money to builders and buyers, to settle the problem of public vs. private development, to solve problems of costs, to attack local development problems, and to handle minority housing. A few mentioned market inflation, tax reductions, housing for the aged, and cabinet status for the industry (Table 3).

TABLE 3

HOUSING ISSUES BY NUMBERS OF TIMES MENTIONED
BY 55 LEADERS, 1956 *

Issue	Number of Times Mentioned
Urban redevelopment, renewal, and slum clearance	14
Shortage of mortgage money	11
Private vs. public housing	10
High cost of housing	8
Scarcity of land, and other local problems	5
Minority housing	4
Inflation of market	2
Tax reduction	2
Cabinet status for the industry	1
Housing for the aged	1

* A few mentioned more than one policy.

As I talked with the leaders, it was interesting to note that many of them were concerned and troubled about the redevelopment of urban communities. This was as true of the ones who could surely be classified as conservative in their attitudes as of the labor leaders and others who had long taken a position to the left. The conservatives were convinced, however, that the best way of eliminating urban blight, getting low-cost housing for slum families, and meeting the demands for housing on the part of disadvantaged minorities was to expand and extend the arrangements of the FHA type of financing, which was considered the private enterprise solution. The contradiction with government's role in this solution had been resolved through years of experience in working with government and of fairly well established lines of control. Those at the extreme opposite of the conservative interests contended that the problem was too big for private financial interests acting alone, and they pointed to the fact that there was in 1956 an extreme shortage of mortgage-lending money. The insurance companies and the larger lending banks were very defensive in this matter. John Jewett, vice-president of Prudential, assured me that there was plenty of mortgage money available in banking and insurance funds to meet housing needs. He emphasized that he had supervised the lending of approximately one and a half billion dollars during the past two years for mortgage purposes. The company had nearly 38 percent of its listed ratio of assets in mortgage loans. The mortgage figure had to be discounted somewhat, however, because the company also lent large sums of money to enterprises engaged in erecting city skyscrapers and industrial plants. The experiences of the Mutual Benefit Life Insurance Company, which had headquarters in the same city as Prudential, and the Metropolitan Life Insurance Company of New York, where I talked with Milford Vieser and Norman Carpenter, have been similar. The Mutual Benefit listed more than 50 percent of its assets as mortgages. None of the men, however, could explain quite how the private lending companies could do the immense job of refurbishing American community housing. They thought private industry could do the job, but the details had not been worked out. They would like to have had a say in the matter as it progressed toward solution.

The so-called warehousing of mortgage money was a device created by some of the larger financial institutions to relieve the tight money market. The warehousing scheme essentially had

been a device by which a central office was set up by some of
the banks and other financial institutions to pool mortgage
money so that it could be channeled quickly to recognized
builders waiting for FHA, VA, or other governmental insurance loans. Thomas Coogan, an ex-builder, operated an
office in New York that served about one hundred builders.
He was helped considerably by John Scully and the insurance
men mentioned. One government agency, FNMA, popularly
called Fanny Mae, had the potential of conducting itself as a
warehouse for builders, but there was a hassle over whether
or not it should. Direct loans by banks were another way that
many housing starts had been made. These schemes seemed to
indicate, on the whole, a modification of the extreme views
expressed by those who cried socialism at every turn a few
years before.

It is not my intention here to get beyond my depth in
analyzing the issues raised by the housing leaders. It was evident that the issues named were of prime consideration to the
industry, and many elements in them presented problems that
remained unsolved. Study, conferences, hearings, pressures,
and power manipulations will continue to involve the men in
housing. One by one the issues will be resolved, they said. I
was interested in knowing how the men thought they could
come to solutions. I therefore asked and probed for the answers to the ways in which things get done.

Those who believed government should go little further in
helping to develop the industry said that government regulations had proved too restrictive on private enterprise. They
pointed to the fact that the regulations on returns from invest-
ments, through a control of interest rates, had kept the money
market tight.

I should like to repeat that the men in the housing industry,
like others, did not operate on a basis of collusion and conspiracy in getting things done, and I do not believe that many
power processes, in the long run, are effective on this basis.

Not all motivations in power are pure nor actions always carried on in a blaze of publicity, but in most power struggles sides must be taken, and resolutions of conflict most often come after the facts are taken into account.

Several of the men interviewed said, "I am a voice crying in the wilderness," in relation to the ideas for resolving a particular issue. It was a statement revealing a thwarting of the will, and power deals with willing that things get done. Those who wring their hands helplessly in a wilderness are not men of power. I thought the despair expressed was less than hopeless. The men making such statements would then tell me what they had done about getting their ideas across to others. Twenty-four men said, in many ways, that their activities in relation to public issues entailed committee or association work, 7 indicated that they thought their most effective work had been carried out in appearances before Congressional committees, and 3 thought that widespread speech-making had been effective. These were the activities that came readily to their minds when I asked, "What, specifically, have you done about issues?" Most qualified their remarks and indicated that association work meant the use of considerable time in study, research (in some cases), preparation for lay and professional responsibilities in associations, attending meetings of commissions and committees, and making their ideas known through individual contacts, speeches, and writing. They could not reveal much beyond this. They operated in their local communities. They related themselves to other lay leaders in the status scheme of things and felt comfortable in this. They used the knowledge of professionals. They took insoluble problems to committees of government. And "this," they said, "is all I really do."

I probed to see whether they did more—whether they connived with others to force their views on still others. I could make no such connections. When pressed, some would become a little exasperated. Their own actions were above board, they felt, and the implication of collusion and coercion was absurd. In many cases they had espoused their points of view for years, and their views were often a matter of public record. They knew that others might disagree with them wholeheartedly and even violently, but most considered this part of the democratic way. They were willing to try with all their might to make their own points of view prevail, but their ways of acting were generally in accord with the procedures outlined in the previous explanation of association activities, procedures sanctioned by custom in our society and utilized by the leaders with sureness and confidence.

It was perhaps no accident that many of the men listed as a part of the power structure in housing had appeared as members of major committees related to governmental activities. "Because of its unique authority," I have said in one of the hypotheses of this study, "government is of special concern to the rest of the power structure, and segments of the informal structure, tacitly supported by the whole structure, act through and upon government in relation to specific problems." Men in the housing industry have centered many of their activities within recent years in two major efforts. The President's Advisory Committee on Government Housing Policies and Programs has constituted an extremely important body of policy makers.[3] Another group of men has appeared before Congressional committees.[4] A majority of these men in both the President's Committee and in the Congressional hearings were put forward by their associations. They expressed their own views,

3. See "Recommendations on Government Housing Policies and Programs: A Report to the President of the United States" (U. S. Government Printing Office, December, 1953).

4. See especially "House Amendments of 1955, Hearings before the Committee on Banking and Currency, House of Representatives, Eighty-fourth Congress, on H.R. 5827"; "Investigation of Housing, 1955, Hearings before the Subcommittee on Housing of the Committee on Banking and Currency, House of Representatives, Eighty-fourth Congress, on H.R. 203, and Parts 1, 2, and 3"; and "Housing Amendments of 1956, Hearings before a Subcommittee of the Committee on Banking and Currency, United States Senate, 1956."

but they could not be considered average-citizen witnesses speaking spontaneously about housing needs. They had points of view related to their primary interests, some of which seemed to coincide and certainly did coincide in their eyes with the public interest, for the most part. Some men would emphasize that their activities within their own businesses were the real ways of power. What they did daily had important policy implications. One of the insurance company executives expressed this when he said, "My primary responsibility in matters of policy is to see, with our corporate board, that the trust funds of our insurance company are invested wisely for the protection of our investors. I feel that we have a responsibility to do whatever is necessary to achieve this end. I have been in Washington very few times. I have always felt our company to be above the sort of things that go on down there." He continued with some disdain, "When I appeared before one of the subcommittees in Washington recently, I was contradicted in one of my statements by a Congressman, who cited the testimony of some obscure builder out west. When power is thought of, one usually considers the source of it. I had always thought of our company as representing some weight. I was shocked by what I heard in Washington. . . . Maybe I should get down there more often."

DURING the course of this study, it may be repeated, I was seeking to learn whether there was a definable national power structure decisive in shaping the general policy course of the country. With modifications that will be made later, I have found that there is such a power superstructure, generally with a coordination of goals and a resolution of unavoidable conflicts by the same types of individuals in roles and status positions similar to those found in communities. Utilizing the familiar sociological concepts of role and status analysis, together with questions related to group action patterns, I found it increasingly clear that the formulation of national policy and its ultimate execution by these individuals also were processes in a structure of action not unlike that found in community power situations. The broad framework of action can be outlined as power elements:

1. Establishment by power group of claims of status
2. Use of selected personnel to put forward ideas on new policy or to reinforce existing policy claims
3. Use of quasi-formal organization to shape policy
4. Use of formal organization to promote policy
5. Use of institutional organization to sanction and execute policy

In thinking of these elements it is necessary to recognize that we are dealing with people acting in relation to policy direction. Thus one must hold in mind conflicting ideas—fluidity and stability, specifics and generalities. Let me illustrate the meaning of this by taking element number one, the establishment of claims of status.

The social roles that a man plays and the importance of the roles determine a man's status. If his roles are generally power-oriented, the man becomes a power figure. This is true first locally and then nationally. The habitual assumption of a policy-making role where vital subjects are under consideration gives a man power prestige. It also gives him an expertness in handling policy problems and, through recognition gained by his activities, opens for him further opportunities for utilizing his skills. Social responsibilities are delegated to those deemed trained and qualified to handle them. Power exercised according to determined policy is effective when it is localized, whether the localization be from the national scene to a county or town, or from a corporate board chairman to an operating field supervisor. Policy must be translated into the living activities of individuals moving in accord with the requirements and directives of higher authority. Social organizations devoted to controlling the activities of their members develop gradations of status for the implicit or express purpose of exacting obedience of all individuals within them. By custom, regulation, and law, men become habituated to following the patterns of activities agreed upon by the directors of an organization. These patterns of action are, then, structured. They give form and stability to organization operations. In a very real sense, those who top the various pyramids of power in society are status symbols. They stand as points of localization of power direction.

Specifically, Ben X. Russel of U.S. Motors in 1956 stood for liberalized credit in the national economy. His policy stand was dictated apparently from his desire to sell more automobiles. His stand was a symbol for every man in the organization to rally around. It gave direction to the day to day decisions of vast bodies of men, within and outside the corporate structure of U. S. Motors, who cued their activities according to dictates of the top policy maker, Ben Russel. Russel, obviously, could not tell every man in the country what to do. He could tell him what he wished would be done. What he wished was shocking to those who had been devoted to a sound dollar economy, but the world knew that Russel was willing to set aside what had been considered a stable policy direction for a policy that then fitted his company's needs. One had to view Mr. Russel's actions and statements in terms of fluidity and stability. He was operating in a stable corporate structure—a structure in which he held the highest status position—but his role demanded a fluidity of policy direction to meet changing operating conditions. He could not have fixed indefinitely upon any given course.

In general, Mr. Russel had committed himself to a hard money policy. He had not given any indication that he believed in a policy of inflation, but specifically he was of the opinion that liberalized credit terms were not inflationary. I am not here arguing the merits of the man's case nor singling him out for attack. His situation merely illustrated the fact that fluidity and stability, specifics and generalities may be operative in any given set of policy considerations.

Mr. Russel's corporate status was generally known. His claims for status had been recognized locally, within his corporation, within the community, within the state, within the general business community, within the nation, and abroad. This recognition was not static, although his position was relatively stable. He was in no immediate danger of losing his position if his guesses about the economy happened to have been wrong. Conceivably, he could have lost status as a national spokesman if he was too far wrong on too many issues, but there was an element of stability within the total policy-making structure that helped to stabilize his own individual position and prepare the way for a changed position on his part at the appropriate time.

Mr. Russel's position also was relative to other stands taken by other important men in the general policy and power structure of the nation, and when the final choice of position was made, his position in the status structure would rise or fall according to the final direction of policy. Because of the size of his operation, thousands of men were weighing his stand on liberalization of credit and watching with interest the outcome of the conflict between him and certain government officials.

The fact that there were voices in open, firm opposition to Mr. Russel's position made his national position different from his corporate and community position in Detroit. Within the corporate structure of U. S. Motors it would have been a brave soul indeed who spoke and wrote in open, public opposition to liberalized credit. Less so, but true, it would have been a courageous man who consistently, openly, and frontally attacked the policy in the community of Detroit. Several good rationalizations could have been available to anyone who might have felt privately like doing so. I had spoken to several Detroit leaders who deemed Mr. Russel's stands on almost any question worthy of deep consideration.

Prestige from local status and power is a vital element in national power status. This does not mean that a man cannot become a national power figure without a local following, but without exception the men with whom I talked and who were designated by their peers as national power leaders were men quite stable in their positions as key figures in a localized configuration of activities. According to interests and capabilities, individuals are tapped from such positions for wider service in the cause of policy development. Few, indeed, are rootless men. Top leaders within basic, local power organizations are drawn into ever-widening circles of associations devoted to policy development.

It became apparent as national leaders were interviewed that all engaged in a kind of watchful observation of the movements of others. For example, all would know who recently had been elevated, demoted, or retired in any one of the larger corporations. If a man was about to retire in any of the larger enterprises, there would be a certain amount of speculation as to the man's successor. A man in the ascendance was called a "comer." Related business establishments would cultivate the goodwill of a comer, through channels.

In the local community, a man about to be elevated in an individual company is encouraged by his superiors to engage in one or more civic activities to enhance his community reputation. Such a man is aided in this endeavor by other members of the community, who become fully aware of the fact that he is being groomed for bigger things. It becomes expedient for many to go along with the grooming process, sometimes even when they may entertain doubts about the fitness of a candidate.

This is also an important element of the informal national structure of power-wielding and policy-making. Entry into the circuit (not a tight circle) is by doing and sometimes by thinking. A man who is a doer is one in the upper ranks of leadership who actually may not do much of anything but talk with people and express his opinions on many different matters of public policy. He is often a person who earlier served varying periods of apprenticeship on national committees or in government service of the dollar a year variety, or who has come to be regarded as a lay expert on a specific topic such as education or international relations.

Inclusion in the upper power circuit is not a hard and fast, rigidly ruled process. Neither is exclusion. But there are some men known as recruiters of policy-making personnel. This is especially true in relation to government appointments. Two men, not a part of formal government, were mentioned very frequently as recruiters for key committees and government posts. But inclusion and exclusion, as processes in forming a trusted circuit within the national power structure, are not concerned only with the limits of government appointment.

Many of the men were persons who had achieved recognition by scaling the ladder of corporate success. James X. Clancy was one of them. Mr. Clancy began work as a salesman of food products. He progressed to a position comparable to that of a division or territorial manager and was then taken into the general management of his company. One day the president of the company said to him, "What would you say to our having another vice-president in the company?" "We've got two too many already," replied Clancy. "I heartily agree," said the president, "I've just fired two and want you to take over the work they have been doing." From the recognition of his ability within his own company has come, step by step, general recognition of his abilities in the country.

National recognition had come to P. X. Fisher in a somewhat different way. After coming into his father's business, large scale pulp manufacture on the West coast, reaching the top of a local corporate pyramid was relatively easy. "From this position," said Mr. Fisher, "it was rather natural that I would be called upon to do things of a civic nature in San Francisco. I got to know a lot of people not only in my home community but along the coast. Leadership out here tends to be coast leadership anyway. I began to be called into things in the East and got to know still another circle of people, and from that I began to move on the international scene. I was a postwar economic administrator abroad with the rank of ambassador. Each move meant knowing a widening circle of people, till I guess I could go anywhere in the world now and know somebody."

Between Mr. Clancy and Mr. Fisher there are at least two apparent differences. The corporation headed by Mr. Fisher is considerably larger than that headed by Mr. Clancy. This is a factor in sizing them up. The inherited position of Mr. Fisher also weighs in his favor. The weighing process has to do with the social roles of men. Other factors concerned with a man's religion, his associates, and the nature and scope of his activities are also decisive, such as the fact that Mr. Clancy has been a very active participant in national affairs for many years.

Speaking of international affairs, one of the top leaders said that he was invited to an off-the-record meeting with representatives of other nations to discuss what might be done about the German problem by a prince of one of the smaller Western European nations. "The meeting was unofficial. While representatives of several nations sat and observed and heard our discussions, there were no official minutes taken, no protocol prescribed. It was a let-your-hair-down session." The honor accorded this man was duly acknowledged by members of his local club, who invited him to a special dinner to tell about the results of the trip upon his return. Communication, particularly the personal, face-to-face variety, is as important nationally as it is locally.

In the process of evaluating a man's social status, there will have been much weeding out before a man reaches national prominence, and national groups are tolerant of numbers only to a point. The general top power structure is a cross-section affair, and any overload of representatives of minority groupings is avoided. With certain groups, inclusion is only token. Although ranking and exclusion are abhorrent to egalitarian concepts, they are functional to any power system.

The status claims of individuals have valid currency nationally if they bear the various seals of local approval. The right business, profession, style of life, manners, and morals are prerequisites to entry into the group of top level national policy makers. A leader may be a self-made man, a leader by achievement, or a leader by inheritance of status; he may be a leader by ascribed status, he may be a professional or a business enterpriser, and he may not be particularly rich; but to be on the inner councils of policy-making he must establish a claim of status as a leader in, or having vital connections with, an organization of men. He must also recognize the validity of the status claims at the national level of a broad range of other men active in key corporations, committees, government posts, and other institutional settings. If he does not recognize such claims, the general structure may discount his own claims and aid in tarnishing the brightness of his star within his own primary group. One man, a demoted executive of one of the national corporations, said as he looked over a list of leaders in the upper group of policy makers, "If I had played footsie with the guys on this list, I'd still be top man in my company. I should have got around to see them more, but I refused to believe they could shake me. I was twenty years younger then. I wouldn't make the same mistake now."

For this study to nail down the fact of recognition in status evaluations, three things were necessary to establish. First, men designated as top policy makers should know each other. I did not consider that knowing about others would be sufficient to contend that a power structure of top policy makers exists. Consequently, I asked those who were chosen by association groups as leaders to tell how many persons they knew on a list provided them. Secondly, they were to rate, by status, the persons they knew. And last, but most important, they must have acted with these others in developing specific policies. I have devoted a separate chapter to the last point and I deal here with the question generally.

An analysis of the results of cross-country interviews, mailed questionnaires, and leadership polls conducted during the course of study showed that by 1956 out of several hundred persons named from all sources, between 100 and 200 men consistently were chosen as top leaders and were considered by all informants to be of national policy-making stature. One hundred of these received more votes proportionately than all others. These were also judged in the status-rating process as number-one power leaders. A second hundred were designated by the same informants as second raters. The remainder were either third raters or did not count at all in the opinion of the persons polled.

Utilizing a one-in-three sample of persons for test purposes, I demonstrated that number-one leaders were generally personally known to each other (Table 4), and second and third raters knew fewer and fewer of the number-one group (Tables 5 and 6). Again, a mere personal knowledge between persons does not prove a power structure, but it was considered axiomatic that if persons presumed to wield power were unknown to one another, it would be very difficult to have said that any sort of structure existed. Correspondence or hearsay knowledge hardly would be the basis of power activities. It must be remembered here that all questions related to leaders in the various polls were aimed at selecting top policy-making leaders in the many categories of persons polled. Thus, such national organizations as the American Association of Social Workers contributed names, along with the National Association of Manufacturers. Consequently, when the next questions were asked, such as "Pick the top policy-making group in the nation from our list" or "Rate the names on the list on a one-two-three power scale," many of the lesser power-potent figures fell by the wayside. It should be repeated too that the 100 number-one leaders do not represent the total power structure of the nation. Nor do the second and third raters necessarily represent an understructure of the number-one policy makers. These facts are stressed to avoid the charge that I believe that these 100 men ever act in total concert. It is incontrovertible, however, that a nucleus of a power structure is contained in the 100 number-one leaders, and their activities fan out in various ways that I have continued to describe as fully as my facts have warranted.

The 100 number-one men actually represented a measuring device at a point in time in this study. Each individual on the list was named repeatedly as a person of power. Each individu-

TABLE 4

33 NUMBER-ONE
LEADERS KNOWN PERSONALLY TO EACH OTHER, 1953-54 *

	10	23	25	55	62	63	81	90	91	98	102	182	202	204	208	230	266	292	308	315	321	322	351	353	371	373	396	398	403	435	445	453	456
10					X			X	X	X	X	X	X	X	X			X					X					X	X	X	X		X	X
23	X		X					X		X	X	X	X	X	X				X	X	X	X	X	X	X	X			X	X		X	X
25		X		X	X	X				X	X	X	X	X		X			X	X				X		X		X		X	X	X	
55			X		X		X			X	X		X	X				X	X		X		X	X		X		X	X		X		X
62	X		X	X				X	X	X	X	X	X	X	X	X		X	X	X				X	X	X		X	X	X	X	X	X
63	X		X				X				X	X		X		X		X						X				X		X	X	X	X
81	X				X	X			X	X	X	X	X		X	X		X	X	X				X				X	X	X		X	X
90	X				X	X			X			X				X			X	X	X		X	X		X		X	X	X	X		X
91	X	X			X	X		X				X	X			X		X	X	X	X		X	X	X			X	X	X	X	X	X
98			X		X						X					X		X	X									X	X	X			X
102	X	X	X	X	X	X			X	X		X	X	X	X	X	X	X	X	X	X	X	X		X			X	X	X		X	X
182	X	X	X	X				X	X	X	X		X		X	X	X	X	X	X	X	X		X	X	X		X	X			X	X
202	X	X	X	X	X	X	X		X	X	X	X					X	X	X				X	X	X	X		X	X	X	X	X	X
204	X	X	X		X						X	X	X		X	X		X	X		X			X	X	X	X	X	X	X	X	X	X
208	X	X			X	X					X	X	X	X			X		X	X	X	X	X	X	X			X	X	X	X	X	X
230		X	X	X	X		X		X	X		X	X	X			X		X	X	X							X	X	X	X	X	X
266	X										X			X										X	X	X		X		X	X	X	
292	X	X	X	X					X	X	X	X	X	X					X	X			X	X	X	X		X					X
308		X	X	X	X	X	X				X	X	X	X			X				X			X	X			X	X	X	X	X	X
315	X	X							X		X	X	X				X				X			X				X				X	X
321	X				X					X		X	X			X		X	X	X						X	X			X		X	X
322	X				X						X		X					X	X													X	X
351	X	X						X	X			X	X	X		X	X		X	X				X				X	X			X	X
353	X	X	X	X	X			X	X			X	X	X	X	X	X	X	X	X	X				X		X	X		X	X	X	X
371	X											X	X				X			X								X			X		X
373	X	X	X	X	X						X	X		X			X	X	X					X			X	X		X		X	X
396	X				X									X	X	X					X	X						X					X
398	X	X		X	X		X		X	X		X	X	X		X	X	X			X			X	X	X					X	X	X
403	X	X			X		X		X		X		X	X	X	X		X	X	X						X		X		X		X	X
435							X					X	X			X			X														X
445	X										X					X			X					X				X					X
453	X	X			X	X					X	X	X	X	X			X	X	X			X	X	X			X	X				X
456	X	X	X	X					X	X	X	X	X	X	X			X		X				X				X	X			X	

* All numbers in Tables 4, 5, 6, coded and disguised, represent individuals.

TABLE 5

33 SECOND-RATE LEADERS
KNOWN PERSONALLY BY 33 NUMBER-ONE LEADERS, 1953-54

	14	24	34	47	59	78	96	110	127	132	153	176	190	212	227	244	251	275	282	299	317	327	333	339	362	368	386	397	405	420	442	449	470
10																x				x		x			x	x	x			x			x
23		x																													x	x	x
25		x				x	x	x												x		x											
55															x						x								x				
62	x	x	x						x				x	x						x	x	x	x		x				x			x	x
63		x	x								x		x		x	x													x				x
81								x														x	x										
90		x					x	x	x											x	x		x		x					x		x	x
91				x									x							x			x										x
98																																	
102			x				x	x	x					x							x	x			x					x	x		x
182						x	x													x			x		x								x
202	x		x				x													x		x	x		x								x
204															x									x							x	x	
208	x																					x			x						x		x
230			x			x	x					x						x		x	x		x		x								x
266							x	x										x		x				x	x		x	x					x
292		x					x	x												x									x				x
308		x	x				x	x						x						x	x				x								x
315																	x															x	
321																								x								x	
322																						x											
351															x	x					x				x						x		x
353		x				x	x	x										x		x	x		x		x								
371																																x	
373						x	x				x		x	x		x				x	x				x	x	x						
396		x							x														x	x					x	x			
398						x	x						x		x	x												x				x	x
403	x									x									x		x			x	x	x							
435																																	x
445								x																							x	x	
453								x															x	x									x
456						x	x	x			x	x		x			x		x	x												x	x

TABLE 6
33 THIRD-RATE LEADERS KNOWN PERSONALLY BY 33 NUMBER-ONE LEADERS, 1953-54

	8	28	40	85	113	119	143	158	168	177	191	196	199	218	220	260	261	284	325	328	346	359	379	380	404	407	410	423	429	434	451	455	463
10																						x										x	
23																																	
25											x	x						x															
55																																	
62					x											x				x		x											
63										x									x														
81																																	
90																																	
91																				x													
98																																	
102																																	
182																																	
202																	x										x						
204													x																				
208																				x				x									
230				x				x																									
266																																	
292																	x							x									
308																																	
315																																	
321																																	
322																								x									
351																								x									
353																								x									
371																									x								
373																															x		
396																																	
398																																	
403																								x									
435																																	
445																			x														
453																								x									
456				x														x															

al's power varied in relation to others on the list and in relation
to vast numbers of people not included in the listing. The system of analysis employed here, then, like that in Chapter 7,
can be termed a system of comparisons in which the leaders
themselves rated others. In its inception it avoided the pitfall of
subjective evaluation on my part. Even although I may have
thought so in the beginning, I did not say Mr. John X. Smith
was a power figure. His peers said that he was. After many said
so and he had been added to my list, I began to listen for statements about him, scanned news releases, interviewed him, and
finally came to conclusions about him. As evident from the ex-
cerpted materials presented in Chapter 5, judgments about individual power leaders varied.

With few exceptions, the tables (pp. 169-71) readily confirm
the fact that mutual recognition existed between the top leaders. This was underscored and verified in the interviews held
with members of this leadership bracket. It seemed quite
natural to these men that they should know each other, and
likewise few expressed any surprise that they knew so few of
the second and third rank. Asked to pick out top, second, and
third rank leaders from the list, almost universally the top men
could readily perform the task, and many said that they
habitually thought of others in a rough and ready system of
rank order. As members of organized civic life, they are used
to such evaluations.

From the point of view of the power structure concept, we
are dealing here, in part, with a belief system. Because of their
observations of acts, positions, or reputations, men begin to
believe that power resides in this or that man. Power is imputed
to him. He is then observed in the company of others; or, as
importantly, he is believed to be in league with others; or,
further, it is believed that if he is not consorting with others
of his imputed power rank, he could be if he so willed. It is
functional to the structured community system of order that
men so believe. The man or men, as the case may be, begin

themselves to believe their own or others' estimates of themselves and they weigh others in the balance with themselves and others of their kind. "He is my kind of man," they say, or "Birds of a feather. . . ." The social psychologists have given us a useful scientific term, "reference group," meaning the group to which one refers in his thinking and in relation to which he acts, even though he may not physically interact with every member of the group. To the community at large a recognized power group becomes a psychological point of reference, to which the majority defers.

The structure of top number-one leaders tended toward closure. The number-one men knew number-one men. They recruited rising number-one leaders into their orbit and excluded those who did not fit. They knew generally the pattern of policy development, and they knew well and specifically how to go about getting what was good for them and for their individual enterprises. Their names appeared repeatedly in the national press.[1] (Only twelve on a research list of 100 top leaders did not receive one or more press notices during the course of study up to 1956. It is likely that these twelve may have received notices that were missed.) They knew and were known by elected and appointed officials, from whom they tended to hold themselves somewhat superior and aloof. They represented a cross-section of national civic life. They belonged to clubs and associations in common membership across the nation. Their operating bases were located essentially in the large cities. They included the politicians, the men of wealth, and the military elite of whom Professor Mills speaks.[2] None of these things can be said about the second and third raters, nor about all leaders examined in this study. In the cities, small towns, and states studied, connections between the upper leadership structures could be made, but the little fellows were ex-

1. Some of these objected to local publicity, but did not resist national news releases about them.

2. C. Wright Mills, *The Power Elite* (New York: Oxford Univ. Press, 1956).

cluded from the top leadership structure. The exclusion was made on a power status basis, not primarily on the basis of class position or institutional status. Inclusion in the top group of number-one leaders was, then, a rough measure of a man's power potential.

Let it be clearly understood again that I am not suggesting that the top leaders in the nation ever sit face to face around a table and decide in solemn judgment what will or will not be good for the nation. Such a view would deny the whole notion of process that is contained in the social power structure concept. Nor do I believe that much policy is ever wholly decided in smoke-filled rooms, nor in club leadership outings of the Aspen, Hot Springs, or Bohemian groups. No one-factor analysis is ever satisfactory, even though some articles that suggest this may appear from time to time in the sensational press. Yet, there is a selective process of agreement and habit patterns related to leadership recognition that can be observed. There is a kind of reservoir of leadership on tap from which men are chosen to perform the important tasks of policy-making and/or to give status to any major policy proposal. As one said, "Of course there is a group that's recognized as national leaders. They quietly put their stamp of approval on most of the things that go on. They're big men. You don't send a boy to do a man's job, you know."

I probed the notion that the men of family, wealth, and society prestige might be the true leaders of power in American society. I asked whether the managers had taken over. I questioned concerning the status of professional politicians in power-wielding. I wanted to know whether the country is run by powerful lobbies of labor and other special interest groups. I was interested in determining again whether the narrowed circle of men about whom I questioned represented a conspiracy of interests bent on doing the nation out of its birthright.

The answers to all of these questions were qualified. "Yes,

there is a definite number of men looked upon as being more powerful than others, but that answer is too simple. It does not explain power as a total thing." "Yes, some men of family and wealth are included, but there's more to a man's inclusion than being born on the right side of town." "Yes, managers have taken over in many areas of influence, but they never act alone." "Yes, professional politicians and their political parties are important factors in policy-making and power, but they are a part of something bigger than pure politics." "Lobbies and their professional secretaries are very meaningful in decisions, but they are not always useful." "No, there is no conspiracy of interests. It is just natural that some men act the way they do, and most have the good of the country in mind."

Continuing to utilize the model of a community power structure in my interviews, I found certain common elements among the top leaders, whom I began to look upon as a national power structure, as they look upon themselves. I have already mentioned the facts that they knew each other, that they could rate each other in a status scale, and that they tended to include and exclude others from their company. They were not known to the little fellows on my lists of names nor did they know the little fellows, as pointed out. They represented a cross-section of national civic life, and active recruiting into the circuit goes on continuously to fill vacancies, geographic and otherwise. For the most part they tended to know certain persons in Congress and other national government policy posts. Their names appeared repeatedly in the national press as newsworthy spokesmen—particularly in crisis situations. There was a kind of amiable tolerance among them toward the world—a world that had been pretty good to them during the past few years. Importantly, they knew the patterns of the policy-making process and generally agreed on the content of such patterns. In the final analysis, of course, it is at the point of getting things done that a power structure is proved.

It will be remembered that I said hypothetically that at the national level of affairs, as in a local community, there is a power structure inside and outside government (but not synonymous with government or any other formal organization) acting in relation to policy development and that the national power structure could be identified in various ways. It is not a single pyramid of influence and authority. It is a kind of informal, potential group, representing many of the major influence groups, that acts on specific matters of policy as the need arises. And finally, although disagreements may occur in relation to specific issues, the basic values and aspirations of dominant interests, traceable most often to the larger corporate interests, will bring about a workable unity within the total power structure.

It was abundantly clear that the men interviewed did not think of government officials exclusively as top policy makers in the country. This does not say they did not recognize the important roles played by politicians in the process of getting things done, but universally, government was thought of as an instrument of extending policy rather than a primary source of policy development. It was taken for granted that government is extremely important. It was also taken for granted that organized government was but one of many power structures with which the men of national influence worked. Key men in government represent an apex of power, but in general it was assumed that these key men would act in concert and in accord with one or more other power groupings to formulate and extend policy.

Classification of the occupations of the responding top policy makers revealed the categories given in Tables 7, 8, and 9 on pages 177-78 and suggests, in general, that the number-one leaders are drawn largely from industrial power structures, and second and third raters are professionals in a broad sense of the term. Public political figures have been added to the list later, when the specific issues of the textile industry are discussed.

TABLE 7

OCCUPATIONS OF 29 NUMBER-ONE LEADERS BY NUMBERS, 1956

Occupation	Number of Leaders
Manufacturers	
Heavy	9
Light	5
Publishers	3
Military	1
Banker (Commercial)	1
Lawyer	1
Industrial Construction Engineer	1
Merchant	1
Miller	1
Mine Owner	1
Oil	
Processor	1
Producer	1
Transportation	
Railroad	1
Ship	1
Utilities Executive	1

The top policy makers do work inside and outside government in many ways. They help elect government officials. In the earlier stages of this study I submitted a list of 112 persons to Professor Alexander Heard, who has made a study of contributors to national political campaigns.[3] Among the names listed, 69 were considered, at that point (1956), number-one. Of this top group, 57 percent contributed $500.00 or more to political campaigns, while 44 percent of the 43 second raters contributed like amounts. As a matter of fact, campaign soliciting has many of the earmarks of a well-run Community Chest campaign. The top givers figure prominently in this activity, as they do in community drives for funds.

The Senate elections and the election of the President, especially, are of vital concern to many top policy makers. The men in these elective posts are relatively accessible to personal

3. "Money in Politics," *Public Affairs*, No. 242 (October, 1956), p. 19.

TABLE 8

OCCUPATIONS OF 33 SECOND RATERS BY NUMBERS, 1956

Occupation	Number of Leaders
Bankers	
Investment	4
Commercial	3
Advertisers	4
Educators	
College Presidents	2
College Vice-President	1
College Dean	1
Manufacturers	
Heavy	2
Light	2
Insurance Executives	2
Lawyers	2
Chamber of Commerce Executive	1
Churchman (Lay Leader)	1
Merchant	1
Dental Laboratory Executive	1
Foundation Executive	1
Meat Packer	1
Publisher	1
Rancher	1
Transportation (Aviation)	1
Women's Organization Executive	1

TABLE 9

OCCUPATIONS OF 20 THIRD RATERS BY NUMBERS, 1956

Occupation	Number of Leaders
Educators	
College Presidents	2
Administrative Officials	3
Merchants	3
Editors	2
Manufacturers (Light)	2
Industrial Services	2
Research Services	2
Transportation (Aviation)	1
Banker (Commercial)	1
Churchman (Bishop)	1
Meat Packer	1

influence and are often decisive in matters of policy. A few Congressmen are considered key leaders in governmental affairs and are cultivated and helped more than others, particularly when they are in decisive positions by seniority in the governmental apparatus.

The famous stag dinners of President Eisenhower were one important, informal gathering for hammering out a line for various policies. A large majority of the number-one leaders and second raters on my lists had attended these dinners. Such meetings with the President had not been confined to the Eisenhower administration. Mr. Truman had entertained many of the men on the number-one list. A high ranking Senator said that not too many people were aware of the fact that when Truman was President, informal, off-the-record gatherings were held at the White House. The guests went in the back door on regularly scheduled evenings. The Senator had met most of the top leaders outside and inside government, at one time or another, at these meetings.

The development of policy requires such informal hashing. The process is the same as that which goes on in informal committee sessions daily in thousands of American communities. It is a part of a meeting of minds. Those who wished to be invited and were excluded were prone to say that something sinister was going on behind closed doors. It was insisted, however, that the White House discussions were open and not decisive. However, it was also apparent that some individuals in such meetings were listened to with considerably more interest than others. Labor was tolerated by some, for example, and second raters "sometimes talked too much."

The larger power interests had direct contact with government through the placement of dollar a year executives in key government spots. The same interests tended to find their way to key government committees, and there were close ties between these interests and the key cabinet posts.

A 1958 analysis of 99 number-one leaders in terms of their

business and government connections showed that 17 of them had made a career of politics, 36 had never held either appointive or elective political office, but 46 had been in both business and government during their careers. The interchange between business and government was apparent, and the statistical findings were borne out by qualitative data.

"I have always considered myself above government and politics," said an executive of one of the largest service companies, who had just returned from a trip to Washington. "I do not go down to Washington very much. Not nearly so much as you might think," said another of the men in one of the biggest banks on Wall Street. "I was amused by one of the Texas newcomers the other day," he continued. "He came breezing into my office saying, 'I have just been down to see the President'—as if he had done something wonderful!"

"If I wanted to get something done through Washington, I would call up about six Senators that I know," said another man in a metal industry, "and I'd go down to Washington and see them. I'd also see a couple of cabinet members, as I did recently in relation to getting a fast write-off proposition through. I'd see two or three Congressmen, and come back home and wait for things to happen." He went on to say that he would not wait passively but would have some of his key men within his corporation follow through on the proposition. In other words, he would operate through several structures of power. He would not call for help from sources outside his immediate sphere of influence, he said, unless the situation got "sticky," i.e., unless he were thwarted—then he might begin the long process of building up pressure through committee activity, association work, political party pressure, and the like.

The top policy makers can communicate with each other easily enough. In testing the fact of communication among the number-one leaders I found that four men knew and could close a communications net with 29 others. Their mutuality of acquaintance was such that at one time or another all had been in contact with approximately two thirds of the circle. The four, shown by center circles in Figure 1, could communicate directly with nearly any man in the larger circle.

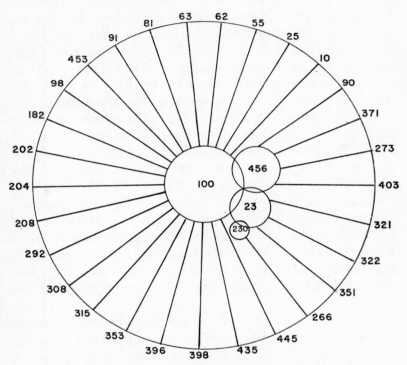

Fig. 1. Communication Net Showing Relationship of Four Top Leaders to Twenty-nine Other Top Leaders, 1954. Numbers are code numbers used in this study to refer to top leaders.

I believe that the basic values and aspirations of these men are such that they would go along with a majority of the desires of any combination of men of like status, but there are often enough conflicts of interests that clearly and almost always keep some of these men from agreeing with others. The matter of tariffs is a case in point. Some men in the auto industry, among others, would like a liberalized, free trade policy for the country. It would be exceedingly difficult to get members of the watchmaking industry or the cotton manufacturers to go along on any such policy arrangement. Both groups are working with all their organization skills and resources to make their own point of view prevail. In this case, as in many others, government has been a mediator through a series of compromises. In a discussion with one of the men in the auto industry, however, on the tariff problem as it related to a specific issue in the textile industry (Chapter 10) it was brought out that the top man in one of the largest automobile companies had made many very forthright statements on the tariff issue, but "this does not mean that the nation followed him." This is quite true in a limited sense. On the other hand, the top man in question was a member of a group that had associated itself for the express purpose of promoting free trade. The man's status in the industrial community was such that many would listen to him. How much influence he had personally in the matter may have been problematical, but it weighed in favor of the free traders, and many on the other side of the question have expressed the notion that they wish the man had been on their side for "prestige reasons—if no other."

It must also be said that not all issues are decided by weight of numbers. Votes are not always counted in relation to issues. It is therefore important to policy makers to know whose word, timed right and spoken to the proper ear, will produce results. One man's making the right call to another may be more influential than countless ballots. This is especially true in those cases where elections are decided only on the basis of personalities and when such personalities will later decide the issues about which the voters did not trouble to inquire.

However, disagreement on a specific issue such as tariff did not mean that there was a lack of general accord on many basic matters of policy, and the mere fact that there was a show of strength on one side or the other helped to keep individuals within the general circuit of the top structure of policy-making.

Many men said that some of the top listed men represented the "committee person." The editor of a famous national daily newspaper, a paper that has a knack for choosing top names for its institutional articles, was one of those who recognized the validity of the executive committee status of many of the number-one leaders. The committee persons are the type found on policy-making executive committees in communities and at the national level. They are opinion leaders, and they represent a reservoir of talent in policy-making. They may be asked to serve on important policy committees or to send representatives to them. They are tapped and they serve according to their interests in given subjects. They represent a cross-section of geographical groupings and formally organized groups.

The assumption that leaders coming into the power structure were recruited largely from the dominant urban centers was borne out. Of the number-one men, nine were from Chicago; six from New York; four from San Francisco; two each from Detroit, Los Angeles, Minneapolis, and Washington, D.C.; one each from Boston, Bridgeport (Conn.), Cincinnati, Dayton, Houston, and Pittsburgh. In the group of second raters, St. Louis led with six members; New York had five; Chicago, four; two members each came from Boston, Buffalo, and San Francisco; and one leader each was named from Birmingham, Denver, Fairmont (W. Va.), Glencoe (Ill.), Lexington (Ky.), Memphis, Minneapolis, Newark, New Orleans, Philadelphia, Poughkeepsie, and Washington, D.C.

The concentration of leadership in the major cities was noteworthy in the number-one group. In the second-rate group it tended to spread and reach down into the smaller cities. The third-rate group was even less concentrated and more diffuse. In this group, three leaders were from Chicago, and two each from Ann Arbor, Austin, New York, Oklahoma City, and

Washington, D.C. The remainder of the third raters came from Birmingham (Ala.), Buffalo, Cambridge (Mass.), Casper (Wyo.), Dallas, Greensboro (N. C.), Indianapolis, Knoxville, Louisville, Maders (Calif.), Memphis, Morgantown (W. Va.), Newark, New Orleans, Rochester, Seattle, University (Miss.), Wake Forest (N. C.), and Washington, D.C.

The tendency toward decentralization of industrial complexes may have served to disperse national leadership, but with the example exceptions of the Dupont empire in Delaware and the Armstrong Cork Company of Pennsylvania, the large port cities and inland trading centers dominated the leadership picture. The dominant corporate groups within these cities furnished a large proportion of the top strata of policy makers. Figure 2 on page 185 shows my general routes of travel between cities, during the course of study. The routes followed the addresses of leaders.

In one cross-country tour in which I stopped in a sample of twenty towns, large and small, by taking every tenth town designated on a road map, I found that the little fellows in the little towns knew directly scarcely any of the top persons listed, either personally or by hearsay. The returns of this investigation were so meager that presenting them in tabular form would be meaningless. The little fellows expect their political representatives or some local lawyer or corporate executive to do for them what they think they need done on matters of policy. They had little notion of the processes of power that go on in Washington, New York and abroad. Each little community had a miniature power structure within it—a stratification of local policy makers who by and large did hook up with top interests in their states. They recognized their own state industrial leaders, but the larger picture of the dynamics of policy development being outlined here was generally beyond their ken. Their outlet to the national power structure would appear to be through the restricted channels

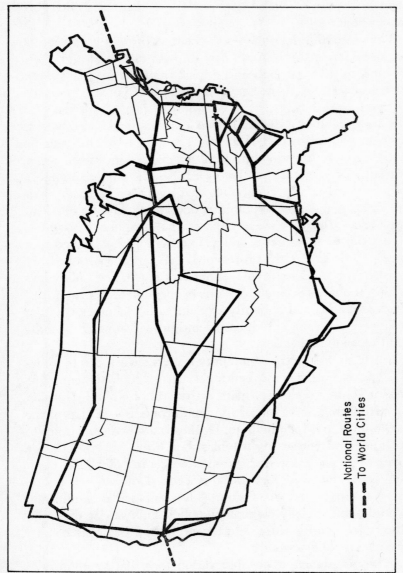

Fig. 2. Areas Covered in Field Study, by Travel Routes between Connecting Cities, 1949-58.

described in our model of state power and through association connections.

The sense of isolation from the centers of policy decision is one shared by many in American life—as a matter of fact, even by some of the very top leaders. Each thinks he is acting alone on many matters. Some feel that they are "voices crying in the wilderness."

There are sharp breaks in the communication networks. Even in well-organized industrial groupings like housing or textiles, communication through association meetings, letter writing, or trade bulletins always leaves some who claim never to have heard of a specific policy that might have been long in the making and finally put into operation. The bane of an association executive's existence is the member who cries, "How did we ever get a policy like that? Who cooked that one up?" Groaning, the professional association leader is likely to ask himself, "Doesn't this fellow ever read? The policy he's talking about has been on page one of the bulletin for months!" Then aloud he will patiently explain to his member that the policy went through all the usual and proper steps of committee discussion and action.

Isolated or not, most community leaders have access to someone concerning specific issues that may trouble them. One way or another the policy matters that trouble John Q. Doakes get to the attention of one or another of the liaison leaders of the community in which he lives. Doakes is advised sometimes to go home and forget his troubles, but often his troubles are carried to some associated group as a case in point. The community policy needs become the seedbed of national policy decisions in a cumulative fashion. The chain of communication is crude, but socially significant policy impulses at the community level consistently light the circuits of the upper reaches of national policy-making.

It would appear upon observation that the community is the most focussed power unit in American society. Local coercion in the power framework is very obvious in case after case. However, as one moves out from individual community power structures into state, regional, industrial, or national power networks, the ability of small groups of men to act in strictly coercive relations to others outside the law seems more and more remote. The major coercive organs of power at the national level are two major configurations, formal government and the economic corporation. Both have organization structures that can reach down to the local level and exert coercive direction on individuals. In combination with other elements of organized community action the members of these two leading organs of power formulate national policy. Because of the decisive influence of the corporations in American life, I have discussed the subject in the last chapter in more detail.

Generally speaking, the Chamber of Commerce, various trade associations, and certain local leaders with some national prominence saw more clearly the dim avenues down which the majority of small town people viewed the larger national scene. Yet, what they read said that what happened at home was much more important than what was happening in New York or Washington. Some of the smaller local papers carried very little national news. How the news came to be news was a mystery beyond their comprehension and considered to be mainly outside their interests.

In looking over the list of top national leaders, one top local leader in Tennessee, a Chevrolet dealer, came to the name of Walter Reuther. He had passed over many other names with no comment. When he came to Reuther's name he said, seriously and earnestly perplexed, "It occurs to me I've heard that man's name somewhere, but I cannot rightly place him." When I told him of Reuther's auto union connections, he replied, "I guess I should have known that, selling automobiles. The name must have escaped me." The significance of the name Harlowe Curtice escaped him too. This case illustrates

our hypothesis that "A large portion of the total power structure is not seen in operation because of its diffuse and informal
characteristics," and the illustrations could be compounded.

Above the little fellow, at the leadership level of community
life, a model of tangible, outward, extra-community relationships can be traced. The network through which at least one
group of little fellows had to move to make their national

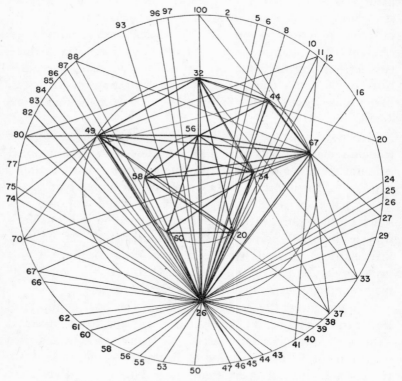

Fig. 3. Working Relationships of Top Community, State, and
National Leaders in the Development of National Public Policies, 1958. Numbers refer to leaders. (Key: Small circle is community leaders who have worked together on a public policy.
Middle circle is state leaders who have policy-making relationships to the same community leaders. Large circle is national
leaders who have relationships to state leaders.)

policy wishes known can be graphically illustrated. Figure 3, page 188, was drawn from data given by top community leaders (middle circle), and finally by 100 top leaders in the nation (outer circle). Let it be stressed that the sociogram embraces general working relationships, which go beyond the personal knowledge and communications networks previously mentioned. I have later illustrated a similar set of relationships concerned with the development of a single policy matter.

The general range of policy matters of interest to the top national leaders and the leaders' general orientation to each other at the interest level are illustrated in Figure 4, page 190. The policies were those mentioned most frequently by leaders during the study and those that were finally designated as those upon which individuals had actually worked, on a test questionnaire.

The general pattern of action or the steps in process in the development of a given national policy, as given by the leaders, are these:

1. Establish the policy purpose and secure a dedication to this purpose by interested individuals.

2. Seek an unselfish working together of individuals and groups to achieve what they believe to be a policy direction for the good of the country.

3. Recruit successful men to help in furthering the idea.

4. Widen but restrict the circle of informed men.

5. Enlist the services of an established national organization in the cause, or set up a new organization if the existing organizations cannot embrace the new policy in their framework of action.

6. Utilize research to develop a factual base of operations.

7. Use a small but technically qualified group to give objective consideration and criticism to the facts.

8. Have facts and strategic problems analyzed by competent citizen groups.

9. Enlist public opinion through publicity of general news and special media.

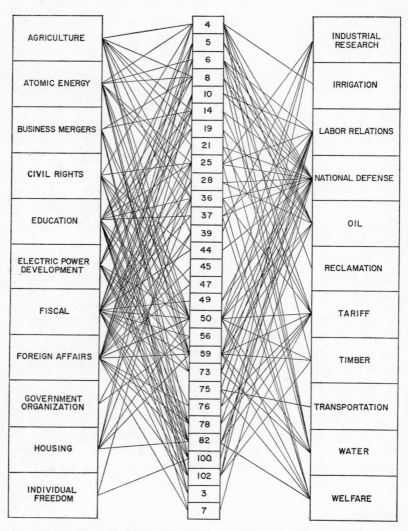

Fig. 4. Twenty-nine National Leaders Related to Policy Interests, 1958. Numbers are code numbers of top leaders.

10. Urge and re-urge vigorous support of all men who have knowledge of the program.

11. Use personal contact methods on other national leaders, the national administration, and Congress.

12. Appear publicly before committees of Congress or request hearings before administrative tribunals.

13. Be resolved to get action from the national administration.

14. Be resolved to get action from the houses of Congress.

15. Be prepared to use varying combinations of the above steps, and to begin over if not successful the first time.

From the other end of the matter, that is, from the men in the administration and Congress who are being pressured, at least three principles are guides, even though not always followed: (1) in advance of a decisive meeting, written recommendations should be circulated for study by the authoritative body, (2) all interested parties should be heard, and (3) the opportunity for rebuttal and appeal should be jealously guarded.

The nation's power system is a series of interlaced and coordinated power structures. Those at the apexes of power in communities, states, regions, service organizations, and industrial complexes become generally known to each other. Some of the leaders in the larger units of power become symbolic power figures in the nation. When such leaders think of policy directions and alternatives, they think of interrelated and weighted factors. Although individual units within the power system may appear to act in isolation, it is well known that major changes in pace and direction of any single power unit have profound effects on the whole.

Part III

TRACING THE ISSUES

I HAVE said, to begin with, that a large portion of the total power structure is not seen in operation because of its diffuse and informal characteristics. Very often one reads that decisions related to specific policies have been made in smoke-filled rooms, behind the scenes, or by an unholy alliance. Even men who are supposed to be political seers do not profess to know how many of the issues come to be or how they are finally resolved. Many who are conscious of the processes of policy development, however, may know a great deal about a single issue, and they may know personally many of the men behind the proposition.

Determined to have the study of policy-making completely empirical, I took several polls of national leaders to get their own choices of those whom they consider to be their peers. The results of some of the early polls have already been given and discussed. Each new poll added a few names to the list, but also many names were dropped in the process. A careful check was made of all early and late culls, and it was clearly evident that neither group qualified as finalists in terms of active policy development.

The third and fourth polls of national leaders in 1957 and 1958 revealed that a basic core of names continued to be nominated for national leadership positions. In the 1957 and 1958 polls the names of public politicians were included. The leaders were nominated from the following list by receiving votes according to the instruction, "Please indicate by a check before the names below those *persons whom you consider to be top leaders in the development of policies affecting the nation.* Leave all others blank." At the end of the list, as in all previous polls, they were asked to add names that should have been included to make it a more representative cross-section of leadership.

J. B. Adams, Jr.
Sherman Adams *
Leo E. Allen
William M. Allen
Stanley C. Allyn
Clinton P. Anderson *
Robert B. Anderson *
Leslie C. Arends
Jacob M. Arvey
Melvin H. Baker
Frank Bane
Graham A. Barden
Stephen D. Bechtel *
Daniel W. Bell
Laird Bell
Ezra Taft Benson *
Harry Betters
Barry Bingham
James B. Black *
Jacob Blaustein
Roger M. Blough *
Charles R. Blyth
Harold Boeschenstein *
Arch N. Booth
Ruth A. Bottomly
Ernest R. Breech *
John W. Bricker *
Styles Bridges *
Clarence J. Brown
Howard Bruce
Ralph Budd
Harry A. Bullis *
Arleigh A. Burke *
Arthur F. Burns *
Vannevar Bush *
Harry F. Byrd *

Clarence Cannon
William G. Carr
Clifford P. Case
William J. Casey
Emanuel Celler
Norman Chandler *
Walter Chandler
Colby M. Chester
Lucius Clay *
William L. Clayton *
Francis C. Cocke
L. L. Colbert
W. Sterling Cole
John S. Coleman
John L. Collyer *
Karl T. Compton
James B. Conant *
Eugene P. Conser
Jere Cooper
George Coppers
John Cowles *
Charles R. Cox
Cleo F. Craig
David Crawford
Frederick C. Crawford *
W. W. Crocker
Hugh Roy Cullen
Harlow H. Curtice *
Robert Cutler *
Horace Davenport
Donald K. David *
Frank R. Denton
Richard R. Deupree
Thomas E. Dewey *
Charles P. Dickey
Charles H. Diefendorf

* Members of 1958 test group of 100, discussed below.

Joseph M. Dodge *
James H. Doolittle *
Paul H. Douglas *
Henry H. Dudley
John Foster Dulles *
Dwight D. Eisenhower *
Sam Erwin
Benjamin F. Fairless *
William T. Faricy
Muriel Ferris
Charles T. Fisher, Jr.
Ralph E. Flanders *
Lamar Fleming, Jr.
Robert V. Fleming
Fred F. Florence
R. G. Follis
Marion B. Folsom *
Henry Ford II *
Clarence Francis *
John M. Franklin
A. J. Gock
Gordon Gray *
Crawford H. Greenewalt *
F. E. Grier
Fred G. Gurley *
John Hancock
John W. Hanes
Robert M. Hanes *
Lewis G. Harriman
W. Averell Harriman *
H. J. Heinz II
Christian A. Herter *
Lister Hill
Mrs. Oveta Culp Hobby *
Luther Hodges
Paul G. Hoffman *
Howard Holderness
Eugene Holman *
John Holmes
George V. Holton
Charles R. Hook *
Herbert Hoover, Sr.*
Herbert Hoover, Jr.*
Clifford R. Hope
Arthur A. Houghton, Jr.
Hubert H. Humphrey *
H. E. Humphreys, Jr.
H. L. Hunt
Irving M. Ives
Lyndon B. Johnson *

Olin D. Johnson
Eric Johnston *
Walter H. Judd *
Estes Kefauver
W. P. Kennedy
Robert S. Kerr
Meyer Kestnbaum *
J. H. Kindelberger
Robert Kleberg
William F. Knowland *
Walter J. Kohler, Jr.*
Hugh C. Lane
J. L. Latimer
Frank J. Lausche *
Fred Lazarus, Jr.
Herbert H. Lehman *
William Levett
John L. Lewis *
James A. Linen
Henry Cabot Lodge *
W. I. Longsworth
Mrs. Oswald Bates Lord
George H. Love
J. Spencer Love
Henry Luce *
George F. Lull
J. Wesley McAfee
Hughston M. McBain
Thomas B. McCabe *
John L. McCaffery
Harold C. McClellan
John L. McClellan *
John McCloy *
John W. McCormack *
L. F. McCollum
J. Frank McCrary
Neil H. McElroy *
Keith S. McHugh
James Francis McIntyre
Paul B. McKee
George Mahon
Thurgood Marshall
Joseph W. Martin, Jr.*
Oscar G. Mayer
George Meany *
Richard K. Mellon *
Kenneth R. Miller
Eugene D. Millikin
R. L. Minkler
Broadus Mitchell

James P. Mitchell *
George G. Montgomery
Walter Montgomery
Joe E. Moody
Ben Moreell *
deLesseps S. Morrison
W. C. Mullendore
Clint W. Murchison
Timothy J. Murphy
Hershell D. Newsom
Aksel Nielsen
Richard M. Nixon *
H. Bruce Palmer
Randolph Pate
W. A. Patterson *
Neil Petree
Howard J. Pew
Paul Pigott
Henning W. Prentice, Jr.
Gwilym A. Price
Clarence B. Randall *
Sam Rayburn *
Philip D. Reed *
Walter P. Reuther *
David Reynolds
James Richards
Sid Richardson
Reuben B. Robertson, Jr.
Thomas Robinson
Nelson A. Rockefeller *
William P. Rogers
Roy G. Ross
Richard B. Russell *
Edward L. Ryerson
Leverett Saltonstall *
David Sarnoff *
Hugh D. Scott, Jr.
W. Kerr Scott
Fred A. Seaton *
Merle E. Selecman
Louis B. Seltzer
Carrol M. Shanks *
James E. Shelton
Henry Knox Sherrill

Boris Shishkin
Allan Shivers
Charles B. Shuman
C. R. Smith
Howard W. Smith
Carl Spaatz
Joseph P. Spang
Francis Joseph Spellman *
Herman Steinkraus
Adlai Stevenson *
Arthur Hays Sulzberger *
Arthur E. Summerfield *
Stuart Symington *
Gardiner Symonds
John Taber
Maxwell D. Taylor *
Charles Thomas
J. Strom Thurmond
Roland Tibbets
George Bell Timmerman, Jr.
Juan T. Trippe *
Harry S. Truman *
Nathan Twining *
Carl Vinson *
Francis E. Walter
Earl Warren *
Thomas Watson, Jr.*
James B. Webber, Jr.
Sinclair Weeks *
Sidney J. Weinberg *
Ernest T. Weir
Frederic Whitman
John Hay Whitney *
Roy Wilkins
Walter Williams
Charles E. Wilson *
Robert E. Wilson
Thomas E. Wilson
P. G. Winnett
R. W. Woodruff
Ben H. Wooten
Howard I. Young
J. D. Zellerbach *

At the conclusion of the polling process in 1958, it was apparent that there was stability enough in a portion of this list to use it as a test to get at questions on working relationships of top national leaders on matters of public policy (names on foregoing list indicated by asterisks).

Consolidating the type of information one can easily obtain regarding these leaders, in 1958, according to data at our disposal, the average age of the leaders in that group was 62, about ten years higher than that of leaders examined in previous power structure studies in individual cities. This group was also heavily weighted with industrial leaders (23), followed in order by: 15 U. S. Senators, 10 cabinet members, 6 professionals (3 attorneys, 2 professors, 1 scientist), 5 bankers, 5 publishers, 5 Congressmen, 4 assistant cabinet secretaries, 3 labor leaders, 3 military officers, 4 Presidential assistants, 3 transportation executives (2 air, 1 railroad), 2 ambassadors, 2 governors, 3 United States Presidents (2 retired), and 1 each, chief justice of the Supreme Court, communications executive (radio-TV), religious leader, utilities executive, United Nations representative, and the Vice-President of the United States.

Of those who could be identified by political party affiliation, 20 were Democrats and 50 were Republicans. Most of them were born in the Northeastern quarter or in the Middle West of the country. Six were born abroad; four of these were born of American parents who were living abroad at the time of their birth.

Many had memberships in private clubs in cities outside their own. One man had ten such memberships. The most favored clubs were the Metropolitan, Links, Century, University (N.Y.), Bohemian, and Pacific Union.

College degrees had been earned by 73, but 27 had no degree. Several of these, however, had graduated from fashionable schools that do not award degrees. Degrees are more often earned by those who assume that they will work for a living and who need to gain status by achievement. Many had been awarded honorary degrees.

With the work that had been carried forward in 1957 and

with the leadership polls completed, I was prepared to move into the final phase of study, determining working relationships between top leaders and various groups of persons in a specific national issue. However, before the results of this can be put down, it has been necessary to go back a step and review the policy factors taken into account in the process of selecting and isolating issues which finally led to a choice of an issue to be intensively studied.

Most of the men interviewed were vitally interested in one or more national policies. They made no secret of their interest. Some of them had held specific policy interests for several years and had written or spoken publicly about them. As already indicated, various policies were of common interest to several leaders.

Whenever differences of opinion on details of policy occurred, each leader would begin to cast about for others who agreed with his point of view and would aid in organizing opinion and action in his favor. He would begin to pick up men who would be most helpful to his cause. His process of thinking, as I heard it expounded repeatedly, would go something like this:

1. "What is the real problem here that needs to be solved in relation to me, my company, or group?"

2. "Who do I know that might also be interested in this problem, or who would know where and how to tap and call upon people who could be helpful in solving it?"

3. "Where does the man or men fit in the power scheme of things in relation to me" (assuming, of course, that he had received suggestions related to whom he should tap). Using his own conceptions of organization based upon a corporate or community hierarchy of authority, he might ask himself, "Are these men on a level with me or are they up or down a few pegs? How much experience have they had working with others, and have others gone along with them? Do they carry weight with their peers? How

many times have they been picked up, and by whom on other occasions?"

4. "How much will getting at this issue cost me in terms of
time and money?"

5. "Will the issue be so controversial that I will lose friends and
business?"

These are questions that determine, to some extent, how active a man will be in relation to moving on an issue. If he
believes that the issue is worth consideration by any large number of people in the top rungs of business and other nationally
organized groups, he will engage in activities designed to
achieve his ends. If the end necessity is to modify an existing
law or get a new one, he will involve professional politicians
in the process. In any event he will begin to make moves
designed to elevate a specific problem to one of national significance by establishing its relevance to the general welfare.

In the process of choosing up sides on any issue, it is normal
procedure to choose men one knows, to choose those whom
one can trust to stand firm when the going gets rough. Many
of those chosen may not be well known to the general public.
The public often has to be educated in different ways regarding its interests. The education process involves press releases
on front personalities and on the ideology of the issue at hand
and personal contact with top leaders who may ally themselves
with the cause. The front personalities are those who will be
most actively engaged in public appearances in relation to
helping others form their opinions. Personalities who shun
publicity in relation to controversial matters may receive
generalized publicity about their achievements, and word may
be quietly passed along that these persons are privately for a
given matter.

I think it rather rare that direct personal pressure is put on
an individual to be for or against an issue while it is in a forma-
tive stage of development. If one or another of the leaders at
the top level of affairs does not wish to be engaged in one of

the policy issues that have been put before the country, he needs to say merely, "This matter is no affair of mine," and remain quiet. The issues tend to be local, regional, or industry-wide in nature, and no man is expected to jeopardize his own position by jumping into an issue that does not directly concern him and about which he may know little.

The pressures that men may put on one another are always a potential threat, however, and subtle pressures are brought to bear on many persons if an issue has jelled to the point where it has got into national politics. Certainly the politicians at this point must stand up and be counted.

During the period of policy development, a cueing process is evident. A clothing manufacturer had this to say about getting cues: "My company is not one of the biggest operations in the country. We're a large outfit of our kind, but we cannot compare with U.S. Steel, for example. In a matter of general business policy and pricing we make our own decisions. We would not do something just because U.S. Steel thinks it is good for business or the country. But this does not mean that we are unaware of what is going on in steel. We would listen quite carefully to what some of the most able leaders in the steel business say, and the chances are good that we would often be in accord with them. Certainly, they have been price leaders for the past twenty years!" Many others expressed the notion that direct collaboration on issues was less frequently found than is generally assumed. Men in the business community do not have to be told directly where their interests lie. They have a general and specific knowledge of this matter that they use daily. It is built into their thinking through experience.

Data were collected on several issues and on men related to the issues. The issues most frequently noted, in the order of their frequency, were those of fiscal problems and taxation, foreign policy (including tariffs), electric power development, civic improvement, individual freedom, labor relations, mergers and anti-trust, national resources, education, agriculture, national defense, housing, welfare, atomic energy, political party organization, and minority rights.

More than half the leaders in a sample drawn on the subject were interested in taxation and fiscal problems, while nearly half of them were interested in foreign affairs. These issues were viewed differently by individual leaders, but most of them agreed that corporation and income taxes were too high. This is certainly no secret, and none of the men would be loath to make his views public on the matter. Nor would most of them object to saying that our country is deeply involved in the affairs of the world and that matters of foreign policy are of grave concern to them, although if one got down to details of foreign policy, such as tariffs, there might then be wide differences of opinion, which would call forth the questions and activities described above (pp. 200-2).

The third item in the list of issues is electric power development. This issue reached the stage of national policy decision during the period embraced in this study. The roots of its development went back to the Samuel Insull days, according to Harry Truman, who said that to understand the present conflict fully, one would need to look at the record of hearings held before a Congressional committee on which he served. I cannot go into the details of the controversy here, but essentially the issue is public versus private development of elecric power. As of 1958, the matter was still at issue. From the point of view of its development as an issue, three relatively large groups of business interests have acted together in the power struggle. These groups represent a geographic spread of interest.

In the case of policy development related to electric power, a combination of Western electric companies, Eastern banks, and Tennessee Valley developers was instrumental in leading others. In general, most top leaders in the country were sympathetic to the desire of the electric companies to make electric power development a private matter rather than a public one. The desire was in accord with the general ideology of free private enterprise, but there were large groups of men who were inactive in the matter. Only a few were extremely active, most of whom testified in public hearings in Washington. The administration in Washington in 1956 had resolved the issue temporarily by granting private companies the right to develop the Hell's Canyon area. Ex-Secretary McKay of the Department of Interior, with a group of businessmen, led the way in accomplishing this end. Paul McKee of a Portland, Oregon, electric company and W. C. Mullendore of a similar company in Los Angeles were active spokesmen, among others, on the private company's side of the issue for several years. A great deal of money was reported to have been spent by all concerned to educate the public and Congress in the matter.

The power issue was not one-sided, of course. There were those in various business communities who did not believe that the private development of power would benefit them. These men organized committees and groups opposing the temporarily successful group. The process of organization was essentially that already described. Now, in 1958, there are rumblings to indicate that those who won in 1956 may finally lose, and the issue remains unsettled.

Of the other issues mentioned, I should like to touch briefly on a few of them to clarify their meaning. These were (1) civic improvements, (2) individual freedom, (3) mergers and anti-trust, and (4) atomic energy.

1. There was a growing recognition on the part of many national leaders that the larger urban centers were drastically in need of remodelling. Civic center development in Detroit, the redevelopment of the Golden Triangle business area of Pittsburgh, and the UN development on the east side of New York are dramatic examples of bold initiative in refurbishing large city sections that had been community eyesores. In hundreds of communities city planning was a well-established

community activity looked upon with favor by some of the most powerful leaders in them. There was a formal movement (called ACTION, American Committee to Improve Our Neighborhoods) on the part of the national leaders to relate themselves to each other in a kind of unified planning group across the country. There were several other private associations that had done an excellent job in getting response from individual groups, community by community, in redevelopment. It was a grass roots movement with considerable national significance. Academic people, like Professors Catherine Bauer, Coleman Woodbury, and John Parker, were among scores of professional leaders who had educated community leaders along these lines. At best, the policy problems in urban redevelopment will require a generation of work to make a start at lasting solutions. Even with goodwill on the part of the national leaders in relation to the problems involved, the difficulties of blanket solutions are so great that much time in finding adequate plans will be required.

2. During the course of this study Senator McCarthy was in his ascendancy, and before his death he went into political eclipse. The issue that he forcibly brought to the attention of the public was that of individual freedom. I was interested in finding that relatively few of the top leaders mentioned Senator McCarthy, and most of those who did, even during the time that he seemed to be the spokesman for a very potent force in the nation, felt that he was doing the country a disservice by conducting himself unseemly. Many agreed with his thesis of anti-communism, but they would have got at the matter differently. For the most part, the professional people with whom I talked during my community visits were quite disturbed about McCarthyism, none more so than the late Walter White of the National Association for the Advancement of Colored People, but most of them thought that McCarthy was too firmly entrenched with the larger interests to be moved. In an article in *Fortune* magazine during this period,

Charles Murphy pointed out that businessmen were divided on the issue.[1] I was interested in the fact that 9 out of 23 men *Fortune* had polled were persons who had at one time or another been named to me as top national leaders. (Incidentally, I asked one of the editors of *Fortune* how they secured lists of men for polling purposes, and was assured that they had no single list of top leaders but "get to know many persons in the course of their work.")

Before the Senate had gotten around to reprimanding Senator McCarthy, a famous Texan had begun to discount his importance. When asked about his interest in McCarthy, the Texan is reported to have said, "I sent $10,000 to help beat Senator Tydings in Maryland and $15,000 to help beat Senator Benton in Connecticut at McCarthy's suggestion." But as for using McCarthy's influence in Washington, the Texan snorted, "Hell, I've got 10 men in Congress who are better thought of than McCarthy. I don't need him for influence."

The Senate, of course, did something about the whole matter by censuring Senator McCarthy for "breaking club rules." It was interesting to note how quickly the Senator's opinions dropped from the national press as unnewsworthy. The country, by and large, did not want McCarthy. The top leaders were still guided in large measure by what they believed "will go," and neither McCarthy nor his issue of a domestic communist threat was needed by the upper policy makers.

3. Some of the men with whom I talked were in the process of merging their companies into larger production units. They were looking two ways in the process. They were looking at a mass of detail in effecting the mergers and were casting a wary eye at the Attorney-General's office. They mentioned with apparent pride the growth of their particular companies and did not dwell on the merger aspects of the activities in which they were engaged. One man asked me if I were connected

1. Charles J. V. Murphy, "McCarthy and the Businessman," *Fortune* (April, 1954), pp. 156 ff.

with the Department of Justice. The political climate had encouraged mergers, and most of them had gone on apace with
little interference. The activities related to "letting the public
in on what is going on" were being handled by public relations
experts.

4. There was evidence that a great deal of jockeying for
position was going on between individual businesses in relation
to the development of atomic energy, but only one leader
talked with me about this matter. General policy had been
determined by government monopoly of control of this vital
power potential. There had been much secrecy in the whole
activity, and it had not been amenable to the usual processes of
discussion in policy development. It represented a departure
in policy-making in American life, one about which I did not
feel free to probe. It was evident from news releases that the
larger production enterprises in the nation had got a head start
in producing buildings and equipment for future production
of atomic materials.

During the early stages of study no single issue was pursued
as a centering device for study. It was my intention, however,
finally to select one issue and see whether or not it would provide a medium for tracing activities of leaders at all levels of
national life. As the study proceeded it was evident that the
settling of policy matters would not be adequately explained
in any single frame of reference such as political party decision, business domination, pressure group influence, labor control, or ideal democratic process. After a word on political
party alignments and the political ideological setting in which
issues were forged, I have presented in the next chapter an
analysis of a single issue and the national leaders related to it.

The 100 number-one leaders in the research list were not
listed in appreciable numbers as members of the national committees of the major political parties, although 15 of them had
been members of some political party committee at some stage
of their careers. Some of the leaders expressed an interest in one

of the two major parties, particularly the Republican party, but by the time they were recognized national leaders they had restricted their activities largely to helping raise political money and to conferring with others on the suitability of national candidates. For the most part, the leaders of the larger enterprises did not wish to put themselves forward as politicians. Although they were policy makers, with rare exceptions they did not wish to run for public office, and they held themselves superior to the men who seek office. By asserting claims of superior social status they could strategically demean themselves when necessary with various legislators to win them over by this subtle flattery. The procedure worked with some. It was best observed in Congressional hearings. When paid lobbyists were on the stand, the committee members might evidence a detached, bored interest. The same lobbyists, however, might have helped to create a status aura around some of their organization members, or they might represent members whose status claims were well established, such as in the larger industries. When these principals appeared, alert, gracious, and courteous behavior was manifested by the chairman and other members of the Congressional committee. There was flattery and politeness on both sides of the hearing table. There was a notable absence of the surly, condescending kind of questioning from committee members that characterized some hearings when lesser status citizens were called to testify.

When stripped of the glamour and aura of publicity that often surrounds them, the men who are elected to public office are quite ordinary men going about tasks prescribed by the society around them. There is a routineness in much that the politician does which grows out of the stability of the political structure and the general climate of opinion in which he operates. Because so much activity in society is related to men who organize working groups, the politician is compelled to understand and be sympathetic to employers and labor union officials who are powerful in determining industrial policy, which in turn affects public policy as previously shown. He listens sympathetically, of course, to other groups, but his attention is centered most often on industrial policy makers.

Big labor organizations, like big business organizations, have usually been content to tend to their own interesting and admittedly profitable business and let the politicians run politics. Their rewarding of their political friends and punishing of their enemies have not been radical departures from any standard political practice in our culture, and their contributions in money and sometimes in votes have been both welcomed and damned.

The political party organizations are not unlike temporary social organizations pulled together for a host of special purposes. They are comparable to any other organization that requires widespread activity from time to time, whether that activity be devoted to charitable purposes or to drumming up a crowd for a sporting event. Party organizations provide a social structure through which men may vote en masse.

With a few exceptions the leaders are drawn from strata below the top leaders at local and national levels. They help to screen issues and provide candidates upon whom the electorate votes. Each party leader is fully aware of the lines of communication between him and those business and civic interests whose policies concern him. In most instances, the politician is thus in sympathy with an upper stratum of his constituency. Those men who thought in terms of democracy at work in 1958 were fully aware of the reality of what I have just said. There was no indication that political party organizations were instruments by which every man in civic life had a say. The top leaders of community life inside and outside these organizations determine their course of action and activity. Of course, through ignorance or cynical pettifogging, some obscured the basic relationships between the men who were elected and those few who had the most to do with their elections. The politicians who had the wholehearted backing of the top leaders in their communities were the most successful in remaining in office. The exceptions were a few politicians who were supported by labor unions and by groups of reform voters and those who represented self-conscious racial and ethnic minorities. If such a politician was successful over a long enough period of time, a process of accommodation ensued between the unacceptable politician and the top community leaders. "Accommodation" does not imply that candidates of minority groupings were bought off. Many of them, as well as politicians acceptable in the first instance, were men who easily identified with social principles related to the development of human and natural resources and held by most leaders in all communities of the nation. Should individual differences of background have stood in the way of understanding between elected politicians and their community mentors, there were many acceptable ways of getting together and thrashing out individual differences in the name of democracy and the common good. This practice held true, too, in single-party, factional disputes.

For the most part, the national leaders thought of the run of the mill politicians as nerveless men. They knew that some of the politicians could make life uncomfortable for them by investigations and controversial publicity, but they were generally assured that their basic interests were in accord with their own.

The politicians who had been repeatedly elected to the national legislature or to executive positions and those who had had wide and important appointive powers were looked upon with special interest by those who needed their services. These men were considered statesmen and were accorded more deference than newer and less advantageously placed politicians. Policy, however, rarely originated in the legislative halls, as already stated. Legislators acted decisively on policy matters that were originated in one constituency or another by those who were the most active in producing goods and services in society.

The questions put by those who would choose men to run for office for their first time were similar to those asked about anyone chosen for civic tasks, i.e., "Who knows the proposed candidate?" "Has he performed any service that shows that he is sympathetic to the problems that confront the leaders of the organized community, state, or nation," and "Do others go along with him?" "Will he go along?"

Once in a great while, a man who had filed as a candidate without the consent of party leaders was successful in a campaign. But it was exceedingly difficult to conduct a successful campaign for a major public office without the backing of those who contributed heavily. Aspirants to the major elective offices in the nation had to have thousands of dollars, sometimes hundreds of thousands, available to their campaign managers. The money had to come from the same kind of larger organized groups which successfully put over charitable drives. There was little basic difference in the social processes entailed. I speak here partly from experience as an observer in Community Chest operations and in local and state political party organization.

Obviously, one cannot agree to the myth that only impecunious and low status persons of humble origins found their way into politics. A few exceptions come quickly to mind: John F. Kennedy, Henry Cabot Lodge, Averell Harriman, Adlai Stevenson, Herbert H. Lehman, Leverett Saltonstall, and Franklin D. Roosevelt. The man of ascribed social status, in distinction to achieved status, stands a good chance of being politically successful if his social eliteness is not overplayed in press releases about him. Wealth, too, is certainly no bar to a political career, for when wealth and politics are combined, I believe they are hard to beat.

Returning to the question of policies that seemed important to the men interviewed in this study, it must be pointed out that some of the policies I have listed are those that came quickly to their minds when questioned. This did not indicate a complete range of policy interest of any given individual. Responding quickly to a question, a man might have said, for example, that he was interested in taxation problems. This may have been his momentary interest or only one of many interests, but in any case, the answers arrayed here are what a majority of number-one leaders thought of as primary problems in policy development. On a questionnaire a larger number of people were given the opportunity to express a range of interests, and the results did not vary greatly from those obtained in interviews.

Looking at the range of problems cited by the whole group, it is apparent that none of the men considered welfare and minority problems as important, prime considerations. That did not mean, however, that individual leaders necessarily were completely disinterested in these topics. Some were not particularly interested in them, but when asked toward the end of some interviews, others indicated that their interest in these matters was that of the average citizen. Such men professed a superficial knowledge of the problems. Others said that such matters, particularly those related to community welfare or social work problems, were handled by subordinates as a part of the public relations programs of their individual companies. Thus, many suggested a delegation of such policy responsibilities.

In a large scale, bureaucratic operation the size of any one of the major national corporations, it is well known that responsibilities for specific items of policy are delegated. The top officer may choose from among a variety of activities those in which he wishes to engage, but the bulk of work is delegated to subordinates. In any case, however, the top executive keeps in touch with developments of most policy matters delegated by him. His views on any policy handled by subordinates are usually taken into account by them as any activity proceeds.

Some executives are vitally interested in political matters, and in such cases they probably will be openly identified with partisan activities. Or the executive may recognize the importance of having someone in the organization engaged in political maneuvering.

In one community in which I went into the matter of delegation of political activity with some thoroughness, it was evident that a bank president acted as a liaison between his own business and county politicians, that a lawyer for one of the larger corporations was a contact man for his company with the governor of the state and with selected state officials, and that a mortgage broker was a key figure for a superior officer of his company in getting certain things accomplished in Washington. These men were well versed on procedures and personalities in their three levels of government. Because of their knowledge, not only their own company personnel tended to look on them as experts, but other leaders in the community looked to them for advice in matters of politics. I have observed this to be true in other communities less intensively studied. As a matter of fact, I feel strongly that the old concept of the local political boss had been superseded in most cities by a concept of business bossism that related in interlocking fashion to all levels of government. The functions of the political boss in most communities had been taken over by certain local businessmen, who divided responsibilities according to personal interest and to the assumed effectiveness of individual members of the group. From what I have been told, I do not believe that such a division of tasks was done by nefarious plot and calculated design. Rather, it seemed that the scheme was pragmatically useful in highly organized communities. It also appeared to some to allay the popular suspicion of authoritarian control exercised by the single boss system. Because the newer method of political control is more diffuse and less concerned with pure patronage, it is a system of authority which operates outside the knowledge of the average citizen.

In Chicago I had the opportunity of a long discussion with a leading banker, A. X. Brown, who had been prominently identified with the Democratic party for many years. I asked Mr. Brown how he had got so far in politics. His reply ran something like this. "My father was a judge under a Democratic regime in Chicago. I believed in his political convictions, and when Woodrow Wilson was up for election I supported him. I was a lower grade employee in the bank at the time. When Wilson won the election, some of the top officials in the bank realized that they had put too much emphasis on their Republicanism, and they began to look around for a Democrat in the organization. I was the only one they could find, and I became the bank contact with officials in Washington. Needless to say, I rose in the bank hierarchy, and I got acquainted with a lot of Democrats around the country." He named a few.

I asked him why he thought the list I carried with me was so heavily weighted with Republicans; was it because the Democrats were out of power in Washington? He replied, "The Republicans have all the money. That's the only reason they ever get into power, but it certainly helps them to do so. The Democrats have to depend mostly on the little fellow to carry their campaigns. Even with this handicap, however, you must remember that the Democrats were in power for several years recently. The men on your list are powerful people regardless of party lines. Many of them are big businessmen. They're Republicans, and you have to work with them whether the Democrats are in or out of office." An ex-President put the matter in a slightly different way by saying that some of the men in the larger enterprises "are above partisan politics; some of them try to work for the good of the country."

To continue the example of Mr. Brown as a businessman-politician, it may be said that there were many men in Chicago who would not work directly with the reputed Democratic boss in that area on matters of political policy. They might send a subordinate to talk with the Democratic boss, but the same men would have gone directly to talk with the Democrat Brown. The difference in such behavior lay in the fact that Mr. Brown was identified in their minds with his role as a bank chairman, whereas in spite of the fact that he was a lawyer by profession the boss' political role was only too well known. Mr. Brown was thus a mediator strictly among partisans. He was a part of Chicago's business bossism which could and must have operated in relation to the controlled Democratic machinery of that city.

It had been my observation that, although most of the top leaders professed a strong liking for the Republican party, I found no evidence to suggest that they felt they could not work with Democratic politicians if the need arose. They had done so, uncomfortably perhaps, but they also had been effective in achieving many policy goals under Democratic regimes. From a policy point of view, life was a little less strenuous under the Republican administration. The leaders probably would continue to push consistently for policy goals of their choice, however, regardless of election returns or their own individual party preferences. The late Jesse Jones, Texas financier and well-known Democratic leader in the administrations of Franklin D. Roosevelt, had a large oil painting of President Eisenhower at one end of his outer offices and a relatively small, tinted photograph of President Roosevelt at the other.

Needless to say, politics is an important side of the equation of policy-making, but not the only side. The intertwining of interest groups, particularly those discussed here, cannot be discounted in the social process of policy development. Mr. Brown thought of himself as a policy maker. He had the same assurance about this fact as had others of equal business stature. When asked what matter of policy interested him the most, he said, "Naturally I am interested in money. I am a banker. I guess the most interesting policy job I've had was as a member of the Federal Reserve Board. When one has something to do with the control of money and credit at that level, he is a policy maker!"

The control of the money market is of prime consideration to many policy makers. It represents a precise and key point of control of the flow of goods and services, and is of concern to those who operate inside and outside the confines of government. It touches everyone. It is often said, by political theorists, that the control of the military is the key to power in a state or nation. I shall not discount that proposition radically, but in our nation in its relatively tranquil periods the power processes have revolved around the control of divisions of land and the production and distribution of goods and services, and in all of this, the control of money and credit has measured activities. It has lively implications for those with small or fixed incomes as well as for those with unlimited ones. The big issues have revolved around its control, and the banker and the larger industrial policy makers are those who chiefly have shaped and continue to shape the course of events by the direction of its flow.

The ideological framework for the whole structure of top leadership action with which the people appeared to have been in accord was capitalism—or the system of economic production directed toward maximizing individual profit. Between 1953 and 1958 this did not appear to be a partisan issue in the United States. On the contrary, those partisan on many issues had joined together in taxing the people and spending vast sums of money at home and abroad to defeat leaders and peoples expressing the ideology of Communist socialism.

IN order to verify the general finding of this study, a detailed discussion of a specific policy in the making was undertaken. This chapter therefore presents a final, critical test of the process of work which included the previously mentioned specific studies.

In examining various national policies that had been mentioned as important by the national leaders, I found that certain of the policies remained unsettled over a sustained period. Taxation, tariff, housing, electric power development, inflation-deflation, oil, and other national resources policies such as those related to water, minerals, and timber had a way of cropping up periodically or in some instances of never quite dying down. I wished to choose one of these issues and follow its ramifications on an intensive basis, utilizing the methods previously employed in the pilot study of housing. I further wanted the issue to have geographical extensiveness, i.e., to reach from the community level of affairs, to the state, to the nation, and if possible to other nations.

While working through some sessions of a University seminar related to communities in western North Carolina, questions arose about what ties could be found between a series of isolated communities there—isolated in the sense that there were forty to one hundred miles between them along the lower Piedmont mountain range. To answer such questions, one must

further ask, "What do the people do?" Or, as the anthropologists suggest, "Around what is the culture of the area built?"
"Is there a definable culture complex there?" Once the questions were formulated, they could be answered quickly. There
were two major activities in the area around which Piedmont
North Carolina life revolved—textiles and tobacco. This provided the answer to the problem of choice of a policy configuration for study. The textile industry in 1957 was quite involved
with a tariff question, particularly in regard to imports from
Japan. The national policy of reciprocal trade agreements was
up for debate on the extension of the program, and the textile
leaders of North and South Carolina were on record favoring limitations on further tariff lowering. The policy had all
of the elements necessary for study. The two states that I had
already studied, North and South Carolina, contain the largest
concentration of textile plants in the world. Tariff had been
an issue that had repeatedly appeared in the study to that date.

That the tariff issue was of general interest to some of the
top national leaders is graphically shown by Figure 5, page 219.
Six leaders in the test group of 100 (see previous chapter) who
had indicated an interest in the tariff question also indicated
that they had a working relationship with all other leaders,
as shown in the figure.

Preparation for research on the problem entailed working
on several fronts simultaneously. It was necessary to bring
leadership lists from both North and South Carolina up to
date. The South Carolina list remained essentially the same as
in the study outlined earlier. The North Carolina list was also
relatively stable.

Exploratory interviews were held with the secretaries in the
American Cotton Manufacturers Institute to get written records, verbal accounts, and leads for interviewing top policy-
making leaders in the textile industry as they acted on the
Japanese import policy matter. As one might suspect, in the
region under study an overlapping of names of textile leaders

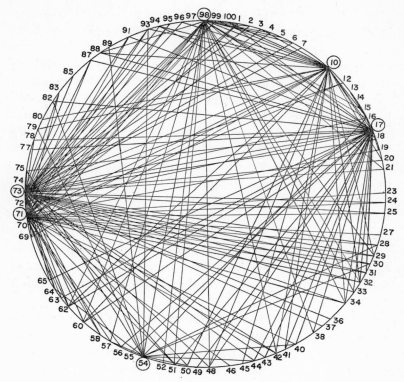

Fig. 5. Working Relationships between Six National Leaders and Seventy-seven Peers on the Tariff Issue, 1958. Numbers are code numbers of top leaders.

with state leaders' names resulted. Even though not textile leaders, other persons on the list of state leaders had a vital interest in the welfare of the textile industry.

A thorough review of the literature, including reports of hearings before Congressional committees and federal administrative bodies, was made. Textile mills were visited, and owners and operators interviewed. Government leaders were interviewed in the states involved in the study, in Washington, D.C., in the Embassy of Japan in Washington, and in the associations and business community in Tokyo, Japan. A long-distance telephone-panel system of interviewing was put into use.[1]

A questionnaire was sent to top national, state, housing, and textile industrial leaders to ascertain their involvement in various matters of national policy-making and in the specific policy matter under scrutiny. The research reasoning behind all of this activity was simply this: If the policy of limiting imports from Japan was a significant national problem, certain leaders in a national power structure would be involved in modifying, furthering, changing, or stopping this policy. Further, there would need to be working relations between the leaders of the various groups involved, even at the international level. If none were so involved or engaged on any level, no power structure could be said to exist, and modifications in the hypotheses would have been quite in order. The policy, therefore, was to be used as a critical test of a process of previous work.

In order to compare and contrast the top national leaders with groups previously studied and to get data to yield intergroup relationships, the questions on the questionnaire were designed to get data on the degree of personal knowledge that all levels of leaders had of each other; on whether or not they had worked together on the development of national policies; on what particular policy was of interest to each and how active he had been in relation to it; on what major associations all the categories of leaders belonged to in common membership; and on related questions. A final set of questions related to the specific policy of Japanese import limitation.

The resulting statistical evidence revealed the structured re-

1. The research technique of using a telephone-panel system of interviewing allowed the researcher to check facts in the policy under study as events were happening. Thus this section of research was compounded of reconstruction research plus data collected in the heat of policy development. It saved many man days of travel and was economical. It was used, of course, after the basic portions of face-to-face interviews were completed.

lationships in the qualitative and quantitative case materials gathered.

In relation to the general questions asked, we learned conclusively that the top national leaders habitually work together on projects and that as one moves away from the core of leadership the number of contacts and relationships drops markedly. Given a list of the 100 top leaders, respondents had been asked to check the names of those with whom they had ever communicated on any matter, business, professional, civic, or otherwise. The top 100 had indicated that they had communicated with an average of 65 others on the list in the ways mentioned. Given the same list and asked the same question, the textile leaders had an average of only 9. North Carolina leaders outside the textile industry claimed an average of 23 such relationships, while South Carolina leaders outside the industry (mainly residing in rural areas) averaged 10. The housing industry leaders, whose statistics are those of a comparable national group, shared an equal number with North Carolina, 23. On a more specific question, "Please check the names of those with whom you have *worked* on any matter of the development of national policy," answers by groups and in average numbers were as follows: top 100's with 100's, 40; textile leaders, 3; North Carolinians, 8; South Carolinians, 3; and housing leaders, 7.

On specific matters of public policy related directly to a man's interest, we asked all leaders polled to respond to this:

Please name here a matter of national policy that is of prime interest to you _____
                    brief name of policy

a. Check below the names of those with whom you have communicated in relation to the policy you have named. [The list of 100 followed.]

In response to this question the answers were: 100's with 100's, 28; textile leaders, 4; North Carolinians, 6; South Carolinians, 2; and housing leaders, 6. The ratio of these numbers remained relatively constant in responses to other related questions. We have concluded from this evidence, coupled with other observations, that all national, functional groups, like that in the housing industry, are likely to have similar patterns of contact with the general national leadership group. Even though the actual number of contacts may be small, liaison leaders from local and state groups are always present to hook into the national network of policy and decision makers.

In a question designed to get relationships related to more than the temporary or committee organization, we asked the leaders to indicate to how many corporate boards (defined in the responses as any incorporated board, not just business organizations) they belonged in common with the 100 top national test group. The average results: 100's with 100's, 6; textile leaders, 0.3; North Carolinians, 0.4; South Carolinians, 0.8; and housing leaders, 2.

More than 50% of the 100 had belonged to the Department of Commerce's status-bearing Business Advisory Council, while only 17% of the leaders in all other categories had held such membership. A similar ratio was found between the 100's and the Committee for Economic Development and the Industrial Conference Board.

All groups were in essential agreement that Washington was the top city in which they had worked on national policy matters, but 70% of the 100's had also been engaged in national policy development in New York, while half that number in the other categories had used New York as a meeting place. A few mentioned Chicago and San Francisco as national meeting places. The more favored specific meeting places within the cities for all leaders were, first, and the overwhelming choice, conference rooms, followed by convention hotels, and finally private offices. Club rooms and private dining rooms, favored meeting places of local leaders when at home, fared badly in the poll.[2]

The types of contact considered to be most effective in policy development were, in order of their weight in the poll, first by a wide margin, personal contact; working on association committees; appearance at hearings; telephone contact (only for the 100's); letter writing; lending one's name to worthy causes (by the 100's only); and, for very few, publication of ideas. The 100's favored official hearings and association work much less than the other categories. They used the telephone more in working on national policy questions.

How often do these men work on the development of national policy? The 100's: 40% daily (mostly but not all government leaders), 20% weekly, and 39.5% occasionally, 0.5% seldom. The textile leaders: 16% weekly, and 50% occasionally, 34% seldom. North Carolinians: 10% daily, 10% weekly, 25% occasionally, and 55% seldom. South Carolinians: 0.5% daily, 0.5% weekly, 66% occasionally, and 33% seldom. Housing leaders: 15% daily, 33% weekly, 33% occasionally, and 19% seldom. The correlation of the ratios with those previously given is apparent.

A final, general question asked of all leaders related to how much they were influenced by policy decisions of the top 100 men—100's by 100's, 22%, textile leaders, 11%, North Carolinians, 12%, South Carolinians, 16%, and housing leaders, 10%. We have no data on the way in which they were influenced nor the item about which the respondent was influenced.

In the light of these composite figures it should be apparent that members of the top leadership are better known to each other than they are to others outside their circuit. They act

2. A special study of the club system of San Francisco was made for the larger national study, but the club relationships were so tenuous in national policy development that the data of the sub-study have been deleted from this writing. Clubs are excellent meeting places for local leaders and are of real significance as exclusive grounds upon which local leaders meet. They apparently do not serve a similar purpose nationally.

together in much greater numbers on general policy matters than do others not in their circuit. The same is true in lesser degree in relation to specific policies of the individual leader's interest. There is, therefore, an element of closure in the circuit described. They are, indeed, a reference group.

In the summer of 1957, in order to see whether it would be possible to trace the lines of communication in a power structure in a foreign culture and whether one could relate the structure to a policy problem in our own culture, I flew to Tokyo. Within a few days and with Mr. H. Usawa acting as a capable interpreter, I was interviewing persons of top organization, government, and business status, who led me to believe that a definable power structure existed in Tokyo and that, further, the leaders contacted were quite aware of the policy problem that I was investigating—the limitation of textile exports to the United States.

I was curious also to know whether the top people in Tokyo were personally acquainted with some of the top leaders in America. With the small sample of people tested on the matter, it was my impression that few knew personally many of our leaders, nor did they know the names of many. They readily identified the names of major companies and in the case of the textile industries knew the employed foreign representatives of our own companies who contacted them on business matters, but they failed to recognize the owners, presidents, or chairmen of boards of the major companies. From brief acquaintance with the question, the network of relationships certainly did not seem to be top industrialist to top industrialist.

Aside from the custom of sitting at a low table with a small cup of tea before me, the interview process and the response, even although through an interpreter, were very much like those in the United States. Besides two letters of introduction from business people here, which helped in specific interviews, I was able to arrange others by contacting the Chamber of Commerce, the Employers Association, and one or two other such groups.

Even though there was not much indication of direct communication between top leaders in textiles of the respective countries, there was policy concern in Japan as deep-felt as the concern of our own manufacturers on this side of the world. The long range economic position of the Japanese nation and industries was as much at stake there as here. Whole communities in central Japan had been thrown out of employment by the policy as it was put into effect, and large delegations of employers, employees, and their families had protested to the Japanese government and to our embassy. Policy made in Gastonia, North Carolina, then, reached directly to Tokyo and central cities of Japan, and the ultimate actions and reactions of the Japanese affected Gastonia.

I had hoped to go more deeply into the facets of the policy-making procedure in Japan on a return trip to that country. My only visit, brief and exploratory as it was, had to suffice, since I was on my way to other cities for another piece of summer research, and within my time limits and resources I was not able to return.

The policy matter specifically at issue may be reviewed from the various, conflicting positions of (1) the United States textile industry; (2) the United States government; (3) the Japanese textile industry; and (4) the Japanese government. Presented in its simplest terms,[3] the policy is of interest in this study merely as a vehicle to prove or disprove previous research conclusions, and the content of policy with its pros and cons is therefore of only academic interest.

1. Following World War II, the United States government encouraged the Japanese to rebuild their war-damaged textile

3. For a look at the record see "Foreign Trade Policy," Compendium of Papers on United States Foreign Trade Policy, Collected by the staff for the Sub-Committee on Foreign Trade Policy of the Committee on Ways and Means (Washington, D. C.: United States Printing Office, 1957), pp. 831, 833, 837, 842, 848-9, 850-2, 884-5, 893, 899-900, 917-75.

industry. The American industry contended that money was spent by our government to put the Japanese industry back into operation. The Japanese disputed this, claiming that they received no direct help other than technical advice. Nevertheless, the Japanese industry was rebuilt, and the machines and factories put in place were of modern design and efficient. The Japanese had approximately one half the number of spindles in place (the measuring term for industry size) as the American industry.

Japanese wage scales were approximately one tenth those of American textile workers. In connection with this fact, it was admitted that the American textile workers' wage scale was one of the lowest in American industry generally. Thus, there was little hope that by wage adjustments American industry could meet the Japanese competition.

Immediately after the war, the American industry exported vast quantities of textiles to all parts of the world, but as the Japanese industry redeveloped, the Japanese product began to drive the American product from foreign markets. The American producers could not meet the low prices of the Japanese goods.

The Japanese were also buying large quantities of American surplus cotton at a government-pegged price below the price that American raw cotton consumers could pay.

Textile leaders said, in substance, "When we were in a foreign area with our goods and the Japanese came in, we left. If the Japanese were already in a place, we just would not attempt to enter." The loss of the American export market for textiles was practically complete in certain lines of ginghams, velveteens, and ready-to-wear goods.

Close on the heels of the Americans' loss, Japanese manufacturers began to send high quality, low-priced goods in a rapidly increasing amount to the American market. This fact put in motion the already restive industry leaders, and a concerted drive was made to get the tariff commission, the federal administration, and Congress to give the industry protection from Japanese competition.

Two state legislatures in the textile areas passed laws requiring retail stores selling Japanese goods to post signs declaring the fact. The textile leaders denied that they had any part in getting these laws passed: "They were spontaneous expressions of outrage at the conditions allowed by the federal government to exist in relation to the industry."

The industry leaders were unsuccessful in getting the tariff commission to grant them industry-wide protection. Pressure on the administration brought belated relief to the gingham and velveteen manufacturers, after long delay, by the President's use of powers possessed in an escape clause in the Reciprocal Trade Act. The clause permits him to exact protective duties on certain classes of goods hurtful to American industry. The textile men said the escape clause was used too late to do any good, and the only long term solution to the problem was protective tariffs.

Under the circumstances, the Japanese became alarmed, particularly when the state laws mentioned were passed, and they protested the laws on the legal grounds of prior agreement to our State Department through diplomatic channels. The Secretary of State wrote notes to all parties, to state governors, and to the Japanese, in an attempt to let it be understood that the federal government was not responsible for nor in sympathy with the states' actions. He received a very unfriendly reply from one of the governors and a cordial response from the Japanese.

Knowing that if they continued they might flood the market with their products, the Japanese decided to limit voluntarily exports to this country, said American spokesmen. An agreement along these lines was worked out between our government and the Japanese. The program was also unsatisfactory as a long term solution to the problem, said the textile leaders. The issue, for them, was still joined, they said.

The American textile industry further contends that the current policies (1958) of our government are ruinous to the domestic industry and that continued Japanese competition will make the country dependent upon a foreign nation for our textile supplies—a situation that could be very dangerous in the time of national crisis. They say that the present government administration believes that the textile industry is expendable and is willing to see it disappear.

2. The United States government did take the position that it should help rebuild certain Japanese industries following the war. No direct aid was given the Japanese to buy textile machinery, but other types of aid may have indirectly enabled the Japanese to rebuild the industry. The American government's policy was based on two major desires. They wished to see the Japanese become self-supporting as rapidly as possible, to ease the burden upon American taxpayers of direct aid to them. The second reason, related to the first, was the policy of strengthening Japan as an ally in the Far East, for any threat that would drive the Japanese toward Communist China or Russia was looked upon with grave concern by the administration.

The United States government had also been committed to a policy of tariff reductions in relation to reciprocal trade agreements. Inaugurated in 1934, this policy had become a keystone of American policy in the years following, and the United States has been moving gradually toward a free trade position in world affairs. The disastrous effects of high tariffs in the late 1920's on foreign trade had made most businessmen and government officials wary of high tariff barriers.

Some said to the textile men, "If you cannot compete with goods from abroad, why don't you get into some other kind of business?" Most in government, however, tried to be sympathetic to the distress evidenced by the textile leaders, and the voluntary agreements with Japan were negotiated with the agitation of the textile people freshly in mind. Actually, Congress came within a vote or two of passing a bill giving the industry a blanket protection. Some government officials said, and there was undisputed evidence in the record, that imports from Japan had only amounted to about two percent of the total volume of sales of the whole industry, and consequently they discounted the idea that the industry was about to be liquidated.

It was pointed out by trade as well as government economists that the industry had had a good many other problems besides the Japanese imports. Obsolescent plants and equipment, uneconomical plant organization internally and in relation to integrated production within the industry, poor selling methods, and other factors were a part of the industries' chronic illness. The whole wage structure left something to be desired in the larger American economy, it was said.

Foreign competition with the United States industry had not been limited to Japan. Italy, Pakistan, the United Kingdom, and India were also world competitors. Many of these nations needed to trade goods with the United States, and textiles were a part of their basic economies. A trade barrier set up against them would have been psychologically and financially a wrong move.

The government's position in the matter had not been a comfortable one, but it pressed for and succeeded in getting a voluntary agreement by Japan on restricting exports of certain textile items to the United States.

3. Japan's survival depends upon exports. The textile industry provided a national staple of export.

Since World War II the Japanese had had a policy of producing quality goods as one measure of re-entering world markets. They desired to be represented in the American market because of the demand in this country for quality goods. The prices that Japan could offer, they felt, should be a boon to American consumers, and their goods should reach a market, also, that might be greatly advantaged by bargain prices.

The Japanese manufacturers and government were greatly concerned over the attitudes of American manufacturers and certain state government officials, and both in Japan and in this country I was told by Japanese government and business officials that they "were not requested by the American government to do something about the situation, but it was politely suggested that they consider 'voluntary quotas' on their textile products." A government official of Japan said, "It was a very delicate situation, you see, and we did not want to lose the American market altogether. Thus at great hardship and sacrifice for some of our people we 'voluntarily' restricted our exports." "You know, of course," he added, "Our exporters would not really restrict their exports if they did not have to. No businessman wants to limit his sales, and ours are no exception."

The Japanese made much of the point that the ratio of import sales to the total sales of textiles in the American domestic market had been less than two percent.

They did not understand why the American textile industry leaders were so concerned with the Japanese wage question. They pointed out that the Japanese textile worker was one of the highest paid industrial workers, whereas the American worker was one of the lowest paid. They claimed that the Japanese workers were beneficiaries of many fringe benefits denied American workers, and since the Japanese workers were happy, why should the American textile leaders complain? This argument did not make a very strong case, to be sure, but it was one of their arguments.

They also said that if they could not trade with the West,

they would be forced to trade with the Communist bloc of nations.

They had many figures to prove that, undesirable as voluntary restrictions on exports might be, they had been made to work. They felt hurt when they heard that our American textile leaders doubted their good faith in the matter.

4. The Japanese government officially transmitted information to and from its own nationals to ours. The bulk of the work in the actual arriving at quotas was performed by leaders and professional persons in the larger textile associations. Certainly, many of the technical details were handled within the associations, just as they were in America.

Since it was evident that a balky attitude on the part of either the Japanese government or the industry would undoubtedly have ended in severely restrictive legal sanctions in the United States, the Japanese government officially endorsed the plans drawn up within the Japanese industry for voluntary limits on exports of specified categories of goods.

Both the Japanese government and the United States government became involved in the problem partly because the United States industrial leaders were afraid to negotiate directly with Japanese leaders. Because of possible violations of the Sherman anti-trust act, the American industry could not enter into direct negotiation in the name of the whole industry. The Japanese are not bound by such law, and it is quite possible that their leaders might have negotiated directly with ours without the formality of going through government channels. Since the Americans felt they had to use diplomatic channels, the Japanese government also obliged their nationals.

The American textile leaders were smarting from two or three defeats in getting what they considered adequate legal relief from their own Congress and national administration, and to some of them the notion of voluntary agreements was a poor shift in policy. They did not trust the "voluntary" idea, and without some governmental sanction on the part of the

Japanese government, it was doubtful that these Americans would have gone along with the idea at all.

Feeling on the part of many American textile leaders is yet extremely high (1958). Even though not all attributable to Japanese imports, their troubles make them extremely sensitive to this problem. One said, "All this feeling of world brotherhood that our State Department is trying to promote is a lot of tommyrot. They think that getting a bunch of people around a table to talk will solve all our problems. And this 'nationals meeting nationals' they talk about is more of the same. Recently I was in Washington for some meetings. At a cocktail party before dinner I was introduced to a Japanese man and told that I was to be his partner at dinner so that 'we could get to know each other.' I soon found that he was one of my competitors in Japan, and that furthermore he wished to come down and look over my plant. That was enough for me. I just picked up my hat and left for home on the next plane. I'm not going to pretend I like what is going on, and I'm not going to have any of my competitors poking around my place in the name of international friendship!"

In talking with the head of the Mitsubishi Trading Company in Tokyo, I was told that the Japanese leaders were quite aware of the strong feeling that existed in the United States among some people, and that this was the major reason that first the Japanese industry and subsequently the government had agreed to voluntary quota arrangements. Another Japanese industrialist said, "I'm sorry to say, but I think your fellow countrymen appear psychotic on this subject, and we feel that we must treat them gently as one does in such emotional cases." Under the circumstances, it was necessary for the Japanese government to act as agents for their textile leaders.

We have here, then, a policy matter that affected and affects communities, an industrial complex, two states particularly, and even two nations, if followed through to its logical conclusion. If the power structure hypothesis holds, small, definable groups within each of these larger social units make and extend policy for the total area, and the process is not confined to formal government. The leaders of the larger urban centers and dominant industries are concerned, and they rely on associations to act through and upon government in relation to specific policies. After examining a little the background issue of tariff control, we shall be in a position to go back to our original hypotheses and the research model outlined in this writing, and see how they have fared in relation to this specific issue of trade policy.

Such tariff questions have concerned one segment or another of the nation since its founding. It is now well known that the two major political parties have in the past few decades slowly been in the process of reversing sides on the question of free trade versus high tariffs, with the Democrats becoming more and more protectionist-inclined and the Republicans becoming free traders.

As previously discussed, when President Eisenhower took office he asked Clarence Randall of the Inland Steel Company to head a commission to study the whole question of tariffs to give his administration policy guidance on the matter. The President had hoped that such a commission would help solve many of the problems in this area. The appointment of such commissions is no new thing, of course, but a vital and recognized part of the process of government.

After months of hearings the Randall Commission issued a final report which satisfied few. A majority report seeming to favor freer trade and a minority report on the other, indistinct side left nobody very happy, but in general the administration has followed the free trade line of reasoning. Over the years, the free trade idea has permeated the thinking of the leaders of a large majority of the industrial groups, and with the exception of textiles, watches, and chemicals, the industrial community has seemed to be behind the present administration's policy orientation. As we saw earlier, before his election President Eisenhower had been personally committed to the free trade idea in Detroit.

Thus, when the textile leaders began to question existing policy and to move on the question of change, they faced formidable opposition and they were in a distinct minority. However, since the textile industry employed every seventh industrial worker, since the industry represented a very large capital investment, and because the industry was organized into distinct and vocal national associations, it was bound to be heard. The textile leaders did not finally get all they went after, but they were accorded a respectful hearing on all sides, and they got temporary relief in the form of limitations of textile imports. They are continuing to be heard.

With a great show of activity, however, it was never clear that more than a handful of men worked consistently toward the policy changes that did take place. The leaders said in interviews that "innumerable men" were involved in going to Washington, appearing before committees, and attending association meetings. When pressed for figures and names, the association secretaries were most often cautiously evasive, but the textile leaders in the industry proper were not quite so retiring. A few of them were willing to take their fair share of credit for what had been done and to name those who had also helped. If one were to leave out of the picture the larger annual and regional meetings of such groups, I would say that not more than six or eight men on the average were involved in this policy development at the leadership level of the major associations at any one time. In other words, as in all association groups, there was a group of top leaders who did all the work, while the vast majority of the membership stood on the sidelines and cheered or remained passive.

Actually the leaders most responsible for the partial success of the drive to limit textile imports utilized all of the elements of power tactics outlined in the chapter on national power structures. Recruits were drawn from their major association, the American Cotton Manufacturers Institute, to carry the word to the proper officials in Washington. The Institute's professional staff had been helping for years to educate its members on how to act in Washington. Concurrently, the staff had been building images of status related to the textile men in the minds of others in Washington. Some of the recruits needed little coaching. They had participated in power moves and pressures in community, state, or private power structures long before they ever moved in Washington circles.

In local communities there was informal opinion-gathering on what should be done about the Japanese problem. The economic urgency of the question made the problem easy of definition, and statistics became readily available to all. Some men began to make speeches about the problem. State government people were invited to private and public dinners to hear some of the speeches or were asked to make speeches and during the question period were asked their views on the important economic question before the body present. None of this was masterminded. It fell within the normal pattern of policy determination in the country.

All assured themselves that what they were doing and wanting done was a dedicated enterprise based upon the highest principles. Certainly, it was for the good of the communities from which the leaders came, and with but little rationalization they could say that their actions were for the good of the country. An *esprit de corps* was built up. Men began to inform themselves and others. They had an ongoing association available to them for the prosecution of their purposes.

As they looked around for leaders, they found those who willingly had served the organization well on other occasions in various capacities. Each was assigned tasks in keeping with his capabilities. Some were workers on the technical detail of organization and strategy, others knew the channels of publicity, and others the mazes of bureaucratic Washington. The way was being prepared for getting to members of Congress, elected administrative officials, and various committees and tribunals in official Washington. All the while, of course, a few men were so engaged.

This is not to say that the large memberships of the textile associations were disinterested nor apathetic while their leaders were on the move in their behalf. Far from it: the membership was quite alert to the issue involved. The bulletins put out by the associations were read with care by many in even the smallest textile plants. As some were interviewed, it was surprising to hear them weigh the whole array of facts they had received.

Once the facts were gathered in the research departments of the associations and the special committees of the board put into motion, the familiar pattern of operations took place in Washington. As one government department official put it:

The Association [of textile manufacturers] conducted the usual pressure campaign as any well-organized group would. They worked on Congress, State Department, Commerce Department, Agriculture Department, and the White House.

This meant making acquaintances, by lobby staff members, with as many as they could in Congress (including the secretariat). They also organized lay members of the industry to write letters and to go see as many members of Congress as possible. They arranged for representatives of the industry to appear at hearings before various bodies interested in the question at hand, and, in all of this, they got as quickly as possible to the highest authority possible with their case.

As was noted earlier in this study, almost universally the favored contact with others on matters of policy development is personal contact. As the textile leaders began to contact members of the Washington community, they also began to weigh the effectiveness of all contacts. One member of the contacting group was Walter X. Brush. He had been elected president of one of the major national associations, whose membership was a cross-section of the country's manufacturing concerns. Brush was not by any measure the largest textile manufacturer nor by any means could he be weighed in the same scale with leaders of some of the very large companies of the association to which he belonged. His election followed the association pattern referred to earlier, "elect the little fellow from the grass roots to head the larger associations."

Mr. Brush was a little fellow only by comparison. He was a big man in his own business establishment, in his community, in his state, and to some extent, but in lesser degree, in his primary association of textile manufacturers. It was only when he moved into the big league association that his status became that of a little fellow. During his tenure of office in the larger national association his stature was enlarged in his local spheres of action, and by virtue of his office he had considerable influence in the big league. His status was coordinate with his roles.

As noted, Mr. Brush had several areas in which he had operated. Consequently, he had status associated with his performance of various roles in those different areas. Depending upon the issue, Mr. Brush would be called upon to be active or passive. If a state issue involving organized groups required the presence and advice of a man who knew the textile industry, Mr. Brush might be called on. After his election to the national office of the manufacturers association he would be called upon more often. His status was established. He was in the power structure reserve. His potential of influence lay partly in the fact that he got to know a lot of people in the various positions he held in various power structures.

During one period of activity, Mr. Brush had got to know a man who later became a cabinet secretary, and this fact was known to the other members of the textile association. Mr. Brush was active in relation to the Secretary and not very active otherwise. It was a case of the quality of contact's counting more than quantity, although the association did not neglect the quantitative approach. The qualitative approach utilized in the personal contact method of work with others is almost the antithesis of a mass pressure drive. It has little build-up and no publicity. It is friend speaking to friend. Pressure is present, but it is not the kind easily resisted. Mr. Brush was most willingly and effectively used by the textile association.

The major associations of textile manufacturers are extremely important in the process of industrial policy-making. They get data together in simple or complex form. They act as a point of reference for arguments for or against their position. They are indeed an auxiliary arm of government. No responsible theorist today says that the associations and their informative lobbies can or should be abolished. They are a functional part of representative government.

Some of the omnibus organizations like the National Association of Manufacturers or the U. S. Chamber of Commerce are less effective on questions like tariff than are the smaller, more focussed organizations. The membership of NAM or the Chamber is divided on such issues as tariff.[4] Thus, they cannot take an open stand. However, in recent years both these associations, reflecting the majority opinion of their members, have made cautious statements regarding the advisability of keeping foreign trade channels open. The textile associations did not cautiously circle the question. They were on the side of protection for their members, and the clarity of their position tended to give them force beyond their size and status in the scheme of things.

As the Department of Commerce man rather wearily said, textile industry representatives "conducted the usual pressure campaign as any well-organized group would." The process had a familiar ring and the places to which research interviews

4. Mr. Brush pointed out that during his term of office as executive officer in the national manufacturing association he had removed himself from the chair to steer the group's thinking so it would not go on record favoring the growing sentiment for free trade and would remain neutral.

led had familiar paths, after my having gone through the housing study a few months previously. The route of which I speak led from Capitol Hill to the White House staff of economic advisors, to the office of a ranking secretary to the President, around the long corridors of the executive departments. It is one familiar to any, I am sure, who have ever had to get anything done in Washington or who, like myself, get involved in trying to find out how things get done.

The most productive stops on the route, in relation to the textile issue, were the Department of Commerce and the White House. The Department of Agriculture, the tariff commission, the State Department, and a couple of Congressional committees also had been active on the problem. All but the Department of Commerce and the White House had been rather sternly opposed to any change in favor of the textile group. The contacts with Secretary Weeks, the fact that he came from a textile-producing region, and his sympathetic reception of the textile leaders made him a pivotal figure in the whole process of policy development. Many minds had been made up far in advance of the appearance in Washington of the textile representatives, but not Secretary Weeks'. Sherman Adams of the White House staff was also considered to have been favorable to the textile industry's position.

Policy makers are not as amenable to pressure as the average citizen is led to believe by press stories. Government officials accede to the pressure that fits their own frame of reference, be that frame of reference personal, professional, or commercial. Many legislators are not dependent for a living on political office, or they can straddle issues, or the people forget. At any event, they do not capitulate quickly to mere pressure. They are more easily persuaded by facts and by hearing the facts from friends or colleagues in whom they trust. The grapevine works in the halls of Congress just as it does along Main Street, and in the case of the textile matter, the word was, "Something has got to be done. The textile people have a case.

Weeks is standing firm for them. We're for Weeks for various reasons. The 'voluntary' business sounds logical and a pretty good solution to what could be a bad international situation if we went the whole way with the domestic traders. We'll buy the 'voluntary' program."

It only remained for the proper committees to be put into motion, for the Secretary of Commerce to meet with the textile leaders at one of their large meetings, for the Secretary of State to approve the work of his understaff who had concluded talks with the Japanese, and for a White House aide to make a speech to the textile leaders in a large gathering and on the day before James Hagerty, White House press secretary, announced in the name of the President that an agreement had been reached with the Japanese for voluntary restrictions on their textile exports.

During such a process, the policy position of each actor becomes clearly known. A centering of opinion can be found, and in this case the center was in the Department of Commerce and the White House.

As I interviewed other officials in order to reconstruct the pattern of action, I found that although some spoke as if they were key figures in making a given decision or they intimated that their agency carried a key role, looking at the whole as an outsider, I saw again that the truth given by each individual was relative.

In spite of the appearance that there is little else but spectacular hearings, every year in Washington the serious search for basic policy goes on. As in communities, some policy matters take more time and attention for execution than others. In past years a great deal of effort has been expended on labor legislation, health insurance, housing, and other matters that remain relatively unsettled. When such questions are up for consideration many of the bureaus are caught up in the current swing of events. If the top policy makers of a particular government department are involved or if the President or one of his top advisors becomes interested or involved in a particular matter, the bureau people are eager to get in on the act. Or sometimes they are commanded to get into it.

In the textile case, the power test was great enough to involve the President and top people in Congress, as well as the nation's top lay leaders. For a few months it was necessary for many in government to be concerned in the question.

As the atmosphere cleared following the policy realignment, it could be seen that the Eisenhower Republicanism had scored a victory. The free trade line had been saved through a satisfactory compromise. Congress was breathing easier. The Southern Senators were on record favoring their textile constituents, but many of them had no heart for a long fight on the matter. They are now trying to encourage industrial diversification in their districts, and since some of the industries they would like to welcome as residents are directed by free traders, too bitter a battle would have antagonized them.

The non-textile men who had called upon the administration and Congress, particularly a number of the national non-government leaders who were identified as communicators on the question, were satisfied with the compromise. They had spoken forthrightly in favor of keeping the trade channels open, and had stressed the need to keep Japan in the Western allied policy orbit. The leading national papers editorialized the relief felt by such leaders.

Unless the deepening depression swings allies over to the textile leaders' policy position within the next few months, the interest will die down, as it is now beginning to do, and the textile leaders will be left with the half-loaf (voluntary export restrictions) they have gained. The bureaus, consultants, economists, and news-vendors will be off on the next upswing of another policy quarrel or development. The policy set in Washington was that of denying to the textile men the benefit of protective tariff. They say they will return to Washington with their case.

It is now evident that top policy makers of the textile industry were involved in the policy discussions and actions. It
has been pointed out also that some of these same leaders were
persons we had turned up as state leaders in North and South
Carolina. Government leaders were certainly involved. I found,
too, in looking through the documents and in going through
the bureaus in Washington that I was going into the same offices and meeting a few of the functionaries in relation to the
textile problem that I had contacted in the housing study.
Even three of the names of Japanese leaders and a similar
number of associations listed that I had contacted in Tokyo
appeared in the documents of a visit to Japan by one of our
junketing Congressional groups whose members also were
learning about textile and other Japanese problems.

But what about 100 of the top national leaders, even those
outside of government, that we have talked about? Were they
related to the problem? The answer is, yes.

In the questionnaire sent to the list of 100 top leaders, from
whom we had more than a one third response, each was asked
to respond to a specific question on the textile policy stated
in this form:

About a year ago, leaders in the textile industry, working with
government officials, were able to persuade the *Japanese textile
producers to voluntarily limit their exports to this country*. This
policy has had an interesting response with much favorable publicity. Although it affects one section of the country more than
others, the policy is of national importance.

a. Please check below how you became aware of this policy.
Check any number:

__From a general news source__newspaper__radio__television
__other
__From an associate in the place of my daily work
__From leaders in the textile industry
__From leaders in government

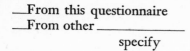

___From this questionnaire
___From other_____
          specify

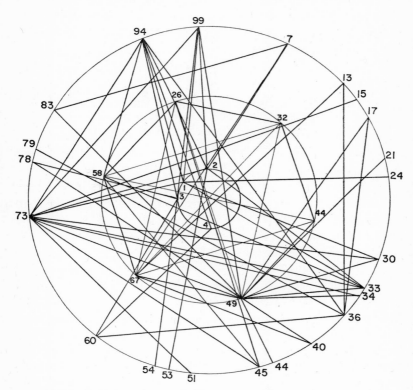

Fig. 6. Four Community, Six State, and Twenty-three National Leaders in Working Relationship on Public Policy Concerned Specifically with the Matter of Textiles, 1958. Numbers are code numbers of leaders.

Besides the general news source which most checked along with other choices, the majority had heard of the policy matter from either leaders in the textile industry or leaders in government. Separating the business and civic leaders from the government leaders polled, we find that 73% of the non-governmental national leaders responding had heard about the policy matter from textile leaders directly. Thirty-six percent were also apprised of the matter by government leaders. There is no doubt in this instance that a chain of communication existed between the leadership groups of textiles and the top leadership group outside.

Within the government group polled, only 10% had heard of the policy from textile leaders, but 80% had heard of the matter directly from other governmental leaders. Not all top-rated government leaders were directly concerned with the policy, but a large proportion had been apprised of the matter directly by government colleagues rather than by general news sources alone. Again the figures point to a communication net that exists, but more important, it was also indicated that 19% of the respondents had worked directly with others on the list of 100 in relation to the problem. Three cabinet members instrumental in this policy development, Secretaries Weeks, Dulles, and Benson in that order, were named more frequently than others by the non-government leaders. These cabinet members, the President, and the Presidential assistant were actively related to the final decision and were key figures in relating themselves to the textile leaders in their problem.

Taking four community and textile leaders in North and South Carolina as a point of reference and tracing their activities in relation to moving other men at both state and national levels in the textile policy issue, I have diagrammed relationships between local, state, and national leaders, both government and non-government. Figure 6, page 243, shows these relationships. The diagram is derived from data gathered at all levels of study, and with proper modifications it points to a segment of the national structure of power. Among many others, the graph relates to Mr. Brush, of whom we spoke, at the local level and it relates to further state and national leaders who would be easily recognized if named.

11 POWER AND THE CORPORATION

NO book on national power would be complete without specific mention of the industrial corporation. These corporations are so interwoven in the pattern of American life that almost no community feels quite complete until it has one or another of the larger production units just outside its town limits.

I happen to like watching the process of manufacture. From the metallic clicking of a small printing press to the crushing roar of a shaping mill, the workings of the machine age have a special fascination. Cranes, earth movers, lathes, jigs, blinking electronic eyes—that is what America is all about, and we are so proud of it! We like it. We want more of it. We want it bigger and better.

At the end of some days in field work, I would go to my hotel room and take a lot of notes on this or that factory. Most of the notes have now seemed irrelevant to this writing. Who would really be interested in the isolated fact that there was an acre of drafting tables in one unit of the San Francisco Bechtel Corporation or that each table had a man working on a tiny bit of a vast project that might finally send miles of steel pipe half round the world? Or what significance does it have that one South Carolina girl could now tend 10 more looms than she could have two weeks before? Or that the total number of spindles in the spinning industry has fallen from 30 million in the past few years to around 20, and yet our over-all production of textiles has actually increased?

Yet, I did see a lot of corporation people. I had preconceptions about them, and I knew that I would finally center on one or another public issue that would involve corporate leaders, as its genesis was traced. It must also candidly be said that I found myself in real conflict as I thought about the corporations and their leaders at the beginning of this study. I had been reared in the tradition of questioning many of the corporate acts that characterize our political system. It had often been evident to me that the leaders of some corporations were narrowly opposed to any activity in civic life that did not produce a product for immediate sale or use, and I have always resisted this opposition.

Also, I have wished to be sure that I did not at any place in this writing paint a false picture of overwhelming arrogated power in regard to corporation leaders. Most top leaders acting as individuals in the corporations do not and cannot exercise personal, decisive public power. Many of the top leaders seem actually to be rather timid and cautious, and one of my social science colleagues who has been studying top leadership in Boston thinks of the men that he has been seeing as "gutless." There often would appear to be much of the "triumph of mediocrity" in policy development. Certainly, it is a social process involving many people, and it does most often involve corporate leaders, among others.

In order to check my facts and opinions on corporate power and to modify them, if necessary, I undertook a brief study of one of the world's largest construction companies, directed by "Ty" X. Tego.

To begin with, the top management people of the Tego corporation were extremely careful not to be tarred with the notion that they were interested in any control of general public policy. All felt that they had a job to do and that it was such an engrossing job that they had little time for moving into the purely political arena to combat social or political evils. Most of the management personnel in this country had little contact with top leaders of other corporations on matters of public policy. They met many corporate leaders in the course of their daily work, but their discussions were technical, generally speaking, and if any matter that might involve political decision arose, it was referred to Ty Tego, who had contacts at all levels of government in many localities, with many in Washington and in the New York centers of finance.

The company generally did not like to contract for work with the government of any country, but preferred to contract with private industrial concerns. Its choice in this matter was dictated, to some extent, by its desire to remain free of purely political entanglements. The company maintained an office in Washington, but its function was mainly that of doing the routine things that have to be done when great numbers of our own nationals are sent abroad to work. During the war the office had a role in getting supply problems unsnarled. In an office reserved for him, Ty Tego sometimes met with people who had business matters to discuss. None of the operations of the office could be construed as lobbying in nature. The company did not work that way. On the rare occasions when a contract was made with the federal government for work abroad, the meetings with government officials were "strictly for business purposes." "It is the government that is being favored, not the company, which seeks no government favors."

Abroad, in those cases where the company had to work with government officials, a very informal set of relationships existed between the company officials and the ruling circles in the particular nation or area. Again, the company took the position, with all concerned, that it was only interested in doing a construction job, and "politics are for the politicians." The policy was one of keeping out of the way of any government, including our own, as much as possible. The hope of the company was, in turn, that governments would put as few restrictions as possible on the company in relation to its need to move great quantities of men and materials in coordinate, logistical fashion. The policy position of the company was as simple as that, and no amount of doubting and probing for hidden methods of operations revealed much more.

Since Ty Tego got around the country a lot, his role as a public relations man for the company had been outstanding. He knew most of the top leaders in the power structure of the country, and the excellence and socially necessary quality of his company's services gave him a base of operations in the power structure that was solid indeed. He had served on major national boards and commissions. He was one of the nation's top leaders. It was good business for him to be related to the upper structure of leadership in the country—just as it is good business for a local leader to be related to civic philanthropic ventures. But too much committee work at the national level of affairs would detract from the job he had to do, and his assignments were not numerous in this area. His opinion was sought on many items of national importance, but he felt that his opinion was just one among many. He knew that his company gave him a springboard for creative activities in many areas, and for many reasons, personal and otherwise, he was devoted to its corporate good. In this, he was like many others.

The strict tending to business of the Tego leaders is typical of the policy positions stated by many corporate leaders. Taken literally, it is a somewhat misleading position. As a matter of fact, the Tego Company was not really neutral on all national and international questions—certainly not on those that directly affected its interests. To the company leaders, all matters of policy discussion outside their relatively narrow range of interests were controversial. To have become openly involved in policy conflict would not have been good business for them. Thus, their interests were partial and segmented. They did not see the nation as a whole, but they were very powerful in relation to the few things that interested them.

None expect the corporations to be the sole keepers of the public interest. Few in American life are interested in a corporate-run state. The truth of the matter, however, is that the larger corporations have a large voice in a great variety of matters and are responsible to few in their views. The partiality of their interests leaves many major areas of policy needs uncovered. Because of their abdication of power in favor of the corporations, other institutional groups in the nation, including government, also leave large areas of policy untouched. None can compete with the corporations as power groupings. Few are willing to call them to account for their actions, whether the actions be in relation to production, pricing, distribution, or other matters in which the public has a real interest.

After the spontaneous laughter died down following Charles E. Wilson's statement regarding the intertwining of the nation's and General Motors' good, everyone seemed to agree that he had inadvertently told the truth. Every issue in public life is measured in some degree in the scale of the corporate good.

To stop at merely discussing the role of the corporation in policy development would be relatively aimless. Such discussion really becomes tangible at the point of tracing out issues and getting at specific matters of public interest that vitally concern the corporations and the general citizenry.

As a social organization, the first task of the American industrial corporation, of course, is to produce goods for manufacture or consumption. In the process of fulfilling this vital function in society many of the individual corporate leaders become spokesmen for their own companies, for a branch of the particular industry in which they find themselves, or finally for American industry generally. Because he has social power and is like the small town millionaire who is presumed by many to be wise in all things because he has money, the modern industrial leader is often asked to give his views, not only on matters of industrial policy, about which he may know very much indeed, but also on matters of national policy about which he may know very little indeed. This division of roles and mixing of functions may create a good deal of confusion in the body politic.

The fact, too, that no single corporation can presume to represent the views of all of the people, but of necessity represents only a small or minority opinion, and sometimes a very narrow one at that, also confuses many issues. For example, the views of the leaders of General Motors or U. S. Steel on matters of commodity or labor pricing may fit the plans of the single corporation, but the same views can be and have been at odds with the views of a majority of people in the nation.

It is a fact, also, that the corporation does not represent a social structure capable of communicating the political opinions of the people from the bottom of the power heap to the top. Thus, leadership opinions in the corporations represent minority views at best, and this fact in itself highlights a major weakness inherent in the American political system. Minority views often override those of the majority.

We are a nation devoted to the idea of producing goods, and many of our national policies revolve around production and distribution problems. We are further devoted to principles of democratic control of policy questions, yet we have devised no machinery of government by which the ordinary citizen can get his views soundly recorded for consideration by our policy makers. Decisions are made at the top, the great debates are carried on at a high level, the meetings on policy formulation are relatively closed affairs, candidates for public office are chosen, often enough, not for their views on this or that policy matter but on very personal factors and, more important still, they are selected for the compatibility of their views

with those of the leading corporate groups in the communities
from which they come.

The corporation is an ongoing problem in American political
life, one that has not been forthrightly faced, I think. It is a
problem that we are reluctant to face because of its size and
because its virtues seem to outweigh its vices. We do not wish
to kill a goose that can produce golden Cadillacs. We assure
ourselves that for every arbitrary corporate decision made out
of pure self-interest, there must be a hundred made for the
good of society. We are also confident that we will get around
eventually to correcting any mistakes we may make in granting
power over the economy to the corporate leaders. In the
meantime, some of us say, the top leaders are doing a pretty
good job, and above all, many of them are in a position to know
much more about most policy matters than the ordinary mill-
hand, cotton chopper, or egghead.

It seems apparent, as one looks out over the nation, that regardless of who makes policy, none of the policy makers will
change the patterns of production of corporate groups quickly
or basically. The system of production is functional to the
social needs of vast aggregates of people, and our policy
wrangles will center, as they have before, on expending time,
money and energy to make more goods available to greater and
greater numbers of people at home and abroad—and to make
profits for some.

It is generally agreed by scholars that as a people we probably need to know much more than we do about the functional
relationships between the corporate enterprises and the policy-
making machinery of state. We go on hunches and half-formed
guesses in relation to our attitudes about them, based on the
subjective literature of by-gone eras as a sufficient model with
which to judge our present policy directions.

The basic questions concerning the activities of the massive
corporations lie in how they exercise power through their
leaders in relation to certain policy matters that confront the

nation. I believe that we wish to be sure that outside their productive confines the corporations do not infringe on any of our political freedoms, that they produce their products in such an efficient manner that they can distribute them at reasonable prices, and that the men who operate the corporations be subject to criticism and restraint when for selfish reasons they abuse the social trust that is allowed them. We wish to be sure, in short, that the corporations are social entities devoted to the good of the country and its citizens, that they conduct themselves in common honesty, through their actions and spokesmen, and that they are not instruments of publicity and propaganda schemes devoted to hiding their shortcomings as producers of goods for the whole people.

I have found that the men with whom I have had contact at the apexes of power did not seem to be devoted solely to absconding with the nation's funds. They were cordial in several hundred discussions. Some have been extremely thoughtful about their responsibilities as citizens. Some appeared to be socially nearsighted, putting their own views of the interests of the corporation above almost any other consideration. None were convinced that labor or any other group should have as great a share in the proceeds of the corporation as it might wish. Each was convinced that the production of the corporation was socially necessary and demanded by society. Consequently, because we deem them so useful, we all join in making the corporations powerful.

From empirical observation it seems reasonable to say that the corporate enterprises are the most potent single forces on the American scene. They reach into every cranny of American life, and their patterns of operations parallel and intertwine with every American institution. Through selected members they collectively control the political machinery at all levels of government, when control is necessary to their functioning. Some of their members hold points of view that seem to many others inimical to the welfare of the people. I think that it would seem wise to have them in every possible way accountable to the public. It would be most difficult in any manner of speaking, to say, however, that they should be abolished or their activities be reduced. Nor has a reasonable substitute been proposed by any to take their place.

Many are impatient with the fact that some of the leaders of the corporate groups have consistently denied the existence of many social problems that are so apparent in American civic life, in spite of our real gains in economic abundance. Some of the leaders have been criticized for putting matters of corporate profits ahead of the wholesome social development of the people of the nation. It has seemed inexcusable to most of us that slums have abounded in American cities and that political expedience also dictated a foot-dragging policy in relation to correcting certain matters of human worth and dignity— notably in relation to the inferior social and economic positions held by racial minorities. But even in these areas, so long matters of policy contention, progress can be seen. Of course, a few corporation executives cannot be held chiefly responsible for the social conditions of the body politic, but none are blind to the fact that the interests of some of the corporate groups have dictated that their leaders take cautious and conservative stands in regard to social questions.

Barely to mention another policy item, I think that it would seem incumbent upon those who are policy makers at all levels of national civic life to be carefully sure that we do not travel again down the road of suppression of civic and academic freedom as dangerously as in the most recent past.

These are policy matters that have seemed to have escaped some of the leaders devoted, in recent years, to the corporate good. More than most other men in 1958, these corporate leaders were in crucial positions in determining the future course of American democracy.

The status system in American life, that so closely parallels the corporate model, seems to spellbind the people. They pay homage to the business and political leaders who profess to serve them, yet, there is also an element woven into the general culture of the nation that abhors power which one cannot control. To confess that another is socially better or stronger than oneself violates the egalitarian values in American society. The way must be left open for achievement and advancement for the able, who may reluctantly concede that at the moment a few have gone ahead of them but believe that, given time, they will prove their equality with the best. This is the American promise that men may freely achieve, and I believe that it must be fulfilled for masses of the people and not just a few. To those few who would deny this urge of the people and claim that what has been accomplished is enough, or those who disdain the relatively powerless individuals and rely on public relations programs to sustain themselves in power at the expense of little people, I would suggest that they reread history and look deeper into the wellsprings of the aspirations in American life.

Most policy considerations are now handled by too few in American society, I think. It cannot be denied that all major policy considerations arising from the needs of the average citizen must be met and mastered and that the lines of communication between the ordinary man and those who make and execute policy for him must remain unclogged. The lines must be open for a free expression and full discussion of all policy matters that confront the nation. Men in America need to speak for themselves more than they do, not to be listeners to only the debates that eddy above them and come to them as ready-drawn conclusions on matters, particularly economic, that vitally affect them. We need to vote regularly and often on issues that affect our daily lives.

In my opinion we must examine thoroughly and regularly the systems of corporate production and power as systems of social, human endeavor and report our findings promptly and fully. In the process we may find elements that we would wish to change. Then, through knowledge and not by blind political shibboleth, we may chart courses of suitable action. Any individual who wishes to oppose corporate, public policy need not act alone. There are innumerable channels of organization open to him through which he may express his views. For example, the labor unions have been able to speak very effectively on many matters of broad public policy. Serious consideration is given to the individual in American community life who aligns himself with the larger association groups. For his views on national policy matters to be effective, they must be expressed, however, through national organization media.

As already pointed out, the corporate pattern of policy operation takes into account clearances and discussions up and down individual chains of command. From a corporate board of directors and its chairman, to the top management team, to divisional executives, to supervisors, to shop foremen, to workers, there are innumerable points at which policy matters may be brought to focus. Through the lowly suggestion box, conferences, committees, sales and annual meetings, political participation, civic enterprise, and countless other ways, the leaders of the larger corporate enterprises learn from others and test policy considerations. Their research departments gather and put forward information. And in all of this, the top corporate leaders are federated in a loose network of personal knowledge of still other national leaders.

The purpose of this discussion of corporations has been to show that, for those interested in getting things done, in moving men and events, it is a requirement that they know the inner workings of the major corporate groups. Those who understand the patterns of the corporate model of power and its ramifications have come a long way toward understanding a model of the dynamics of national power. Those who recognize well the various facets and patterns of power in society believe that there are roughly one hundred of the larger corporate entities that count heavily in the national power scale. It is also generally recognized that these corporations give a continuity and comprehensiveness to power processes not furnished by any other institutional grouping in American life. They are primary forces in organizing the market, and since the market is so large, the corporate leaders are concerned with issues of great magnitude and of concern to all the nation and the world.

The quasi-public character of the larger corporations pushes their leaders into the political—policy-determining—limelight. Their demand for great blocks of capital and credit, in terms of large-scale liens on the resources of labor and materials, usually tends to limit the development of activities demanded by and for the people, e.g., housing and social services, which of necessity must be allotted from the pool of available labor, machines, and natural resources. To resist these latter demands by insisting that existing units of production and distribution should be maintained and expanded puts the corporate policy makers in the position of maintaining the status quo.

The corporate answer to this charge is, "Give us time. Give us the share of men and tools we require and we will produce all that is asked. Look at what we have already accomplished and be prepared for more!" They further insist that government should allow industry a free hand in the allocation of labor power and goods, although during the crises of depression and war the corporate groups have used the preferential position of government to organize and acquire tools and plants of enormous quantity and size.

The use of the government as an instrument of capital levy has not, however, been in contradiction to the requirements of production within the past two decades, nor has it been in discord with long-term credit obligations. No single corporation nor group of corporations could have the social sanction to demand the resources of the general economy that were necessary to prosecute the most recent major war. During such a period, it became imperative that the corporations operate as quasi-public institutions, and their leaders were pushed into the foreground of national policy considerations. During the postwar decade, the issue of war and peace that has involved many national leaders has made a topsy-turvy budget problem for the nation. Consideration of domestic problems has been consistently overridden by costly military programs.

The social value of free private enterprise has been reasserted since the war, and the larger companies have bought, at a fraction of their first cost, many of the facilities built by public subscription and credit. It has been asserted that the control of money and thereby the control of the flow of goods and services should revert to corporate management. Of course these are matters of great importance in the body politic, and are far from settled. Few favor the autocratic central controls of the totalitarian regimes that have risen and fallen within the past two decades in foreign lands. No one wishes to be told in minute detail what he can and cannot do to earn a living, but almost no one is completely satisfied with the scheme of things in which individual corporate groups might make decisions, followed by formal and informal announcements of what they will or will not do in a given situation, and thereafter await any slings and bolts that may come their way. Nor is it enough that smaller social groupings, corporate and otherwise, then adapt their own policy considerations in conformity or in opposition to the pronouncements of the larger, single groups.

Power, in our time, cannot be spoken of in lesser terms than these, nor can decisions appropriate to the needs of the people be phrased in less than national considerations. The problems of public policy in relation to the underlying demands of the people for a continued expansion of productive and distributive capacity vitally affect the actions of corporate leaders who, reluctantly or not, must justify themselves and their actions to the whole people. In communities, in states, and in the nation they represent a power bloc numerically small but exceedingly active, as has been explained.

In spite of their preponderance of power, of course the corporations are composed of men amenable to coordinate pressures of the society in which they operate, and in most recent years they have followed surely many of the dictates of leaders wholeheartedly supported by great masses of the people. In this I feel that there is room for optimism in what otherwise might be a pessimistic view.

As some of the corporate leaders see themselves, it is doubtful that many fear individual malevolent influence of any of the others. I am reminded in this regard of an interview with a man on the West coast. I had been asking about decision makers in the Los Angeles area. The man stopped me politely enough and asked, "What do you mean by decision makers? I think I know what you mean, but in order that we may speak of the same thing, could you define the term?" I replied by illustrating that men like himself have to make decisions on a variety of policy issues. I thought of him as a decision maker.

"Let me tell you my version of decision-making," he rejoined. "There are a lot of policy matters that come before me in our business, but a lot of decisions are already made before any matter comes to my attention. Customers make decisions about our product, its price, its quality, and our service. If anything goes wrong, such decisions very quickly are translated into losses for us. Decisions related to customers are made up and down the line every day in our company. Labor makes decisions on the price and quality of labor given. Stockholders make decisions on how much they expect as a share in profits. My top management team makes decisions in day to day operations. Government makes decisions on taxes. In all of this, from time to time, policy has to be evaluated and changed or reinforced. The decisions are only partly mine. To be sure, I sometimes have to make arbitrary decisions in conflict situations, but this is rare. I'm not a referee very often."

I have since used the term "decision-making" with some care and qualifications. Even as I talked with this man, however, it was evident from what he said that policy development was the kind of social process outlined in this study. It is less of an autocratic process than is assumed in some treatises on the subject, but it always has power elements in it and these elements are related to stratification patterns of status and social prestige. Individuals are looked upon, in a power sense, as reference points in the process. Any individual may deny that he is personally very powerful, and certainly no man of whom I know can universally get his will in the face of conflicting policy forces. Some, however, on the larger issues, get their way more often than others. And many who do not succeed the first time keep on trying. They try most often in association with other men.

The modifications of power structure definition caused by our study of the textile issue and of the Tego Corporation are similar to those made at several previous points in this writing. I do not believe that the men listed in this book represent a circle who can tell everyone what to do and exact his obedience. No great number of them ever met, to my knowledge, as an executive committee in charge of national affairs. Most of them have primary duties in this or that business, profession, or other community role, and in some cases power may be imputed to them in a degree that they do not possess. It does not appear that they have ever made, as one man put it, a broad, concerted effort to influence or control policies.

The men named do serve as a leading circuit in American life. And I believe they do lead in at least the ways outlined as this writing has progressed. They are picked up on this or that level of policy development. They join forces with others on specific issues—not always others entirely of their own rank and status, but in structured relationship. They move in and out of government both as citizens and as officials, as the case may be, and they have a better-than-average speaking acquaintance with those who are at the helm of governing. As I have repeatedly said, I would differ with those who consistently impute wrong motives to all who are in positions of power, or who believe that power is mainly exercised in secret.

When it is deemed necessary by those wise in the ways of power that the American people be led, there is a distinct and recognizable group of men who do the leading, as "Citizen," as "Chairman," or as "Senator, Commissioner, Deputy, or Ambassador." The men named in this piece of research are the principal actors in the drama of power. Others, sensitive to the cues onstage, wait in the wings while the principal actors fret their hour.

To drop the analogy, for none ever fully holds, the leaders form shifting knots of interest, and it is from such interest groups that individuals are selected by others like themselves to man authoritative national policy committees and commissions or individual offices of trust—by others whom they know, with whom they have worked, in whose capabilities they trust, and whose policy views coincide with the selectors'. The best choice, according to some, is the man "who does not really need the job but takes it as his duty." President Eisenhower's cabinet appointments illustrate the point.

To judge objectively where these men lead or whether their leadership has social effectiveness or morality is generally beyond the scope of this writing. It will have been enough, perhaps, to have begun an investigation of leadership and to have focussed in some degree on a national power model.

Most policies are a long time in the making. Those who wish to have their own policy views recognized have to sell their ideas to somebody, to a lot of somebodies as a matter of fact, regardless of the position they hold in society. But there are those, nevertheless, whose policy positions are more respectfully heeded by most than others'. There are spokesmen for this or that interest, and their views are often made public. Along with the public life of the policy makers, there is also an informal private life that helps to pass policy ideas along. There is a recognition of compatible interests and congeniality of ideas by men of like status.

The top power leaders do not always get their way completely. The textile leaders certainly did not, but this fact does not deny the overriding fact that the textile industry contains within its corporate complex a power structure. So within the nation. It has leaders. The leaders relate to one another in innumerable but sociologically definable ways. Policies get decided and moved, not by magic, but by men. They get moved, not altogether by men elected to public office, but through coordinate actions between formal and informal groups of interested men.

INDEX